Studies in Organization Trends
#12

THE HEARTLAND INSTITUTE
www.heartland.org

GLOBAL GREENS

*Inside the International
Environmental Establishment*

JAMES M. SHEEHAN

CAPITAL RESEARCH CENTER

ABOUT THE AUTHOR

James M. Sheehan directs international policy activities at the Competitive Enterprise Institute, a non-profit think tank in Washington, DC that promotes free market and private property-based solutions to public policy issues. At CEI, Sheehan specializes in policies concerning international environmental regulation, trade, finance, and foreign aid.

Sheehan speaks and writes about such international institutions as the United Nations, World Bank, NAFTA, and the World Trade Organization. He has presented his views on television programs for CNN, C-SPAN, CNBC, Fox News and America's Voice. His writings have appeared in the *Wall Street Journal, Baltimore Sun, San Francisco Examiner, Washington Times*, and *Journal of Commerce*. He has testified before Congress and is a frequent guest on radio programs across the country, including National Public Radio. Sheehan holds a B.A. in international politics from the Catholic University of America and is an adjunct scholar with the Mackinac Center for Public Policy, a Michigan think tank.

Copyright ©1998 by Capital Research Center
Photo Credits: UNDPI - Evan Schneider
UNDPI - A. Brizzi

ISBN 1-892934-00-0

ACKNOWLEDGEMENTS

I am indebted to Fred L. Smith, Jr., president of the Competitive Enterprise Institute, whose vision and energy helped me see this project through to its completion. Fred sent me to London, Singapore, Melbourne, Wellington, Canberra and Kyoto in search of the truth. Thanks are due to Patricia Adams, Jonathan Adler, Paul Georgia, Laurel McLeod, Craig Rucker, R.J. Smith and Jeff Tucker for their comments on various parts of the manuscript. Inspiration came from Ray Evans, Henry Lamb, Jeremy Rabkin and Julian Simon. I could not have carried on without the patience and support of my wife Karen. At the Capital Research Center I am indebted to Bob Huberty for his superb editing talents and to Terrence Scanlon for having confidence in me to undertake this venture.

CONTENTS

Introduction ix

Chapter 1. *The New World of the NGO* 1
A New Kind of Organization 2
Working with the United Nations 4
NGO Attacks on Business 6
   The Campaign Against Royal Dutch Shell 7
   The Campaign Against Freeport McMoRan 8
   The Campaign Against Mitsubishi 9
The Shifting Fortunes of International Environmentalism ... 10
"Sustainable Development": New Spin on an Old Argument 13
The Brundtland Report 15
The Earth Summit in Rio de Janeiro (June 1992) 17
Eco-Imperialism: The Priorities of Global Governance 20
The Green Attack on National Sovereignty 21

Chapter 2. *Global Warming: The Politics of Pressure* ... 29
Hell on Earth 30
The Eco-Friendly Solution 32
NGOs and Ozone: The Montreal Model of
   Environmental Policymaking 33
Global Regulation for a Global Climate 37
How the Climate Treaty Was Shaped 39
Kyoto Countdown 41
Carnival in Kyoto (December 1997) 43
The Politics of Green Imperialism 47
The NGO Strategy: Good Cop, Bad Cop 49
Voices for Freedom and Enterprise 52
An Inventory of Greenhouse NGOs 53
"Business NGOs" 56
Appendix: Recent Selected EPA Grants to
   Non-Profit Organizations 59

Chapter 3. *Trade and Environmentalism* 67
Tuna and Trade 68
NAFTA: Linking Trade to Environmentalism 70
To Green the GATT 75
Green Audacity Yields Results 77
The Developing World Fights Back 79
The Rewards of Green Protectionism 80
Tussle over Tuna, Part II 83
The Trade Puzzle 84

Chapter 4. *Building "Sustainable" Cities* 91
Habitat II: How NGOs Planned their Strategy 92
A Calendar of NGO Town Meetings 96
The Clinton Administration's Strategy 96
The Meeting in Istanbul (June 1996) 99
Sexual Morality 100
Economic Growth and Foreign Aid 101
Challenging the UN Message 102

**Chapter 5. *Food Fight: NGO Conflict Over Population Control
and Biotechnology*** 107
Setting the Stage: The 1994 Cairo Conference 109
NGOs Call the Shots 112
World Food Summit: The Path to Rome (November 1996) 113
NGO and Government Paths Diverge 114
Clash over Population Control 115
Gathering Clouds 116
The Campaign Against Biotechnology 117

Chapter 6. *International Forest Regulation* 123
It Started in Rio 124
Looking for Policy Alternatives 126
International Law: An Uncertain Application 127
Understanding Forests and Forest Policy 128

**Chapter 7. *The Yellowstone Controversy:
A Question of Sovereignty*** 131
NGOs Petition the United Nations 131
The UN Monitors Montana 137

Chapter 8. *Seeing Green at the World Bank* 143
The World Bank's History of Failed Reform 144
Enter Wolfensohn 148
The Money Tree 150
What Do NGOs Want? 152
Appendix One: World Bank Funding for NGOs (FY 1996) 154
Appendix Two: NGOs and the World Bank's Global
  Environmental Facility 155

Chapter 9. *The Road Ahead* 159
Mounting NGO Frustration 161
The Future 162

Directory of Environmental Lobby Organizations:
  Funding for International Advocacy 165
Directory of Significant Foundation Grants
  for International Environmental Advocacy 175
Index 201

Introduction

Addressing a black tie dinner of the United Nations Association in September 1997, media magnate Ted Turner shocked the world with the announcement that he would contribute $1 billion to the United Nations. "I've wanted for some time to do something for the United Nations because I think it's the organization with the greatest reach and potential for doing good in the post-Cold War world, for helping children and the environment and promoting peace," he said. Turner's gift – roughly the size of the world body's annual operating budget – will be used to fund ordinary activities of the international organization. But it comes with politically correct strings attached. The billionaire founder of CNN and vice-chairman of Time Warner is a strident advocate of environmentalist causes, and he wants the UN to use his money to promote his agenda.

Turner has created a United Nations Foundation to disburse his money in increments of $100 million every year for ten years. This is an amount larger than the dues of all but three UN member states. Tim Wirth, the former Democratic Senator from Colorado, will oversee the brash billionaire's massive subsidy. Turner says Wirth "shares my vision for the future." Certainly Wirth has very extensive experience in international environmental policy. As Undersecretary of State for Global Affairs in the Clinton administration, he helped formulate policy and led U.S. delegations to international environmental conferences. His new billion-dollar mission is to fight global warming, control population growth, and improve world health.

Wirth has made it clear that he wants the UN Foundation to emphasize the "prevention" of global problems rather than the alleviation of existing ones. This means that directly aiding refugees and the hungry will take a back seat to what Wirth considers more pressing matters of global ecological collapse. To accomplish its aims the Foundation will "tell the UN story" to skeptical American taxpayers, promote birth control and smaller families, and work to restrain energy use by people around the world.

Turner's backing is an enormous windfall for an organization that is nearly bankrupt. Because the UN has failed to undertake needed management reforms, the U.S. Congress cut voluntary U.S. government contributions that were roughly equivalent to the amount of the gift. Consequently, private philanthropy is relieving pressure on UN officials to make changes demanded by Congress. Turner insists that his money not be used for administrative expenses. But UN officials are permitted to take funds from the program agencies he is supporting and redirect them to New York headquarters, site of the organization's most entrenched and top-heavy bureaucracy. They understand that money is fungible.

Turner's money will be funneled through international agencies such as the UN Population Fund, the World Health Organization, and the UN Environment Program. But non-governmental organizations, or NGOs, will be central players in planning and implementing his agenda. Turner understands their crucial role, and he has made sure that his UN Foundation guarantees their ongoing power and influence.

What are NGOs, and why do they figure so prominently in the international environmental establishment?

The non-governmental organization, or NGO, emerged in the early 1990s as a prominent new force in international affairs. Before the Cold War's end, foreign policy was mainly the domain of government officials. Western industrial powers concerned themselves with international security and arms control negotiations, and diplomacy was handled mainly through direct bilateral contacts. Environmental issues had little standing on the world stage, and environmental groups focused almost exclusively on domestic issues and the actions of national and local governments.

Since the 1992 Earth Summit in Rio de Janeiro, the environmentalist credo, "Think globally, act locally," has been permanently altered. Not only do Greens act "locally," they're eager to act "globally" as well. Non-governmental advocacy groups are involved in international efforts to plan global economic development, regulate science and technology, restrict population growth, and intervene in social policymaking. Even in the traditional areas of foreign and defense policy, environmental groups push their issues to the forefront. An all-encompassing Green ideology is now an integral part of the vocabulary of our policymakers.

U.S. nonprofit organizations have played a critical role in transforming the world public agenda. These groups are both critics and advisers of governments, and they have spawned like-minded organizations across the globe. A new and unprecedented force has been created in world politics – the non-governmental organization. NGOs have joined nation-states, central banks and international agencies as institutions authorized to define the world's problems and propose policy fixes. From the calling of United Nations conferences to the negotiation of international treaties, NGOs today exert a profound influence on international affairs.

The United Nations defines an NGO as "any non-profit, voluntary citizens' group which is organized on a local, national or international level." This monograph will examine some of the most politically influential NGOs that focus on international environmental questions. It will review the positions they take, and it will describe their methods of lobbying governments and international agencies.

It is not easy to narrate the story of international environmental groups. The range of issues they pursue is extensive, yet sources of information about them are few and often self-serving. Still, if we want to understand current international environmental policies, we must know more about how these organizations have affected them. This study describes the successes and failures of international environmental NGOs, and it concentrates on the past half-dozen years when they have been most active. I am hopeful that this chronicle of their activities will help the public and policymakers appreciate the scope of their goals and accomplishments.

Environmental groups are achieving their objectives in increments and largely under a cloak of secrecy. Few Americans know that non-profit organizations, staffed by professionals, primarily Americans, and financed by a mix of private and public funds, exercise real power in the conduct of diplomacy and the creation of international policy. A global environmentalist movement is using international law and the assistance of the United Nations and other international agencies to undermine national self-government, economic freedom and personal liberty. This monograph shines light on the behind-the-scenes efforts of this well-funded and ideologically-driven political force.

Chapter 1
The New World of the NGO

A giant Tyrannosaurus Rex constructed of junk metal towers over a conference hall in a mid-sized Japanese city. Thousands of environmentalists have traveled from points all over Europe and North America to be here. Inside, a small group is fanning out across the building to cover every empty table, door, and corridor with propaganda leaflets. Four masked men, disguised as world leaders, play a game of soccer with a large inflatable balloon of the planet. The game is being recorded by several video cameras. Out front, reporters are photographing another group of grim-faced individuals who stand solemnly around three ice carvings of penguins. They are begging the little creatures to forgive mankind for permitting the "global warming" that is now causing them to melt.

Is this is a theater of the absurd? No. It is a United Nations conference in Kyoto, Japan, where a very serious treaty to stop global warming is nearing completion. Lawyers and lobbyists employed by well-funded environmental organizations are huddling in a side room with diplomats and dignitaries, crafting a legal document to curtail energy use in industrialized countries. It is a familiar scene for Green activists, who are accredited by the UN to attend the conference as non-governmental organizations (NGOs).

Welcome to the brave new world of the NGO, where full-time activists attend international treaty-making proceedings as UN-accredited representatives of the public. The UN describes its conferences as sites for "democratic" international governance. But none of the thousands of individuals who participate in these events, save a handful of speech-makers, is elected to public office or authorized to represent UN member governments. Yet by virtue of UN accreditation, members of NGOs are privileged to scold, advise and mingle with the leaders of the world.

Besides participating in UN-sponsored treaty negotiations, NGOs are involved in a wide range of activities. They design and propose texts for international treaties, conventions, and other international law instruments. They monitor governments and private businesses to determine whether they are in compliance with national and international rules. Their attorneys file suit in U.S. and foreign courts against public and private bodies they consider out of compliance with law. NGOs sponsor consumer boycotts and launch media campaigns against policies, companies and governments they oppose. Indeed, the most enterprising NGOs help governments enforce environmental legislation that their own lobbyists have helped write in response to public protests their own activists organized.

NGOs assert proudly that they are independent of governments and private industry. They claim to act in the "public interest," free of outside pressure and influence, and they purport to offer viewpoints that are more objective than the views of private industry. The news media often treats NGOs as unbiased observers.

Yet NGOs have a political ideology. Most believe that the private sector cannot solve environmental problems and that governments must control economic decision-making to protect the environment. This belief may be quite sincere, but it is also rooted in self-interest. Many NGOs depend on governments for jobs, money and power. They seek out grants and contracts from national governments and international agencies. They also bask in the recognition they receive from public agencies, which adds authority to their pronouncements and brings their leaders prestige.

A New Kind of Organization

An estimated 4,000 NGOs worldwide are active in environmental matters.[1] They are not focused exclusively on environmental issues, but include women's associations, consumer groups, farmers cooperatives, human rights organizations, labor unions, private relief charities, policy analysis centers and think tanks, and political action groups.[2] Despite this apparent diversity, however, many NGOs have discovered that "environmentalism" is a winning concept around which they can mobilize support.

Most of the largest environmental NGOs have always had an international focus and some have offices in several countries. Others have deliberately transformed themselves into international organizations. Friends of the Earth International, for example, is a decentralized confederation of over fifty affiliates. Greenpeace, which is based in Amsterdam, has members in 20 different countries. The World Wildlife Fund boasts twenty-eight national affiliates.[3] The World Conservation Union-IUCN is an umbrella organization of private groups and government agencies that comprises approximately 450 members.[4]

All major U.S.-based environmental groups pursue international activities. The oldest conservation organizations — the Sierra Club, National Audubon Society, and National Wildlife Federation — were created at the turn of the century to address domestic concerns, but in recent years they have developed international departments with expanded agendas. The Environmental Defense Fund and the Natural Resources Defense Council were founded in the 1970s to litigate in U.S. courts and influence executive branch enforcement of environmental regulations.

Today, each is active on the international front covering such issues as global warming and ozone depletion. Even the animal rights-oriented Defenders of Wildlife and Humane Society of the United States have gone international. They attempt to influence overseas enforcement of such U.S. policies as the Marine Mammal Protection Act and environmental standards for international trade.[5]

NGOs have different missions. Some identify themselves as grassroots organizations working in cities, villages, or rural areas in developing countries. Many offer special or technical services to other NGOs by doing field work, raising money, or handling litigation and other legal defense work.[6] Policy research groups like the World Resources Institute and the Worldwatch Institute publish books and technical reports that identify problems and propose government policy solutions. And there are coalition-building organizations that assemble and represent other organizations to encourage the formation of still more "grassroots" groups.

By far the most important NGO activity is the written word. Books, papers, press conferences, and news releases fill the arsenal of many NGOs. Environmental groups have become adept at "spinning" stories to the news media to persuade the public that global government programs are essential to its well-being. Ironically, their effectiveness has been enhanced by something that also incites their deepest suspicion — sophisticated technology. Advances in communications allow NGOs to communicate with allies and affiliates all over the world. Fax machines, the Internet, satellite television signals and cellular phones are the international environmental movement's weapons of choice.

A more traditional instrument for gaining attention is what environmentalists call "direct action" — visible public protests, demonstrations and dramatic stunts. This type of activism can range from peaceful picketing and sit-ins by grassroots activists to the well-timed announcement of boycotts and the filing of lawsuits by organizations sensitive to newspaper deadlines. More extreme forms of direct action involve the provocation of violence. Greenpeace is notorious for piloting small boats into the path of massive warships carrying nuclear weapons. Sea Shepherd, a militant group founded by a radical former member of Greenpeace, specializes in sinking or destroying whaling vessels. Earth First! pioneered the practice of eco-sabotage or "monkey-wrenching" against forestry and mining sites.[7] Yet even these groups claim a place at the table when public policy is debated.

The role of NGO coalitions deserves particular notice. Acting as front groups, they can sometimes make support for a cause appear stronger than it really is by temporarily gathering disparate groups together under the banner of a common purpose. NGO coalitions also lay claim to legitimacy by unifying around issues that cross international boundaries. For example, the Climate Action Network (CAN) comprises NGOs from twenty-two countries that have allied to lobby for restrictions on energy emissions. [8]

In recent years NGOs have successfully gained official status as participant-observers at international environmental conventions, conferences and negotiations. While they continue to proclaim their outsider status, NGOs now have the political experience and technical expertise of insiders. With official observer status, they participate in the periodic follow-up meetings to environmental conventions that are known as "conferences of the parties," or COPs. COPs are extended negotiations that build on the basic framework created by the initial convention. NGOs help set the agenda of these conferences by making detailed policy proposals or calling for specific actions. They often use COPs as opportunities to promote the revision or amendment of existing treaty obligations.

Particular NGOs have become experts over time on particular sets of negotiations. Greenpeace, for instance, has expertise in the international regulation of hazardous waste. It has dominated the agenda of the Basel Convention on trade in hazardous waste since the beginning of negotiations in the late 1980s by employing a unique brand of conference participation, report-writing, and lobbying. Greenpeace has managed successfully to impose treaty obligations on the countries of the world that are much tougher than many would have preferred. Its political and organizational skills can only be admired.

The NGO community is a vast resource. NGOs have accumulated deep reservoirs of scientific and technical expertise, but they also can muster large groups of demonstrators and issue a blizzard of press releases to give politicians the protective cover of apparent public support. And they can assemble impressive behind-the-scenes lobbying forces. Officials in national and international environment ministries, who are often very sympathetic to their positions, develop close relations with many NGOs. They rely on the strengths of NGO organizations, and help them obscure their weaknesses.

Working with the United Nations

Nearly 1,500 organizations are registered with the United Nations Department of Public Information. The Department says it "helps those NGOs gain access to and disseminate information concerning the spectrum of United Nations priority issues, to enable the public better to understand the aims and objectives of the world Organization."[9] Such bland language masks the extraordinary political activism NGOs can take on the UN's behalf. According to UN guidelines, accredited NGOs are expected to use their information programs to promote public awareness of UN principles and activities. In practice, this means that NGOs engage in intensive lobbying of governments to support UN environmental policies, while fiercely attacking UN critics.

Amazingly, former UN Secretary General Boutros Boutros-Ghali has called NGO participation in the international organization "a guarantee of the latter's political legitimacy."[10] This credentialling in reverse is clearly demonstrated in the help NGOs give the UN in organizing international summits and conferences. In Rio de Janeiro NGOs galvanized support for a new global policy of "sustainable development;" in Cairo they clamored for worldwide controls over population growth. NGOs publicize these and other activities, boost citizen participation in them, and promote favorable reviews of their outcomes. This legitimating role cannot be underestimated. And it is almost unavoidable when you consider the criteria NGOs must fulfill to be associated with the United Nations. In order to be eligible for formal association, NGOs must:[11]

- *"Share the ideals of the UN;"*
- *"Operate solely on a not-for-profit basis;"*
- *"Have a demonstrated interest in United Nations issues and proven ability to reach large or specialized audiences, such as educators, media representatives, policy makers and the business community;"*
- *"Have the commitment and means to conduct effective information programs about United Nations activities through publication of newsletters, bulletins, backgrounders and pamphlets; organization of conferences, seminars and round tables; and enlisting the cooperation of print and broadcast media."*

Besides registering with the UN Department of Public Information, most NGOs have consultative status with the UN Economic and Social Council. This body is responsible for calling international conferences and preparing draft treaties. As such, NGOs may send observers to public meetings of the Council and its subsidiaries, and they are encouraged to submit written comments and proposals pertaining to the Council's work.[12]

Subsequent chapters of this study will describe in detail NGO activity in some of the most significant UN conferences in recent years.

NGO Attacks on Business

The environmental activist who helps a friendly government bureaucrat may also threaten the hostile corporate executive. NGOs have honed their political attack skills by targeting multinational corporations with overseas investments and manufacturing operations. One survey of 51 large European corporations found that 90 percent expected pressure groups to maintain or increase the intensity of their campaigns over the next five years.[13]

Consumer boycotts are not new, and corporate executives are tempted to ignore them as minor annoyances. But in recent years NGO-sponsored confrontations have increased in number, size and stridency, and they have become more difficult to discount. Consumer-oriented firms are always more vulnerable to attacks on their corporate image. But natural resource industries, while generally more resistant to intimidation, also have reason to fear the skill and ingenuity that NGOs bring to their corporate campaigns.

Oil, gas and mineral extraction industries are directly in the crosshairs of NGO activism today. As environmental regulation checks their activities in the United States, many companies seek economic opportunities in Latin America, Africa, and Asia. But NGO pressure is intensifying there as well. American environmental NGOs are working with foreign NGOs, often forming alliances with groups claiming to represent indigenous peoples who allege human rights violations. This mixing of ecological concerns with human rights questions can confuse the public and take unfair advantage of its concern.

NGOs often minimize the accomplishments of international business and refuse to acknowledge the risk companies face each day. They ignore the massive investment that companies make in the infrastructure of developing countries (transportation, schools, hospitals), which are a basis for future economic growth and the prosperity of local peoples. In some countries, the oil, gas and mining industries provide the primary source of income and foreign exchange for hundreds of thousands, if not millions, of people.

But Green zealots are not likely to be moved by such arguments. No company should underestimate the moral righteousness that motivates so many in the movement. Some may compromise to achieve incremental change, but others believe at heart that industrial progress and economic growth are incompatible with environmental quality. Greenpeace, for example, makes no secret of its desire to shut down nuclear, oil, chlorine, and whaling companies. According to Greenpeace UK, environmental activism is not meant to analyze problems and propose solutions, but to "connect the problem to those who are responsible for it" and then to "hunt them down and eliminate problems."[14] The following controversies demonstrate the brazenness and ingenuity of NGO demands.

The Campaign against Royal Dutch Shell

In 1995 Greenpeace mounted a successful campaign to block Shell Oil from disposing of the Brent Spar, an offshore oil platform in the North Sea. The company had both legal and scientific support for its plan to sink Brent Spar to the bottom of the sea. But Greenpeace waged a publicity campaign against Shell's decision and landed activists by helicopter on the oil installation, effectively taking over the property.

Greenpeace videotaped its assault on the Spar and shared news footage with the media. While television viewers saw a small band of activists confronting a multinational corporation, the reality was quite different. Greenpeace is a highly professional and specialized multinational enterprise. It was spending well in excess of $2 million on a sophisticated public relations strategy to coordinate actions to influence public opinion. Militants on Brent Spar used cellular phones and computers to contact other Greenpeace activists, who initiated protests at Shell gas stations across Europe. Shell's scientific and legal arguments defending its decision proved to be no match for the dramatic incident that Greenpeace staged.[15]

Eventually, it did become clear that the Brent Spar's deep-sea disposal was less a threat to the environment than dismantling and disposing of it on land. Indeed, many oil platforms have become excellent artificial reefs and contribute to a healthier marine ecosystem.[16] Greenpeace was forced to concede as much — but only well after it had sullied Shell's reputation.

In a second 1995 incident Greenpeace alleged that Shell was responsible for the Nigerian government's execution of political activist Ken Saro-Wiwa, a tribal leader and environmentalist. Saro-Wiwa was accused of inciting murder, charges that were denied by environmental and human rights NGOs. Greenpeace accused Shell of failing to use its influence to curb government abuses and also alleged that the company damaged tribal lands by allowing its pipelines to leak oil.

Shell responded that it could hardly intervene in a civil conflict between rival political factions and that any effort to do so would invite attacks on its operations. It had already withdrawn from Saro-Wiwa's home region, Ogoniland, where civil strife created major security problems. Shell officials said no private company could be held responsible for the abuses of a foreign power.

Greenpeace and Friends of the Earth disagreed and exerted international pressure to force Shell to revise its general business principles and incorporate human rights concerns.

The Campaign Against Freeport McMoRan

Freeport McMoRan Copper & Gold, Inc. operates the Grasberg mine located in Indonesia's easternmost province of Irian Jaya on the island of New Guinea. It is the largest gold mine in the world. Environmentalists accuse Freeport of violating the human rights of the indigenous people and of degrading the area's rivers and rainforests with its mine waste. They say the New Orleans-based company abets Indonesia's military suppression of a separatist tribal movement in Irian Jaya.

The campaign against Freeport was launched by three organizations: 1) the Indonesian Forum for the Environment, also known as Walhi, which is an affiliate of the U.S.-based Friends of the Earth; 2) the Berkeley, California-based International Rivers Network; and 3) Partizans, a single-issue group which opposes RTZ, a London-based mining company with a substantial investment in Freeport. An internal Walhi report describes their coordinated strategy against Freeport, which was financed, at least in part, by U.S. taxpayers.[17]

The U.S. Agency for International Development gave Walhi more than $1.3 million for the campaign against Freeport McMoRan.[18] Walhi used its resources to lobby the U.S. Overseas Private Investment Corporation (OPIC), a federal agency that provides U.S. foreign investments with subsidized risk insurance. In June 1995, International Rivers Network lawyer Lori Udall organized a coalition of NGOs to help Walhi pressure OPIC into suspending its risk insurance for Freeport's Indonesian investments. The NGO coalition included the Center for International Environmental Law, Friends of the Earth, Bank Information Center, National Wildlife Federation, Sierra Club, Environmental Defense Fund, and Natural Resources Defense Council. They demanded that independent NGO panels be set up to settle land rights disputes and other issues involving Freeport. They accused the company of moral responsibility for the killing of rebels by Indonesia's military.[19] And they picketed the New Orleans home of Freeport's chairman, Jim Bob Moffet, carrying placards that said "Jim-Bob Moffet Kills for Profit."[20]

Freeport answered that it had complied with all applicable environmental laws and that an audit by the Dames & Moore consulting firm commended the company's $25 million mine waste management program. The company noted that Indonesia's Roman Catholic bishop had cleared it of responsibility for incidents between government troops and rebel factions. Further, the company warned that the proposed NGO panels amounted to a Walhi shadow government that "would be regarded in Indonesia as a usurpation of provincial and national government authority and responsibility."[21]

Freeport failed to stem the international uproar created by Walhi and its American allies. OPIC cancelled Freeport's $100 million insurance contract which protected the company's $2.8 billion in Irian Jaya investments against the possibility of expropriation. This was the first time in OPIC's 25-year history that it had withdrawn coverage because of environmentalist objections. Freeport reacted by offering to give $15 million annually to Indonesian NGOs. This was in addition to the $22 million per year it spent on agriculture and land improvement, schools and hospitals, infrastructure spending on a seaport and airport, and wages for 7,000 local employees who earned almost twice the average national income. After several months of arbitration OPIC eventually reversed its decision, but only after Freeport had pledged to place another $100 million in a trust fund for Irian Jaya environmental initiatives.[22]

The Campaign Against Mitsubishi

The eight-year long battle between the aggressive direct-action group Rainforest Action Network (RAN) and Japan's giant Mitsubishi Corporation ended in early 1998. Accused of degrading tropical rainforests, Mitsubishi Motor Sales and Mitsubishi Electric America agreed to alter their production practices. In a "Memorandum of Understanding," the Mitsubishi firms agreed to conduct environmental reviews of their operations; and they pledged to use more alternative fibers and to phase out tree-based paper and packaging products by 2002. The Mitsubishi firms further pledged to use timber only from sources certified by organizations like the Forest Stewardship Council, an affiliate of the World Wildlife Fund.

Mitsubishi also signed a "Statement of Global Ecological Crisis," which condemned human activities that harm nature, and it promised to fund media advertisements in collaboration with RAN to trumpet the importance of society's transition to "an ecological economy." The firms further agreed to fund a "Forest Community Support Program" administered by organizations acceptable to RAN, such as Friends of the Earth.

One Mitsubishi pledge signaled something new. The companies

promised to incorporate "Natural Step" training programs into their operations. Natural Step is a San Francisco-based environmental organization founded in Sweden in 1989. Its U.S. affiliate is directed by Molly Harriss Olson, the former executive director of President Clinton's Council on Sustainable Development.

The Natural Step notion of what constitutes acceptable business practice includes adherence these principles:

1. *Substances from the Earth's crust can not systematically increase in the biosphere.*
2. *Substances produced by society can not systematically increase in the biosphere.*
3. *The physical basis for the productivity and diversity of nature must not be systematically deteriorated.*
4. *In order to meet the previous three system conditions, there must be a fair and efficient use of resources to meet human needs.*[23]

If a company were actually to abide by these bizarre principles, it could not extract fossil fuels, metals, and minerals from the earth's crust "at a rate faster than their re-deposit." Synthetic substances would be phased out. And land use and consumption would be reduced to levels that nature could sustain without human intervention or work.

What did Mitsubishi get in return for its pledge? For its part, RAN agreed to end its consumer boycott and promised to end its disruptive protest actions at Mitsubishi auto shows, car dealerships, and electronics stores.[24]

The Shifting Fortunes of International Environmentalism

The history of international environmentalism is a story of ideological commitment and political confrontation. Most of the American public was introduced to the movement on the first Earth Day in 1970. But the movement is an outgrowth of America's 1960s counterculture and the radical anti-war movement. It also draws inspiration from Rachel Carson's best-selling 1962 work, *Silent Spring,* and other works which decry the products and by-products of modern industrial society: chemicals, pesticides, radiation, and toxic waste. Many environmental activists are repulsed by modern society, and in seeking alternatives to it they often seem to find in nature forms of spirituality that make their politics seem like a pagan cult.[25]

Groups in other western countries share the same fears and longings of U.S. environmental groups. Philip Shabecoff, the former chief environmental correspondent for the *New York Times*, has observed:

> *"[The Green movement] has tap roots in the Vietnam era peace movement, the antinuclear protests, ecofeminism, Gaian principles of a holistic earth, the ethical insistence on the rights of nature of the deep ecologists, social ecology, and the E.F. Schumacher Small Is Beautiful approach to economics and technology, the successes of environmental activists in the United States, and the inchoate but widely shared sense of dread that late-twentieth-century civilization was on a collision course with ecological catastrophe"*[26]

Inspired by such visions and fears, many environmental groups like Greenpeace and the Rainforest Action Network have relished direct confrontation with corporations. But the maturing of the movement in the 1980s and 90s has led other groups to prefer the leverage of government regulation. The leaders of America's environmental groups are no longer university-based activists. They are weighty players in international public affairs. In the 1990s, they have begun to concentrate their energies on United Nations conferences and international treaty negotiations. Because their world is government-centered (as the NGO acronym implies), they look for political solutions to environmental problems. Says the Worldwatch Institute in the language of bureaucrats everywhere, "If the world is to effectively address the pressing environmental problems on the global agenda, stronger international governance will be needed."[27]

Though they may speak in the passive voice of bureaucrats, there is nothing passive about the environmental lobby. For almost three decades environmental groups have been gathering force in the international arena.

The year 1972 marked the Green lobby's first appearance onto the stage of international governance. The UN Conference on the Human Environment was held that year in Stockholm, Sweden, and it was chaired by Maurice Strong, a wealthy Canadian industrialist and diplomat. This conference brought the environmental movement to the attention of the world's policymakers. Indeed, the commitments made at the Stockholm conference prompted 114 governments to create national environmental ministries. The United States established the Environmental Protection Agency, the Council on Environmental Quality, and the National Oceanic and Atmospheric Administration.

The Stockholm conference also produced the UN's own environmental agency, the UN Environment Programme (UNEP). Headquartered in Nairobi, Kenya, UNEP was supposed to coordinate international environmental protection. It would subsequently convene three environmental conventions: on the international trade in endangered species, on whaling, and on ocean dumping.[28] UNEP's first executive director was Maurice Strong.

In no small measure, Strong was responsible for the environmentalists' first international success. At Stockholm, environmental advocacy groups held a side conference to supplement the official UN proceeding. It was called "the Hog Farm," and it served as a forum for activist speeches, protest demonstrations and the issuance of demands on official conference delegates. This would become a standard practice at subsequent UN conferences. When Hog Farm participants insisted that governments impose an international ban on whaling to "Save the Whale," Maurice Strong acted quickly. Following the Stockholm conference, he flew to London to a meeting of the International Whaling Convention (IWC) and prevailed on delegates to give the activists what they wanted. To this day, Strong credits the IWC decision to the heavy outside pressure exerted by the NGOs in Stockholm.[29]

But the developing countries of the Third World did not welcome environmentalist victories of this kind. Governments in Asia, Africa and Latin America wanted to utilize their natural resources. They were afraid that the international environmental lobby would stymie their efforts to use their resources to strengthen their economies and raise living standards, and they resented what they regarded as patronizing and colonialist environmentalist demands. This attitude hardened, and at later UN conferences it would pose a significant challenge to Green ideology.

Third World governments had their own ideology. In 1974, the UN General Assembly passed a resolution calling for a New International Economic Order (NIEO). It envisioned international commodity agreements, projects for North-South wealth redistribution and other global schemes. NIEO was inspired by the ideas of radical Marxist intellectuals, and it was backed by anti-Western politicians who were attracted to theories of centralized economic planning that promised to increase their power.

Many Western political leaders understood that NIEO was an economic disaster for the Third World and a political weapon for the Soviets. But some environmental activists believed they could use it to enact UN environmental policies. For example, the UN Conference on the Law of the Sea was a massive undertaking to establish an international legal regime for the world's oceans. It declared the mineral resources under the sea to be the "common heritage of mankind" and proposed that a treaty put them under UN control and management to create a "just and equitable economic order." Fortunately, in 1981 Ronald Reagan became

U.S. president just as a draft of the treaty was near completion. Under his leadership, the U.S. withdrew its support for the Law of the Sea. Midway through Reagan's first term the U.S. also left UNESCO, the hopelessly mismanaged UN Educational, Scientific, and Cultural Organization.

The 1970s were boom years for the "limits to growth" philosophy. *Limits to Growth* was the name of a book published in 1972 by the Club of Rome, an influential association that called for government control over economic growth, resource use, and energy consumption.[30] In 1980 the outgoing Carter administration's *Global 2000 Report to the President* took a similar position.[31] Both volumes warned against the twin threats of economic growth and population growth, and argued that the earth's natural "carrying capacity" soon would be exceeded. An even more extreme forerunner of these views, Paul Ehrlich's 1968 book, *The Population Bomb*, predicted ecological catastrophe and mass starvation by the 1980s.[32]

The predictions of Ehrlich and the Club of Rome were answered by reality, and their arguments were refuted by the late Julian Simon and Herman Kahn. In *The Resourceful Earth* (1984), Simon, Kahn and others explained that the earth's most important resource is human ingenuity.[33] History records how mankind has used technology and the market mechanism to overcome every scarcity in natural resources. Simon and Kahn reproached the Carter administration for flirting with ideas that would condemn Third World countries to chronic poverty. Although they were attacked in academic circles, their ideas found favor in the Reagan administration.

The environmental movement persists today despite its intellectual refutation and political setbacks. The 1972 Stockholm conference was an historic first step. During the decade of the 1980s approximately 250 environmental treaties and conventions were enacted. These initiatives have not fully consolidated the movement's power over environmental policymaking. But NGO familiarity with the elaborate framework of policymaking instruments now in place is helping the movement maintain and expand its influence. Environmental NGOs have learned important lessons from their successes and failures in the international arena. Not the least is that rhetoric and public relations are essential ingredients of public policy. Words matter.

"Sustainable Development": New Spin on an Old Argument

The end of the Cold War made things difficult for the environmental movement. Socialism had collapsed as a political movement and an intellectual idea; governments committed to free markets were freely elected around the world; and the emerging global economy was demolishing the "limits to growth" argument that "progressive" thinkers used to justify a new international economic order. If environmental NGOs wanted to rebuild popular support for their positions, they needed a new language and a more appealing core message.

Environmentalist NGOs began to re-package their opposition to economic development and population growth. They could see that gloom-and-doom scenarios were unpopular, and they needed new ways to define and market their ideas to prevent a slowdown in the movement's momentum. In 1980 the International Union for the Conservation of Nature (IUCN), an international network of 450 government agencies, scientists, and NGOs, released *World Conservation Strategy: Living Resource Conservation for Sustainable Development.* This was the first major work to promote a new concept — "sustainable development."[34] "Sustainable development" would become the most important buzz-word in the new environmental vocabulary.

IUCN had been commissioned by the UN Environment Program (UNEP) to prepare *World Conservation Strategy.* UNEP and the World Wildlife Fund (which shared headquarters with IUCN) funded the study, which also was supported by the UN Food and Agriculture Organization (FAO) and UNESCO. With their support and the backing of UNEP's Maurice Strong, the idea of sustainable development had suitable credentials.

A year later, the concept received wider notice when a number of U.S. environmental advocacy groups formed the Global Tomorrow Coalition. The Coalition included the Sierra Club, National Audubon Society, Environmental Defense Fund, Humane Society of the United States, Natural Resources Defense Council, Wilderness Society, and Worldwatch Institute. They stated that their goal was to work for "a more sustainable, equitable global tomorrow."

"Sustainable development" (and its sister term "carrying capacity") gave Green activists an attractive vocabulary, even though its policy agenda was little different from the limits-to-growth philosophy. Like the 1972 Club of Rome treatise, the 1980 IUCN *Strategy* propounds a theory of resource limitation: "the planet's capacity to support people is being irreversibly reduced." The *Strategy* blames an "affluent minority" for consuming most of the world's resources. It demands heightened conservation awareness and more government regulation. And it calls for population control measures to keep the alleged problem of resource consumption from worsening.

While sustainable development is not unlike limits-to-growth, it is noteworthy that nowhere does *World Conservation Strategy* explicitly call for a halt to economic growth.[35] The IUCN volume concedes the harshness of earlier environmentalist positions. "Conservation is positive," it asserts; it is "for people."[36] The *Strategy* also avoids blaming economic growth for environmental problems, and it seldom predicts impending doom. Instead, sustainable development promises to solve problems by managing economic growth intelligently and democratically.

What is most distinctive about sustainable development is the way it combines the goals of environmentalism with those of economic development. Its supporters describe a political system in which conservation measures are integrated into all aspects of centralized government economic planning. Indeed, IUCN says a prosperous economy requires conservation controls: "For development to be sustainable it must take into account social and ecological factors."[37]

Sustainable development also requires large wealth transfers from industrial to developing nations. This merges the two forces that drove the UN agenda in the 1970s — the environmentalism of the Stockholm conference with the Third World's call for global wealth redistribution. The report warns: "Humanity's relationship with the biosphere. . . will continue to deteriorate until a new international economic order is achieved."[38]

The Brundtland Report

"Sustainable development" was just what the international environmental lobby needed. In 1982 UNEP held a conference to review its progress in the ten years since Stockholm. The delegates — a mix of government representatives, UN functionaries and IUCN participants — recommended the establishment of yet another elite body: a World Commission on Environment and Development. The following year the UN adopted Resolution 38/16 to create it, and UN Secretary General Kurt Waldheim appointed its chairperson, Ms. Gro Harlem Brundtland, Prime Minister of Norway and head of the Norwegian Labor Party.[39]

For three years the commission held meetings which produced *Our Common Future*, a 350-page manifesto commonly known as the Brundtland Report.[40] With input from NGOs like the World Wildlife Fund and IUCN,[41] the report sang the praises of "sustainable development," which it defined as:

> *"[meeting] the needs of the present without compromising the ability of future generations to meet their own needs. The concept of sustainable development does imply limits — not absolute limits but limitations imposed by the present state*

of technology and social organization on environmental resources and by the ability of the biosphere to absorb the effects of human activities."[42]

The Brundtland report is based on a model of "market failure." It argues that the free market system is reaching its ecological limit: further relying on markets to allocate resources will endanger the well-being of the world's populations. Instead, governments should make future management decisions about using the world's "finite" resources by consulting a menu of policy options. These options range from environmental taxes to mandating an upper limit on consumption. Population growth also should be restricted by a series of increasingly coercive incentives.[43]

To achieve international "equity," the Commission proposed global taxes to transfer financial aid from the industrial West to less developed countries. Some of its suggested taxes are rather imaginative:

- taxes on revenues from the use of the "international commons" (e.g. ocean fishing, seabed mining, transportation on the high seas, and use of Antarctic resources), and from parking charges for geostationary communications satellites in space.
- taxes on international trade (e.g. a general trade tax; taxes on specific commodities, on "invisible exports," on balance of trade surpluses, and on the consumption of luxury goods).[44]

The Commission asserted that "Sustainable global development requires that those who are more affluent adopt life-styles within the planet's ecological means — in their use of energy for example."[45] This definition of "development" essentially reverses its meaning.

The World Commission on Environment and Development was officially dissolved after the Brundtland report was published in 1987. However, a year later its members then formed the Center for Our Common Future.[46] With headquarters in Geneva, this organization worked to promote the next landmark international conference — the UN Conference on Environment and Development (UNCED) — which was scheduled for 1992. Conference organizers worked closely with the key environmental groups: the Sierra Club, National Wildlife Federation, Natural Resources Defense Council, National Audubon Society, the Wilderness Society, the Nature Conservancy, WWF, IUCN, and the World Resources Institute.[47] The Center also established alliances with 160 organizations in 70 countries to promote distribution and discussion of the Brundtland Report. In the U.S., these groups included the Global Tomorrow Coalition, the U.S. Citizens Network for UNCED, the Environmental and Energy Study Institute, and another umbrella group, the Consortium for Action to Protect the Earth '92.[48] These organizations in effect became an international lobby. Their first opportunity to do what lobbies do — exert pressure by making their presence felt — happened in Rio.

The Earth Summit in Rio de Janeiro (June 1992)

The UN Convention on Environment and Development (UNCED) was a very high profile conference. On June 1-12, 1992, dozens of world leaders, including President George Bush, and thousands of official and unofficial delegates and news media gathered in Rio de Janeiro, Brazil. The Secretary General of UNCED was the ubiquitous Maurice Strong, who reprised his role in Stockholm twenty years earlier. Known as the "Earth Summit," UNCED was the international version of Earth Day 1970 — an event to raise global awareness of environmental problems.

This massive undertaking broke new ground for NGOs. It was the largest gathering of NGOs at a UN-sponsored event. The United Nations accredited over 1400 NGOs to participate in conference activities.

UNCED set an even more important NGO precedent that became the standard by which all future international conferences would be judged. For the first time, conference organizers officially involved NGOs in the lengthy, arduous and extremely important process of preparing the conference agenda.[49] Maurice Strong played a crucial role here in overcoming opposition from Third World countries. They recognized that letting NGOs into the process threatened their own goals and interests.[50]

The UNCED process began in 1990 with a series of four Preparatory Committees — "PrepComs" in UN-speak — that preceded the conference. At these meetings NGOs were able to work with officials in the UN bureaucracy and with delegations from UN member governments. Environmental NGOs and other activist groups joined working groups from the UN Secretariat to draft negotiating text for consideration by the conference delegates. Some were even invited to serve on government delegations. Governments of the United States, Canada, Australia, and several states in Western Europe — countries with the most numerous, powerful and sophisticated NGOs — were the most generous in offering their delegate slots. They also let NGOs participate in UNCED's informal negotiating sessions.[51]

The perks and privileges of the UNCED process attracted nearly 500 NGOs to the final PrepCom which was held in New York City in April 1992. More than twenty NGOs served on the official U.S. country delegation. Many governments also provided financial support so that activist groups could attend the meeting; it has been estimated that one-fifth of the

NGOs at the New York meeting received subsidies from the UN or other government sources to cover travel, lodging and expenses.[52]

Two months later, the NGOs gather in Rio de Janeiro, where they sponsored a separate conference to parallel the official one. The NGOs "Global Forum" attracted 25,000 people from 167 countries. It was intended to remind the official delegates that 1,400 NGO official observers were watching their actions. The activists were on hand to stage protests, hold press conferences, and distribute press releases should their agenda be endangered. More often, however, the participants tried to create the appearance of popular support for official Earth Summit initiatives. UN officials generally regarded them as less a threat than a validation of their work.[53]

Of course, each group wanted to leave a lasting imprint on the proceedings. From vegetarianism and New Age philosophy to animal rights and women's rights, each NGO claimed the mantle of saving the planet. "Our biggest goal is to make sure that the summit recognizes the importance of women; we're planning to lobby that one to death," said former New York Congresswoman Bella Abzug the head of Women's Environment Development Organization (WEDO), a feminist group.[54]

The result was global cacophony. Youth groups organized demonstrations inside conference rooms to demand equal speaking time. Rock bands performed live concerts to support negotiations on biological diversity. Angry dissenters hung a large banner on Sugarloaf Mountain overlooking the city denouncing the summit's slow progress, and throngs of people lined the beaches day and night to dance and chant for their favored cause.[55]

The craziness of the Earth Summit proceedings did not deter President George Bush. He attended official functions and sought advice from America's NGO representatives: Teresa Heinz of the Environmental Defense Fund; Russell Train, chairman of the World Wildlife Fund; Dianne Dillon-Ridgley of YWCA International; Russell Mittermeier of Conservation International; and Elizabeth Barratt-Brown of the Natural Resources Defense Council.[56] They were invited to meet personally with the President in Rio. As proponents of sustainable development, they were privileged to see the President of the United States confirm the importance of their convictions.

The following documents, signed by the world's leaders, contain the results of Rio:

The Rio Declaration: This broad statement of principles affirmed "sustainable development" as the foundation of international environmental policy.

Agenda 21: This detailed 800-page blueprint outlines proposed government actions to implement sustainable development. The document translates the idea of sustainable development into a series of political commitments. It is divided into detailed sections on economic development, energy and resource planning, social policies, and NGO participation. A separate chapter on women's rights was added at the urging of Bella Abzug.

Framework Convention on Climate Change: 150 nations signed this treaty to prevent global warming by curbing the emissions of carbon dioxide and other "greenhouse gases."

Convention on Biological Diversity: 98 nations signed this treaty to protect the habitats of all living species, to manage ecosystems, and to protect genetic resources by regulating scientific research and use of biotechnology.

The Earth Summit was a landmark achievement for the international environmental lobby. The 1,400 NGOs accredited by UNCED not only played an active role before and during the Rio conference but they were invited to the all-important follow-up activities. *Agenda 21*, the UNCED convention document, asserted that NGOs should play a permanent role in policymaking.

There were a number of important and immediate consequences of the 1992 Earth Summit:

• The UN created a Commission on Sustainable Development and gave NGOs a prominent role in its deliberations.

• The World Bank created a permanent Global Environment Facility (GEF), a $2 billion slush fund for Third World environment projects. The GEF was called for by the global climate and biodiversity conventions. Mohammed El-Ashry, a World Bank environmental official formerly with the World Resources Institute, was appointed to head the fund. (See chapter eight on the role of the World Bank.)

• The Clinton administration named James Gustave Speth to be head of the United Nations Development Program (UNDP) and to refocus the Program on "sustainable development." Speth, then president of the World Resources Institute, had been chairman of President Carter's Council on Environmental Quality and he had helped write its *Global 2000* report.

• The UN scheduled additional summits, including a conference on human rights (Vienna, 1993), a conference on small island states (Barbados 1994), one on population (Cairo, 1994), a Summit on Social Development (Copenhagen, 1995), and a World Conference on Women (Beijing, 1995).

(See chapter five for discussion of the Cairo conference.) A conference on human settlements, scheduled for Istanbul in 1996 would be the culmination of the five-year conference cycle. (The Istanbul conference is reviewed in chapter four.)

• The Clinton administration created the President's Council on Sustainable Development to advise the White House on how the U.S. could implement *Agenda 21*.

Eco-imperialism: The Priorities of Global Governance

Third World nations were quick to discover that they did not share the policy priorities of developed governments and NGOs. It seemed that the rich countries of the North wanted to impose green rules on the poor countries of the South. At the Earth Summit American and European environmental leaders demanded that poor countries comply with a schedule of regulations that their own countries ignored during their early stages of economic take-off.

Market-oriented governments in Africa, Asia and Latin America resented this new form of colonialism. They believed the NGOs were fixated on fine points of environmental protection. Instead of the old Marxist shibboleths of social class exploitation, they suspected that the ideology of environmentalism was an "eco-imperialism" that protected rich countries from the competitive energies of poor countries.

The North-South rift was evident in the negotiations over a global forestry treaty. Developing countries, led by Malaysia, the Philippines and India, rebuffed all U.S. and European proposals to limit their use of tropical forests, and called such overtures a violation of their sovereignty. They said the forestry negotiations unfairly focused on restricting tropical forest harvest while excluding North American and European forests. (See chapter six for further discussion of international forest policy.)

The call for global population control policies also generated fierce controversy. Here the Vatican, governments in Latin America, and Islamic states would lobby successfully against *Agenda 21* policy recommendations calling for reductions in Third World population growth. They also forced debate on the morality of abortion and the sterilization of women. (See chapter five on the 1996 Rome summit on world food policy which describes this conflict.)

One Indonesian writer complained that "an imperialistic attitude between First and Third World NGOs" led environmental groups to be more concerned with their "projects and campaigns than with the actual needs of Third World NGOs and communities"[57] The ironic result was that

UN conferences in the 1990s were strangely removed from the real concerns of the world's poor people. They focused on issues NGOs wanted to discuss instead of on the interests of less-developed nations, which are after all the majority of the actual member governments in the world body.

While the environmental lobby has supported more Western aid to lessen world poverty, its promises cannot placate developing countries that fear being left behind in global competition. During the Earth Summit negotiations, they tried with little success to underline the importance of their economic aspirations. Said one official from Ghana:

> *"The very development assistance which comes to us arrives with paternalistic and humiliating conditions ... Basic development technology arrives with price tags that deepen not only our poverty but extends our condition of peonage to our so-called benefactors ... It cannot be expected that, because of the present perverse economic order, those who earn $200 per capita ... are the ones to make sacrifices so that those who — by dint of the massive advantages of technology and an exploitative international economic regime — earn $10,000 per capita can breathe cleaner air or escape the tormenting discomforts that global warming may bring in its wake."*[58]

The Green Attack on National Sovereignty

An attack on national sovereignty is at the political core of the sustainable development agenda. For sustainable development to work, there must be international mandates that governments cannot ignore. There must be a comprehensive body of enforceable international law promulgated by the United Nations, multilateral institutions and international treaty secretariats. Green advocates argue that this system of law will comprise a system of "global governance." Global governance remains largely an idea, but an amazing controversy over Yellowstone National Park demonstrates how it can be used to thwart private rights, local self-rule, and the ordinary give-and-take of domestic national politics. (See chapter seven.)

The concept of global governance is the brain-child of the private Commission on Global Governance (CGG), a successor to the Brundtland Commission. The CGG is a group of twenty-eight world notables co-chaired by Ingvar Carlsson, former Prime Minister of Sweden and head of its Social Democratic Party, and Shridath Ramphal, former Secretary-General of Guyana and former president of the World Conservation Union-IUCN. Maurice Strong is also a member of the Commission. In 1993 the John D. and Catherine T. MacArthur Foundation of Chicago gave

$500,000 to the CGG. It should be no surprise, then, that one of the American members is Adele Simmons, president of the MacArthur Foundation. The other U.S. member is former World Bank president Barber Conable. Besides MacArthur, the Commission's other funders (amounts undisclosed) include the Ford and Carnegie foundations and the governments of the Netherlands, Norway, Sweden, Canada, Denmark, India, Indonesia, Switzerland, Japan, and the European Commission.[59]

In 1995 the CGG released *Our Global Neighborhood*, a 410 page successor volume to the Brundtland report, *Our Common Future*.[60] Following two years of meetings, the Commission members outlined how the United Nations should undertake world economic planning. They proposed a vastly expanded role for an array of global political institutions.

The CGG grandiosely proclaims that it will examine "what the world community may set down as the limits of permissible behavior in a range of areas, and consider mechanisms to encourage and if necessary enforce compliance with these norms."[61] Environmental writer Ronald Bailey, writing in *National Review*, more simply calls CGG a"creeping UN power grab."[62]

"Global governance is not global government," writes the Commission, but it's hard to tell the difference. The Commission suggests that UN agencies should exercise authority that currently rests with national governments. It would add five new permanent members to the UN Security Council and eliminate the veto power currently held by the U.S. and other permanent Council members. NGOs, or what the Commission calls "Civil Society Organizations," would have a direct advisory role in the UN General Assembly.

The Commission recommends that the UN be funded by global taxes rather than depend on voluntary member-state contributions. One proposal, by Yale University economist James Tobin, would impose taxes on international currency transactions, which are "of no intrinsic benefit in terms of economic efficiency." Other tax ideas include special "user fees" on airline tickets, ocean shipping, fishing, satellites, and the electromagnetic spectrum.[63]

Commission supporters say too many world problems — climate change, ozone layer thinning, world trade — transcend national borders. Because national governments can no longer control the flow of capital, trade and telecommunications, they say a new source of political authority must be created. Jessica Tuchman Mathews, currently president of the Carnegie Endowment for International Peace, makes this point indirectly: "The United Nations charter may still forbid outside interference in the domestic affairs of member states, but unequivocally 'domestic' concerns are becoming an endangered species."[64] Less circumspect is Daniel C. Esty, a senior fellow at the Institute for International Economics. He says, "In dealing with global environmental problems, it is only by surrendering a bit of national sovereignty and by participating in an international regime that we can ensure our freedom from environmental harms and protection of our own natural resources."[65]

Global governance is far from attainment. But there should be no doubt that supporters of the sustainable development agenda have it as their goal. Writing in 1992 as a vice president of the World Resources Institute, Mathews applauded the global warming treaty "because it is so potentially invasive of domestic sovereignty." She praised the climate treaty as a way of "forcing governments to change domestic policies to a much greater degree than any other international treaty," and hinted that it might jar Western governments as the Helsinki Accords had once destabilized the Eastern Bloc.[66] Mathews earlier likened the Rio Earth Summit to Allied preparations for a post-World War II economic system, "in the same light we now see Bretton Woods, as one of the places where the rules of a new order were born."[67]

Green groups praise sovereignty-robbing treaties because they have calculated that they stand to benefit. Organizations like the World Resources Institute are already well-funded by large foundations. (It was set up with a $15 million grant from the MacArthur Foundation in 1982.) Any action that empowers the United Nations is likely to empower them. Far from taking "non-governmental" roles, they aspire to be extensions of a global governance system they have helped create.

When they imagine a world of global governance, NGOs are aiming for political control more than global environmental protection. But until their vision can be realized, they will continue to operate through the nation-state, urging it to share authority or act as a partner with international agencies and and nonprofits. Green visionaries Nazli Choucri and Robert C. North admit as much: "We do not know how to manage and regulate the activities of individuals in the absence of institutional requisites of 'sovereign' states."[68]

Will the American public accept an environmental new world order? Elaine Dewar, a Canadian journalist who writes about the connections between environmental groups, government and big business, suspects that environmental issues have been used as a scare tactic:

> *"How do you persuade [citizens in democracies] to give up sovereign national powers to govern themselves? How do you make them hand over power to supranational institutions they cannot affect, control, or remove? You make it seem as if this*

will serve their best interests. You terrify them with the grave dangers national governments cannot protect them from."[69]

Indeed, if all environmental threats are "global," then the environment may become for us what national security was during the Cold War. Jim MacNeill, Secretary-General of the (Brundtland) World Commission on Environment and Development and friend to Maurice Strong echoes Dewar: "The fears of nuclear conflict that once exercised enormous power over people's minds and translated into political support for today's massive defense establishments are declining. But certain environmental threats could come to have the same power over people's minds."[70]

MacNeill describes how a climate of fear over threats to the environment can be politically useful. But his thinking has moved well beyond that. MacNeill was Strong's deputy at the Earth Summit, and he understands that the political importance of UN environmental conferences is *the process* of organizing them:

> *"Part of what we are trying to achieve here is the process; we are trying to get countries to act internationally. The goals of sustainable development involve major compromises of sovereignty. There is no commitment yet to diluting national sovereignty. Before that happens we must have a credible system of international governance. But our job is not to do just what will happen in our lifetime. This process is an important step toward global governance, in which governments will have confidence and will surrender sovereignty."*[71]

NOTES

[1] Gareth Porter and Janet Welsh Brown, *Global Environmental Politics*, 2d edition, (Boulder: Westview Press, 1991, 1996) p. 50.

[2] World Resources Institute, United Nations Environment Programme, and United Nations Development Programme, *World Resources 1992-1993: A Guide to the Global Environment*, (New York: Oxford University Press), p. 216.

[3] Porter and Brown, *Global Environmental Politics*, 1996, p.51.

[4] Thomas Princen and Matthias Finger, *Environmental NGOs in World Politics*, (New York: Routledge, 1994) p. 2.

[5] Porter and Brown, p.53.

[6] Ibid.

[7] Philip Shabecoff, *A New Name for Peace: International Environmentalism, Sustainable Development, and Democracy,* (Hanover, NH: University Press of New England, 1996) p. 73.

[8] Porter and Brown, p.53.

[9] United Nations Department of Public Information, DPI/1438/Rev. 1-07508-October 1995.

[10] Ibid.

[11] Ibid.

[12] UN brochure, "Basic Facts About the United Nations," #E.95.I.31; Press Release ORG/1211/Rev.1.

[13] Control Risks Group Limited, *No Hiding Place: Business and the Politics of Pressure,* July 1997.

[14] *Greenpeace Business,* London, February/March 1996, as quoted in *No Hiding Place: Business and the Politics of Pressure,* p. 12.

[15] *No Hiding Place: Business and the Politics of Pressure,* p. 21.

[16] Michael DeAlessi, "Enhance Biodiversity: Sink an Oil Rig" *Wall Street Journal Europe,* Sept. 18, 1995.

[17] "Moving from Problem Exposing to Problem Solving," Walhi's Concept Paper to Build the Foundation to Achieve Solution for Environmental and Social Problems of Amungme People Caused by Freeport Mining Operation in Timika, Fakfak District, Irian Jaya, Indonesia, submitted by Indonesian Forum for Environment.

[18] Brigid McMenamin, "Environmental Imperialism," *Forbes,* May 20, 1996.

[19] Letter to James R. Moffet from Lori Udall of International Rivers Network and David Hunter of Center for International Environmental Law, November 28, 1995.

[20] Alan Gersten, "Moffett Confronts Strife in Indonesia," *Journal of Commerce,* June 21, 1996; McMenamin, "Environmental Imperialism."

[21] Letter to Lori Udall from Thomas J. Egan, Senior Vice President, Freeport-McMoRan Copper and Gold, Inc., December 8, 1995.

[22] Alan Gersten, "Coverage Reinstated for Freeport Mine," *Journal of Commerce,* April 23, 1996.

[23] www.emis.com/tns/documents/IntroTNS.htm

[24] Rainforest Action Network, "Landmark Settlement Reached in Long-Running Environmental Boycott of Two Mitsubishi Companies," press release, www.ran.org/ran/ran_campaigns/mitsubishi/QT/release.html.

[25] See Jonathan H. Adler, *Environmentalism at the Crossroads*, (Washington, DC: Capital Research Center, 1996).

[26] Shabecoff, p. 69.

[27] Hilary F. French, "Strengthening Global Environmental Governance," *State of the World 1992*, (New York: W.W. Norton & Co., 1992) p.157.

[28] William K. Stevens, "Earth Summit Finds the Years of Optimism a Fading Memory," *New York Times*, June 9, 1992, p. C4.

[29] Shabecoff, p. 39.

[30] Donella H. Meadows, et al, *The Limits to Growth*, (New York: Universe Books, 1972).

[31] *Global 2000 Report to the President* (Washington, DC: Council on Environmental Quality and Department of State, 1980).

[32] Paul Ehrlich, *The Population Bomb*, (New York: Sierra Club/Ballantine, 1968).

[33] Julian L. Simon and Herman Kahn, eds., *The Resourceful Earth* (Oxford: Basil Blackwell, 1984).

[34] *World Conservation Strategy: Living Resource Conservation for Sustainable Development*, (Gland: International Union for Conservation of Nature and Natural Resources, 1980).

[35] *World Conservation Strategy*, Section 1.

[36] *World Conservation Strategy*, Section 1.4-1.5.

[37] Ibid.

[38] *World Conservation Strategy*, Section 1.2.

[39] Matthias Finger, "Environmental NGOs in the UNCED Process," in Princen and Finger, *Environmental NGOs in World Politics*, 1994, p. 187.

[40] World Commission on Environment and Development, *Our Common Future*, (Oxford: Oxford University Press, 1987).

[41] Finger, p. 188.

[42] *Our Common Future*, p.8.

[43] *Our Common Future*; Porter and Brown, *Global Environmental Politics*, 1996, pp. 26-27.

[44] *Our Common Future*, pp. 341-2.

[45] *Our Common Future*, p.9.

[46] Finger, p. 189.

[47] Finger, p. 191.

[48] Consortium for Action to Protect the Earth — EDF, Friends of the Earth, Audubon, NWF, NRDC, and Sierra Club.

[49] World Resources Institute, et al, *World Resources 1992-1993: A Guide to the Global Environment*, p. 219.

[50] Shabecoff, p.133.

[51] Porter and Brown, p.58.

[52] Shabecoff, p.149; Porter and Brown, p.58.

[53] Peter M. Haas, Marc A. Levy and Edward A. Parson, "Appraising the Earth Summit," *Environment*, October 1992. See also Yolanda Kakabadse N., with Sarah Burns, "Movers and Shapers: NGOs in International Affairs," May 1994.

[54] Quoted in James M. Sheehan, "The UN's Environmental Power-Grab," *The World and I*, March 1993, p. 93.

[55] Yolanda Kakabadse N., with Sarah Burns, "Movers and Shapers: NGOs in International Affairs," May 1994.

[56] James L. Malone, "Report on the United Nations Conference on Environment and Development (UNCED)," Rio de Janeiro, June 3-14, 1992, unpublished monograph.

[57] Hira Jhamtani, "The Imperialism of Northern NGOs," *Earth Island Journal*, Summer 1992, p.5, cited in Shabecoff, p. 74.

[58] Ibid.

[59] *Our Global Neighborhood*, p. 376 and Cliff Kincaid, "Making Americans Pay: The MacArthur Foundation's Plan for a Global I.R.S.," *Foundation Watch* (Capital Research Center), September, 1996.

[60] Commission on Global Governance, *Our Global Neighborhood*, (New York: Oxford University Press, 1995) pp. 135-151.

[61] *Our Global Neighborhood*, p. 369.

[62] Ronald Bailey, "Who is Maurice Strong?" *National Review*, September 1, 1997.

[63] *Our Global Neighborhood*, pp. 219-221.

[64] Jessica Tuchman Mathews, "Chantilly Crossroads," *Washington Post*, February 10, 1991.

[65] Daniel C. Esty, *Greening the GATT: Trade, Environment, and the Future*, Washington, DC, Institute for International Economics, July 1994, p. 93.

[66] Jessica Tuchman Mathews, speech to the Atlantic Forum, Federal News Service, May 18, 1992.

[67] Mathews, "Chantilly Crossroads."

[68] Nazli Choucri and Robert C. North, "Global Accord: Imperative for the Twenty-First Century," in Nazli Choucri, *Global Accord,* (Cambridge, MIT Press, 1993), p.492.

[69] Elaine Dewar, *Cloak of Green,* (Toronto: James Lorimer & Co.,1995.) p. 251.

[70] Jim MacNeill, Pieter Winsemius, Taizo Yakushiji, *Beyond Interdependence: The Meshing of the World's Economy and the Earth's Ecology,* (New York: Oxford University Press, 1991) p. 69.

[71] Quoted in Shabecoff, p.157.

Chapter 2
Global Warming: The Politics of Pressure

During the first ten days of December 1997, international negotiators met in Kyoto, Japan to complete a global warming treaty. Officially, environmental groups and their allies in the UN were putting in place the capstone to a decade-long effort to prevent dangerous fluctuations in the earth's climate. But there was a hidden agenda, and it was more menacing. Environmental groups sought effective control over industrial society's supply of energy.

The environmental lobby's crusade against energy began in the 1970s when OPEC oil embargoes dominated the news. The Greens warned that the U.S. would run out of fossil fuels - coal, oil and natural gas — unless the government discouraged Americans from using them. But political pressures for controls on energy subsided when the oil shortages of the 1970s became the gluts of the 1980s. Market forces gave firms an incentive to locate new fuel sources, cut prices and undercut activist demands for government intervention.

However, energy abundance did not deter the Green establishment for long. It found a new reason to restrict energy use: the specter of changes in the earth's climate. In the 1970s environmentalists raised an alarm over "global cooling," a hypothesis derived from evidence that climate temperatures since about 1940 appeared to be in gradual decline. Some alarmists even predicted a coming Ice Age.[1] But by the mid-1970s the cooling trend had petered out. The scare talk, however, did not. Environmentalists now turned their attention to refurbishing a climate theory of "global warming." By the late 1980s, all the major environmental organizations were espousing the theory, and they demanded government action to restrict use of fossil fuel, its purported cause.

The World Resources Institute and the Worldwatch Institute were in the forefront urging action to combat the "greenhouse effect." Their public relations campaign capitalized on the audacious predictions of some environmentalists inside government. NASA scientist Robert Watson had predicted in 1986 that the earth would warm by 1.8 degrees Fahrenheit by 1996.[2] The prediction proved false, but its assertion reinforced Green claims that a change in the weather meant changes to our way of life. "We face the prospect of substantial economic loss and social disruption," said Worldwatch Institute officials.[3]

Sensational predictions by academics also raised public fears that were used to thwart private sector energy use. Sherwood Rowland, professor of chemistry at the University of California at Irvine, warned: "If you have the greenhouse effect going on indefinitely, then you have a temperature rise that will bring about the extinction of human life in 500 to 1,000 years."[4] Such statements were exploited to great effect. The use of computer forecasts generated even more publicity. In 1987, the World Resources Institute programmed climate variables into a computer and devised a model that predicted global warming would raise sea levels by four feet.[5]

The news media echoed these doomsday themes. "The next time someone offers you a hamburger," warned one particularly frantic 1988 press report, "you will not be told that every bite means another step on the road to the ecological destruction of planet earth." How were hamburgers linked to worldwide destruction? Because as ranchers in South America cleared tropical forest for beef cattle pastureland they created conditions for an environmental chain reaction that would irreversibly disrupt the earth's climate system. The article concluded that hamburgers posed a threat "second only to thermo-nuclear war."[6]

Hell on Earth

Environmental alarmists no longer scold us for eating hamburgers. They also now scold us for driving cars, flying in airplanes, manufacturing goods, and for heating and cooling our homes. Energy may be the lifeblood of modern civilization, but the environmental lobby denounces modern civilization as planet earth's greatest enemy.

Pro-environmentalist scientists say that modern industry and agriculture cause gases to be emitted into the atmosphere, and these emissions are producing a "greenhouse effect" that is causing the planet to overheat. Indeed, there is a natural greenhouse effect that does warm the atmosphere: it's what makes possible life on earth. Water vapor causes about 98 percent of this warming. Carbon dioxide and other "greenhouse gases" are responsible for a fraction of the remaining two percent. They are generated naturally and when we burn fossil fuels.

The environmental lobby is alarmed by the man-made addition and insists that it will cause uncontrollable global warming. According to their propagandists, the result will be a world in which the polar ice caps melt and the seas rise; islands will be submerged and coastal plains flooded. Deserts will expand, reducing arable land and the productivity of agriculture. World food supplies will dwindle, causing widespread starvation. There will be plagues of biblical magnitude. The Sierra Club warns that "there are two main ways in which global warming will affect human health — extreme weather events (including heat waves) and infectious disease."[7] Global warming will prompt the spread of malaria, dengue fever, and eastern equine encephalitis. The Environmental Defense Fund (EDF) describes in stark terms how encephalitis can strike horses and humans: "Early symptoms include fever, headache, drowsiness, and muscle pain, followed by disorientation, weakness, seizures, and coma."[8]

The Natural Resources Defense Council (NRDC) predicts "current rates of sea-level rise are expected to increase by 2 to 5 times due to both the thermal expansion of the oceans and the partial melting of mountain glaciers and polar ice caps."[9] "Sea level is projected to rise by six inches to as much as three feet" by the year 2100, predicts the EDF. Flooding will ruin Washington, D.C., "threatening such historic and culturally significant landmarks as the Mall, Georgetown, and the cherry trees surrounding the Tidal Basin near the Jefferson Memorial." Most frighteningly, if sea levels rise only two feet, "a major storm surge would nearly encircle the Washington Monument and completely surround the Internal Revenue Service — Muddy waters would even reach the grounds of the U.S. Capitol."[10]

For Americans who are indifferent to the inundation of the IRS, the Environmental Information Center warns, "Recreational activities like fishing and hunting in the summer and skiing in the winter are vulnerable to climate change." Vacationers should be warned that sea level rise "may cause widespread beach erosion," and because of global warming, "many of the features that make Florida attractive to tourists, retirees, and other residents are threatened."[11]

Some environmentalists admit that the effects of their global warming hypothesis may be less predictable and dire. According to the NRDC: "Warmer temperatures, by increasing the energy of the climatic system, can lead to more intense rainfall at some times and in some areas, but more frequent drought-like conditions in others." NRDC concedes that recent snowfall, rainfall and flooding in the Pacific Northwest "cannot be unambiguously linked to global climatic change." It even conjectures that global warming may cause some agriculture to flourish: "Predictions range from large drops to large increases in crop yields depending on assumptions of the temperature increase, potential benefits of increased carbon dioxide, and adaptation measures."[12]

Yet despite the occasional silver lining, most environmental groups move quickly from computer-generated extrapolations to lurid pictures of global warming's devastation. The World Wildlife Fund describes the grim implications for parks and wildlife:

Many national parks and protected areas are already under tremendous pressure from environmental problems such as encroaching development, overcrowding with cars and visitors, and water and air pollution. The additional stress of climate change may be enough to tip the balance and cause serious damage to ecosystems and the extinction of some of the species these magnificent parks were set up to protect.[13]

The Eco-Friendly Solution

To prevent eco-catastrophe, the global warming lobby proposes drastic government policy changes. Worldwatch analyst Christopher Flavin says even the most modest proposals "would mark a dramatic shift in direction and require wholesale changes in energy policy and land use planning around the world."[14] But American workers and consumers will be big losers if their homes, offices and factories, appliances and vehicles are governed by the efficiency standards that environmental groups demand. Frances Smith, executive director of the market-oriented group Consumer Alert, warns that, "Consumers are direct users of oil, natural gas, and electricity in their homes and for transportation. They are the end users of products - food, home building materials, appliances, furniture, cleaning and personal care products — whose manufacture and transport require energy"[15] American living standards will decline if government regulations make energy more expensive and less abundant.

Green groups' demands have grown increasingly strident. Greenpeace insists that the governments of industrial countries impose regulations to reduce carbon emissions twenty percent below 1990 levels by the year 2005.[16] Other groups say this action, draconian as it may sound, will not avert impending catastrophe. "To stabilize carbon dioxide concentrations in the atmosphere at their current levels," writes Ozone Action, a radical group "would require an immediate reduction of emissions by 50-70%, with further reductions later."[17]

Reductions of this magnitude would require governments around the world to eliminate almost all carbon-based fuel use. What will replace the burning of coal, oil and natural gas, which comprise 90 percent of the world's energy supply? Environmental lobby groups favor solar energy, and they would phase out the automobile, replacing it with railways and other forms of mass transportation. Greenpeace exclaims, "a future without fossil fuels is essential to preserve the environment from the serious risk of climate change."[18] But the drastic changes it proposes will cripple national economies, radicalize individual lifestyles, and dramatically increase government regulation of producers and consumers. The more industrial — and prosperous — a country is, the harder it will be hit.

One economic analysis conducted by WEFA Inc., a consulting firm, concluded that 1997 Clinton administration policy proposals to cut emissions to 1990 levels by the year 2010 would be the equivalent of an energy tax hike that would slash the U.S. Gross Domestic Product by $227 billion per year. As many as 1.8 million jobs could be lost annually and energy-using industries would be particularly hard hit. Global warming controls on energy would raise residential and commercial fuel prices by 55 percent, electricity prices by 40-50 percent, and gasoline by 70 cents a gallon.[19] According to MIT economist Richard Schmalensee, the global warming rules would be like experiencing the "energy price hikes of the 1970s with a massive hangover."[20]

NGOs and Ozone: The Montreal Model of Environmental Policymaking

Today environmental lobbies use global warming to pressure governments and frighten their citizens. But global warming is only the most recent science scare. A decade before Kyoto, there was Montreal. Green groups then demanded stringent government regulations — not to prevent the build-up of greenhouse gases, but to mend the "hole in the ozone layer." The tactics of that campaign were a model for what happened at the 1997 Kyoto summit.

In 1987 a treaty known as the Montreal Protocol phased out the worldwide production and use of chemical compounds called chloroflourocarbons (CFCs). CFCs, the key ingredient in refrigerators and air conditioners, made life better for millions of people around the world. Besides their role in cooling, CFCs had many other industrial applications and were commonly used as solvents, foam insulation and aerosol spray propellants. But environmental NGOs waged a successful international campaign to ban CFC production and use. Without CFCs, industry has been forced to adopt more costly and less-than-ideal alternatives.

The ozone treaty, signed by twenty-five countries in 1987, was the outcome of a lengthy process that began in the 1970s when environmental groups like the Natural Resources Defense Council first clamored for restrictions on CFC use. NRDC claimed CFCs were destroying the ozone layer in the earth's stratosphere. (The ozone layer shields us from the sun's ultraviolet rays.) In 1978, NRDC and other groups prevailed on the U.S. Environmental Protection Agency to ban the use of CFCs as aerosol propellants in spray cans.

Emboldened by their success, environmental groups pressed for more. They called for an international treaty to enforce a worldwide ban on the production of CFCs. In the early stages of the campaign, NGOs and U.S. and foreign government officials formed a Coordinating Committee on the Ozone Layer under the auspices of the UN Environment Programme (UNEP).[21] The committee produced periodic reports that built a case for international regulation. UNEP assisted the lobbying process by supporting scientific and economic research to bolster the environmentalist cause.

How dangerous is ozone depletion? The environmentalists and UNEP could not have taken this question seriously. In fact, they treated it as unimportant. They had initiated the treaty-making process without scientifically verifying that ozone thinning was a genuine problem. Most scientific reports in the early 1980s concluded that the concept was overblown, and almost all member countries on the Coordinating Committee acknowledged that the issue lacked scientific urgency. Nonetheless, the leadership of the environmental non-profits and their UN allies made sure that the process of international policymaking moved forward. Richard Benedick, the treaty's chief U.S. negotiator, observed that when the theory of ozone depletion lacked scientific support, "it is no exaggeration to state that it was UNEP that kept the ozone issue alive."[22]

Why would the UN do that? The major CFC producing nations in Europe and in Japan initially refused to consider international environmental restrictions. Nor was the U.S. under President Ronald Reagan in any mood to impose new environmental regulations. W. Allen Wallis, Undersecretary of State for Economic Affairs, opposed an ozone treaty because he feared it would lead to more international regulation and undercut domestic deregulation. He warned that UN and federal government agencies would use a treaty to suppress independent scientific research that did not conform to the "official" policy findings.[23] Wallis' assessment of the ozone convention and other environment treaties would prove prescient.

Yet despite their reservations, the CFC producing nations yielded to environmental group pressures to "do something." In 1985, they settled on the Vienna Convention for the Protection of the Ozone Layer, a vague statement of good intentions containing no binding commitments. The ozone treaty simply required all parties to exchange scientific information and conduct further monitoring and research. But that was just the beginning.

What started as a non-binding convention evolved into a treaty with regulatory teeth. UN agency bureaucrats and their activist allies operating within the UN system made all the difference. They were responsible for establishing follow-up scientific commissions that were authorized to define the problem further, and they scheduled the meetings to require parties to the convention to review its progress. These regular meetings — where environmental groups were granted NGO (nongovernmental organization) status — gave the activists a forum to maintain a constant drumbeat of lobbying activity. The relentless international process created by the ozone treaty allowed environmentalists to wear down all resistance to a global CFC phase-out. A short two years after the signing of the Vienna Convention, the Montreal Protocol was finalized.

A deceptive 1986 report on the ozone issue was responsible for the rush to judgment. Uncertainty prevailed in the scientific community about whether CFCs affected the ozone layer and whether more ultraviolet rays were reaching the ground. But the report's sponsors, UNEP and the World Meteorological Organization, smothered any doubts. These UN agencies claimed to represent international scientific authority. Their "official" judgment was that ozone depletion was imminent, dangerous, and man-made.

The report built momentum for a CFC phase-out and contributed to the sense of crisis that was cultivated at UN meetings. NGOs used the report as if it were a judicial verdict that validated the "hole in the ozone" theory and found CFCs guilty of opening it. The Environmental Defense Fund timed the release of its own study, *Stratospheric Ozone Depletion: The Case for Policy Action,* to coincide with the UNEP report. It too clamored for "action."[24] No one but a polluter could oppose these international measures to "save" the ozone and life on the planet. The UNEP/WMO ozone report was a bold political move and a masterful example of environmentalist theatrics. The environmental lobby had vindicated its own pre-conceived notions about the science of the ozone layer.

The Environmental Defense Fund played a crucial role in framing the issue and negotiating its outcome. Not only did EDF participate in UNEP's scientific and technical forums, but an EDF staff economist served on the official U.S. delegation to the ozone negotiations. This well-connected NGO pushed for a CFC ban from every possible angle. It was a participant in the scientific assessment process, an inside player in the political and diplomatic process, and an outside self-appointed "watchdog" trusted by its news media contacts. Together EDF and the UN were shaping how the public understood the scientific issues, how citizens perceived U.S. government reactions, and how the news media reported the story.

The lobbying campaign was overwhelming. In September 1986, the Alliance for Responsible CFC Policy, a U.S. coalition of 500 corporate CFC producers and users, endorsed international CFC controls. The group had opposed the international regulation of CFCs at first, but then it capitulated. Arguably, the "pro-business" Alliance was as responsible for the Montreal Protocol as the most extreme environmental NGO.

Why did U.S. industry take this action? The truth is that this was not simply a loss of nerve or a suicidal act. The Alliance reviewed the alignment of political forces and calculated that a treaty could advance its own interests. It reasoned that European corporations would have an advantage if the U.S. government alone succumbed to strong environmental group pressures to regulate CFCs. But an international ozone treaty would force European companies to work under the same restrictions as American companies.[25] American CFC manufacturers decided it was preferable to suppress European CFC companies than defend their own economic freedoms. In this instance, the fate of an international treaty depended on the willingness of private industry to bargain for comparative advantage rather than resist coercive demands.

The environmental establishment was delighted. Its far-reaching amendment to the Vienna Convention had established a powerful new regulatory tool. The Montreal Protocol cut production and use of CFCs by industrial countries in half. It froze production of halons, which are fire-extinguishing chemicals. And it banned trade in CFCs – as well as products made with CFCs — with all countries that had not signed the treaty.

Besides the successful ban, the 1987 ozone treaty also demonstrated for the first time how it was possible to implement internationally what environmentalists call the "precautionary principle." This is the jargon justifying public policies that lack scientific warrant. The "precautionary principle" holds that environmental regulation should not be delayed because of scientific uncertainty or inconclusive evidence. When dealing with potential hazards, the environmental establishment believes it is better to regulate first, ask questions later.

The negotiators had traipsed from Vienna to Montreal; the procession would move on to London and Copenhagen and back to Vienna. The Montreal Protocol stipulated that the parties would meet in London in 1990 to review the treaty. This meeting mandated the complete phase-out of CFCs and halons in industrial countries by 2000. Developing countries were given ten additional years to comply. Meanwhile, other industrial products were discovered to be injurious to the planet and targeted for extermination. Methyl chloroform and carbon tetrachloride were banned under the ozone treaty.[26]

The 1992 Copenhagen conference revised the ozone treaty yet again. Phase-out dates for CFCs, halons, methyl chloroform, and carbon tetrachloride were accelerated in response to technical advice from UN-coordinated expert panels. The CFC ban was moved from 2000 to 1996. Most hydrofluorocarbons (HFCs), which are chemical substitutes for CFCs, were slated for elimination by 2020. And emissions of a widely used pesticide called methyl bromide were frozen at 1991 levels. A 1995 conference in Vienna imposed a phase-out of methyl bromide in industrial countries by 2010.

The Montreal Protocol has been so successful that it replaced the Vienna Convention as the term commonly used to identify the ozone treaty. Environmental groups regard it as a model for the process of:

- developing an agenda of policy issues.
- securing the involvement of government officials and unofficial participants from nongovernment agencies.
- formalizing a regulatory instrument that wields power over countries that don't sign the treaty as well as those that do.

The Montreal strategy used UN-coordinated panels that relied less on uncertain scientific data than on the collaboration of environmental NGOs and UN functionaries. "A handful of tireless individuals," applauds the Worldwatch Institute, "confronted the ozone challenge with the fervor of crusaders."[27]

Can Montreal's success be replicated for global warming?

Global Regulation for a Global Climate

As the ozone hole receded from public consciousness, environmental pressure groups began to lobby governments for an international convention to prevent global warming. Their efforts bore fruit in 1988. A Canada-sponsored "World Conference on the Changing Atmosphere" convened in Toronto to reduce the industrial output of carbon dioxide, a "greenhouse gas."

Conference participants discussed as short-term target reducing carbon emissions by 20 percent by the year 2005. They also considered a number of innovative and comprehensive policy ideas. Some suggested global taxes on the use of coal, oil and natural gas to finance the creation of a global atmosphere fund.[28] Others conceived of a "Law of the Atmosphere," an umbrella-style legal regime similar to the failed Law of the Sea treaty. But the principal players in the environmental establishment decided this was too complicated and unwieldy. They opted instead for an approach like the Montreal Protocol. Its very deliberative and numbingly methodical process might strike some as less ambitious than the other ideas that were floated. But it was just this quality that made the Montreal model successful.[29]

If they were ever to bind countries to an international treaty, the environmental lobby knew they needed to put in place a foundation of procedures and focus proposals. First, they had to create a vague and open-ended framework treaty. In 1990, the UN established the aptly-named Intergovernmental Negotiating Committee for a Framework Convention on Climate Change (INC/FCCC). Administered by UNEP and the World Meteorological Organization, the same groups that nurtured the ozone treaty to fruition, the INC held a series of meetings to develop a treaty in time for the June 1992 Rio Earth Summit. Rio would make global warming an issue of international importance.

The Framework Convention on Climate Change was signed by the representatives of more than 150 governments. But the real policymakers were the UN functionaries who worked on the draft text with environmental NGO activists over the course of two years of "pre-negotiations." The wording of the document is innocuous enough. All countries are exhorted to reduce their carbon dioxide emissions to 1990 levels by the year 2000. Parties to the convention are obliged only to submit national reports to the convention Secretariat.

At the Earth Summit this language was further watered down. Indeed, the final climate treaty was so vague and non-binding that the Bush administration was denounced for sabotaging earlier versions. The final treaty instrument contained no mention of the activists" priority goal — binding "targets and timetables" for reduced emissions of carbon dioxide.

In public the environmental lobby would cry, "Sell-out!" But privately it understood the importance of the process all too well. The Framework Convention lived up to its name: it set the framework, the first stage of the Montreal Protocol model. Without prescribing binding mandates, the Convention set a timetable for subsequent regular meetings at which its interim commitments could be further interpreted and elaborated. Pressure politics thrives in this setting. These meetings are called "Conferences of the Parties," and each one gives environmental lobbyists a chance to add something onto an earlier proposal and to build new expectations. At every meeting NGOs can either a) declare a small victory for the planet or b) attack national governments for failing to save the planet. In any event, the framework convention process sets the stage for progressively manipulating "soft law" treaty promises into binding "hard law" international obligations.

The climate treaty that was signed in Rio was weaker than what environmentalists would have preferred. But they always intended to add tougher and more binding commitments at follow-up international conferences and in later UN pronouncements. Jessica Tuchman Mathews, then vice president of the World Resources Institute, astutely observed in 1992,

"[The climate convention] is going to start a process that isn't going to be walked backwards."[30]

How the Climate Treaty Was Shaped

The Bush administration signed the Rio treaty but never took it seriously. That changed in 1993. Early in his first year in office, President Bill Clinton declared, "I reaffirm my personal, and announce our nation's commitment to reducing our emissions of greenhouse gases to their 1990 levels by the year 2000." In October 1993, the Administration completed "The Climate Change Action Plan," a comprehensive strategy of federal government policies and voluntary actions by industry to achieve climate treaty objectives. These actions included energy efficiency measures, research into alternative technologies based on "renewable energy" (i.e. solar power), and promotion of nationwide tree planting to absorb atmospheric carbon dioxide.[31]

Many environmental activists were pleased with the Administration commitment, but unimpressed by its mostly voluntary emphasis. And when its BTU tax proposal and national health care plans failed, the Administration's focus on environment policy seemed to slacken. The Natural Resources Defense Council issued a report in 1994 predicting that in the year 2000, the Clinton plan would exceed its own 1990 emissions target by five percent.[32] The Climate Action Network estimated that the U.S. would exceed its Rio target by ten percent.[33]

In March 1995, the first Conference of the Parties met in Berlin to extend the requirements of the climate treaty. But there was a lack of consensus and weak U.S. support for further negotiation of a follow-up treaty. The 1994 elections had brought a Republican majority to Congress, and the Clinton administration pulled back from the issue of global warming. Instead of a strengthened treaty, the 1995 conference produced the "Berlin Mandate," a statement that merely declared the Rio convention inadequate and exhorted industrial countries to take action. Even worse, the developing countries took advantage of the listless proceedings to exempt themselves from future emissions targets. Any later binding protocol to the climate treaty would apply only to the industrial powers.

The issue of global warming could easily have lost all focus in Berlin were it not for an extraordinarily persistent environmental establishment which refused to give up. The Berlin Mandate committed governments to meet in Kyoto, Japan in December 1997 to negotiate targets and timetables to reduce carbon emissions. The NGOs would have another chance.

The Berlin Summit also demonstrated how thoroughly the environmental lobby had infiltrated the world of international diplomacy. Roughly 1,000 NGOs attended the Berlin Summit, and from the outset they lobbied hard to expand their rights of access to the proceedings.[34] The *Earth Negotiations Bulletin* aired NGO complaints about their treatment:[35]

> *Environmental NGOs expressed surprise and disappointment that they were not allowed access to the main floor of the Plenary and the [Committee of the Whole]. Several NGO representatives said that this lack of access to delegates had not been the customary practice in meetings of the [Intergovernmental Negotiating Committee], particularly given the contribution of environmental NGOs to the work of the Convention. A group of NGOs plan to appeal to the President and the Executive- Secretary to reconsider this matter.*

Finally an activist from the Climate Action Network, a coalition of 160 global warming pressure groups around the world, was granted speaking time to address the delegates.[36] Environmental NGOs salvaged the stalled Berlin conference by drafting the "Green Paper," a document produced with the cooperation of sympathetic governments.[37] The principles in this paper formed the basis of the Berlin Mandate.

While the conference was in session, the pressure groups also influenced the proceedings by publishing daily newsletters. *Eco*, produced by the Climate Action Network, and *Earth Negotiations Bulletin*, from the Canada-based International Institute for Sustainable Development (IISD), were diary-like journals that made editorial comments on the proceedings, targeted matters that activists cared about, and proposed compromises for deadlocked issues. Bombarding the negotiators with daily tips and admonitions, these and other newsletters provided the rhetoric and ideological tone that gave credence to radical ideas that delegates might not otherwise have considered. They also helped document the status of the issues being discussed, and they reminded delegates that their positions were being monitored.

Despite their name, NGOs are not always "nongovernmental." In fact, environmental pressure groups work hand in glove with governments that appreciate their work. This is apparent in the funding of the NGO newsletters. The Environment Ministries of Germany and the Netherlands contributed an undisclosed amount to the Climate Action Network to publish *Eco*. In her book *Cloak of Green*, Canadian journalist Elaine Dewar reveals that the publisher of *Earth Negotiations Bulletin* "is almost entirely dependent on governments for its existence." During the year-long period ending in March 1994, the IISD spent $530,000 to publish *Earth Negotiations Bulletin*. Over half that amount came out of the pockets of Canadian taxpayers. All told, the IISD received $23 million in taxpayer dollars over a five year period; in some years it had no other source of revenue. Moreover, it did not hurt IISD that its board of directors included Maurice Strong.[39]

Clearly, international environmental groups do not represent grassroots citizens. They are well-connected and well-compensated advocates for increasing the regulatory powers of government bureaucracies. Global warming lobbyists shower delegates with constant written and personal attention, and this usually has its intended effect in international treaty negotiations. Delegates begin to think that radical proposals have strong public support. *Eco* explains, "NGOs contribute to the success of these regimes at every level by developing the science, informing the public, marshaling political support, prodding recalcitrant negotiators, and providing front line troops to implement and monitor these regimes."[40]

The Berlin Summit was also important because it encouraged NGOs to rethink the identity of a non-governmental organization. According to *Eco*, "NGOs have turned out in record numbers, from mayors and other local officials to church and youth action groups to various shades of business and industry."[41] In other words, environmental pressure groups can increase their numbers and influence once they understand that any group of persons or organizations can be a potential recruit to their cause.

Kyoto Countdown

To prepare for Kyoto, NGOs cemented their relationships with national and international environmental agencies. Of particular importance was the UN Intergovernmental Panel on Climate Change (IPCC). This UN scientific panel was funded and controlled by environmental agencies, and they were not afraid to use their power. In early 1996, the IPCC published a report on climate change. When the scientists who were the actual authors of the report failed to link variations in climate temperature to human activity, the lead author, who favored the global warming hypothesis, simply re-wrote the parts with which he disagreed. Frederick Seitz, the former president of the National Academy of Sciences, called the incident the most "disturbing corruption of the peer review process" he had ever witnessed. He warned that the effect of the re-write was "to deceive policy makers and the public into believing that the scientific evidence shows human activities are causing global warming."[42]

The IPCC played its role well. "Almost without notice," commented Jessica Mathews, "governments created an institution [IPCC] that practically forces them to follow the science and to change their views as it changes."[43] The re-written report approved a politically distorted interpretation of science that benefitted the UN's global regulatory aspirations and that could be used to steer the Kyoto climate treaty negotiations.

The IPCC final report asserted that human activities have a "discernible" influence on climate. The environmental pressure groups used the lead author's editorial revision to distort the report's meaning. Now they announced that science had "proved" the need for drastic energy policy changes, and they smeared as dishonest industry shills any climate scientist who disagreed with an official UN finding. "The IPCC report serves a clear warning: Humans have begun to influence earth's climate and the outcome could be disastrous for many people and natural places," said EDF's Michael Oppenheimer.[44]

Patience and determination were paying off for the global warming lobby. In 1996 the planets of international policy and domestic U.S. politics came into alignment. As the UN report was being drafted, the Clinton administration was searching for issues that could be advanced without congressional interference and that would help mobilize the Democratic Party's base of environmental supporters. Global warming lobbyists were energized by the knowledge that the Administration would go to Kyoto if it was re-elected. A tightly coordinated coalition of activists began preparing a multi-million dollar two-year lobbying campaign on global warming.

Under the aegis of the Climate Action Network, pressure groups like EDF, Natural Resources Defense Council, Sierra Club and Environmental Information Center sprang into action. They scheduled a series of "town meetings" in Austin, Boston, Miami, San Diego, San Francisco, and Seattle.[45] The meetings featured Clinton administration scientists and environmental officials, and their purpose was to generate scare stories in the media about how global warming would devastate local economies and the lifestyles of area residents. This gave rise to the many absurd and frightening stories about how global warming would destroy local tourism, fishing, skiing, real estate and forestry.[46]

As the public campaign for Kyoto was underway, environmental groups privately offered the Administration their advice. On September 15, 1997, President Clinton, Vice President Gore, and Interior Secretary Bruce Babbitt met with leaders of fourteen environmental lobby groups to finalize plans for a pre-Kyoto White House conference on global warming.[47] Clinton and Gore would sell the treaty to the press. The environmental lobbyists advised them to take a hard anti-industry line.

> **ENVIRONMENTAL NGOs MEETING WITH CLINTON**
>
> Environmental Defense Fund
> Environmental Information Center
> Green Group
> Izaak Walton League
> League of Conservation Voters
> National Religious Partnership for the Environment
> National Wildlife Federation
> Natural Resources Defense Council
> Physicians for Social Responsibility
> Sierra Club
> Union of Concerned Scientists
> U.S. Public Interest Research Group
> World Resources Institute
> World Wildlife Fund

Carnival in Kyoto (December 1997)

On December 1, 1997 an estimated 10,000 people began gathering in Kyoto, Japan. For the next ten days they would witness or participate in the international negotiations that would lead to the signing of a treaty to reduce the emission of greenhouse gases. The global climate treaty was the culmination of over a decade of effort by members of the international environmental establishment. They now came to Kyoto determined to make certain that the world's politicians endorsed their conclusions. Commented Senator Joseph Lieberman (D-CT): "It is as if a large chunk of the lobbying community from the capital has been transported from Washington to Kyoto for two weeks."[48]

While the world's governments sent delegates to negotiate a serious agreement, the world's non-governmental organizations assembled to stir the pot of activism. Over 3,500 people attended the Kyoto conference as NGO lobbyists, more than double the 1,500 official delegates. About twenty American environmental organizations were represented, and each had pockets deep enough to pay for several participants. But the American activists were easily outnumbered by Greens from Europe and Asia. A Japanese NGO confederation, the Kiko Forum, alone deployed 385 participants.

The global environmental lobby was determined to demonstrate in the most graphic ways possible the significance of the climate change treaty. For instance, activists demanded that conference organizers impose "climate discipline" on the negotiations. This led to the distribution of a notice informing delegates that they would have to tolerate a cooler indoor climate in order to reduce greenhouse gas emissions. Said one flyer, "It will be required that we accept a new lifestyle, including wearing warmer clothes, which enables us to live comfortably in spite of lower temperature in winter."

NGOs convinced the Kyoto International Conference Hall to set the temperature of heating equipment "at no higher than 20 degrees Centigrade [68 degrees F]."[49] However, they failed to take into account the conference hall's inadequate insulation, which lowered temperatures in many parts of the building and forced the ten thousand shivering conference-goers to don coats and scarves. Conference staff distributed 100 shawls to women delegates; they featured the words "Smart Life with Energy Saving."

Outside, the Korean Federation of Environmental Movements arranged attention-getting props. Its members covered trees and shrubbery with signs reading, "Cool the Earth, Save Us," "Please: Gas Masks!" "No Nukes, No Fossil Fuels for Us," "Silent but Angry," and "Reduce GHGs [greenhouse gases] 20%."[50] It didn't occur to the demonstrators that more fossil fuel use meant less use of wood or that global warming could benefit agriculture. Economist Thomas Gale Moore wisecracked, "Don't these bushes know that 95 percent of all plants will grow bigger, faster in a world of enriched CO2?"[51]

In front of the entrance to the conference hall activists placed three ice statues carved into the shape of penguins. The statues were supposed to melt during the day, dramatizing before television cameras the "warming" of the earth's climate. However, Mother Nature would not cooperate and the sculptures remained standing. When a warmer day did arrive, activists held a prayer meeting around the melting penguins and prayed for forgiveness. (Greenpeace's solar-powered coffee maker was just as luckless. Rainy and overcast days thwarted the alternative fuels solar cell panel in the Greenpeace $20,000 "kitchen of tomorrow" display. Those seeking free solar-brewed coffee were turned away when the sun failed to shine for three days.[52])

A massive Tyrannosaurus Rex constructed of junk metal stood at the back door to the conference hall – a symbol of the obsolescent wastefulness of modern society. Yet the conference itself generated three tons of waste paper in its first four days.[53] NGOs covered every table in the conference hall with so many fliers and pamphlets that journalists in the press center complained.

Some green antics were foolish but funny, while others revealed the fanatic's self-righteousness. Most NGO representatives traveled to Kyoto by plane from North America and Europe. But some believed the claim that one plane passenger caused as much global warming as eight persons traveling by train. This led three dozen purists to travel for three weeks on board the "Climate Train" from western Europe across Siberia, then by ferry over the Sea of Japan and on to Kyoto on bicycle.[54] "We felt it important to travel to this conference in a way that has as little impact on the climate as possible," said Richard Scrace, a director of Great Britain's Green Party. Climate Train passengers criticized their Japanese hosts for not establishing bicycle lanes to make their pedaling easier.[55]

While silliness is perhaps inevitable in all large public gatherings, civility was also a casualty of the global warming policy debate. Activists wearing masks of prominent politicians ridiculed the world's leaders; someone defaced a Nuclear Energy Institute display; and about thirty activists stormed an Esso gas station in downtown Kyoto. While chanting protests against Exxon, Esso's corporate parent, they stopped station employees from approaching gas pumps and raised a banner denouncing gasoline.[56] Jeremy Leggett, a Greenpeace activist and solar power advocate, characterized opposition to the climate treaty as "a new form of crime against humanity."[57] A Leggett seminar open to "accredited press and invited NGOs only" was entitled "History of the Fossil Fuel Disinformation Campaign at the Climate Talks."

UN officials and representatives of the American government abetted the activists' sense of self-importance. Members of the U.S. delegation, many of them former environmental activists, had close working relationships with the Greens.[58] Every day, the U.S. delegation briefed NGOs on the state of the negotiations, but they made a point of hosting separate ninety-minute meetings for environmental NGOs and industry NGOs. There were many more environmental NGOs than industry groups.

When Vice President Al Gore arrived in Kyoto on December 8, the eighth day of the conference, he left no doubt where he stood. In a five-minute presentation to a small, handpicked group of U.S. delegates and reporters, Gore publicly instructed American negotiators "to show increased negotiating flexibility" on the treaty, "one with realistic targets and timetables, market mechanisms, and the meaningful participation of key developing countries." "The most vulnerable part of the Earth's environment is the very thin layer of air clinging near the surface of the planet," Gore intoned. "We are altering the relationship between the Earth and the Sun." Changing mankind's behavior would require "humility because the spiritual roots of our crisis are pridefulness." Gore urged his NGO compatriots to be patient. "This is the step-by-step approach we took in Montreal ten years ago to address the problem of ozone depletion. And it is working."[59]

S. Fred Singer, an atmospheric physicist and founder of the Science and Environmental Policy Project, described the spectacle of press coverage surrounding Gore's long-awaited "16,000 miles for five minutes" address. Only fifty handpicked reporters were allowed inside the conference hall, while the rest were dispatched to watch the Vice President on large screen televisions:

> *As Gore's giant image appeared on screen, hordes of reporters crowded around each video projector, taking photographs of the TV, pressing their microphones up to the speakers, and straining to catch every word emanating from this New Age Big Brother.*[60]

At a news conference immediately after Gore's remarks, the environmental NGOs attempted to characterize for reporters the meaning of his cryptic, emotional speech. But their "spin" was mixed. Some lashed Gore with the catcalls normally reserved for political enemies, while other welcomed him as a passionate partisan for the planet.

European Greens were unanimous in denouncing Gore as a traitor and lackey of Big Oil. Greenpeace International said "the speech was strong on rhetoric but basically full of hot air."[61] World Wide Fund for Nature attacked Gore as "unwilling to commit to a meaningful target for reductions in line with the other industrialized nations."[62] Friends of the Earth International reverently read aloud excerpts of Gore's 1992 book, *Earth in the Balance*, and challenged the vice president to re-read the book himself.[63] The group distributed leaflets that depicted Clinton and Gore as wooden dummies sitting on the lap of a wealthy Texas oil man in a cowboy hat. "The White House must now make a choice between protecting people from climate disaster or letting a few big companies make massive profits at our — and our children's — expense."[64]

U. S.-based NGOs were more loyal to their champion. The National Environmental Trust gently nudged Gore, reminding him of his own 1992 remarks criticizing President Bush's trip to the Rio Earth Summit. "[This issue] is about far more than hopping on a plane for a quick photo opportunity ... and then flying back with a meaningless treaty that has no commitments in it." The Union of Concerned Scientists praised Gore for demonstrating the "significant leadership we are looking for."[65] Fred Krupp, director of the Environmental Defense Fund, commented that Gore "has significantly raised the environmental expectations of the conference and provided the key to unlocking the global gridlock which has paralyzed the negotiating process."[66]

The negotiating process had been extraordinarily convoluted, and it was conducted in the jargon bureaucrats often use to avoid questioning. Perhaps this explained the mixed signals that the environmentalists were sending and receiving. The Hoover Institution's Thomas Gale Moore attended the Kyoto conference. The former economic adviser to President Ronald Reagan recalls:

> *We were informed that the modality of evolution was stymied, but that it would be taken up by a contact group; that, for unknown reasons, the European Union wouldn't budge on the bubble; and that the United States supported limited differentiation. The QELROs group debated the number of gases to be covered, and the United States insisted on joint implementation. Note: If you understand the previous two sentences, please go to the next conference in my place.*[67]

The Politics of Green Imperialism

Environmental activists were united in their demands. They insisted that the world's most advanced economies undertake major reductions in the emission of greenhouse gases. The most drastic demand came from a Korean activist group, which carried a sign with the threat: "Delegates, we will make you Rowing Boats Slaves in the Water World if you fail to stop global warming." The Sierra Club called for a 20 percent cut in 1990-level emissions beginning no later than 2005. Other organizations liked the idea of starting with the European Union proposal of a 15 percent reduction by 2010 – and ending with zero emissions.

But here's the rub. If the United States, the European Union and Japan restricted their economies' use of energy, then competitors from less-developed countries would have an advantage in international markets. American labor unions, in particular, feared U.S. industries would have every incentive to relocate their operations to Third World countries not covered by the treaty's mandates.

The Clinton administration, ever-sensitive to domestic political considerations, reacted by asking Third World countries to accept binding emissions reductions on their own economies. It pledged to secure the "meaningful participation" of major Third World economies in emissions reduction. The U.S. Senate, which would have to ratify the Kyoto

Protocol, also took a stand. It passed the Byrd-Hagel resolution in July 1997 by a vote of 95-0. The resolution specified that any climate protocol not damage the U.S. economy and not exempt developing countries from emission reduction requirements. The Administration seemed to concur.

This, however, would be no easy task. Led by China and India, Third World countries adamantly opposed actions that would slow their economic progress to solve what they perceived as the West's environmental problems. Currency devaluation, capital flight, and economic collapse were threatening Thailand, Indonesia and South Korea. Other countries could succumb to the "Asian flu" unless the region's economic problems were addressed.

The Chinese government's position was particularly strong. It rejected any limits on its own emissions, and it opposed any reference in the treaty to voluntary restrictions.[68] All other developing countries supported the Chinese. Third World negotiators even deleted a proposed treaty provision that would have allowed developing countries to undertake emissions cuts at a later date.

Though the Kyoto talks were classified as a negotiation on the environment, delegates were actually hammering out an accord over energy, the life-blood of a global economy. Whether people can heat or cool their homes, cook meals, and drive vehicles to productive jobs depends on the availability and cost of energy. This was well-understood by UN officials, who affirmed, "The key is to put into place effective national policies to influence the behavior of the industry and consumers."[69]

After eleven days of private negotiations, the conference settled on a final treaty. It looked very different from what the Clinton administration had first proposed. The original Administration proposal would have cut carbon emissions to 1990 levels by 2010, a 34 percent reduction from what they otherwise would be in that year. But this position was contingent on getting Third World countries to agree to cut their emissions too. The treaty that was agreed to by 167 countries contained these major provisions:[70]

- Six "greenhouse gases" were targeted for emissions reduction.
- The U.S., Japan, the EU, and other industrialized countries made commitments to cut their aggregate emissions of green house gases by an average of 5 percent below 1990 levels by 2012. The U.S. would curb its emissions by 7 percent below 1990 levels, bringing emissions roughly 40 percent below what they otherwise would be in 2012.
- The Third World would not cut emissions at all.

- A framework would be established to permit the U.S., Canada, Japan, Russia, Australia, and New Zealand to trade emissions credits. This "umbrella" concept allows countries to buy and sell credits to one another in the hope that each will discover particular economies that will help achieve overall emission reduction targets.
- A "Clean Development Mechanism" would be created. It would allow industrial countries to earn emission reduction credits when they gave energy efficient technologies to Third World countries.

Because the treaty did not meet the requirements of the Byrd-Hagel resolution, U.S. Senators Chuck Hagel (R-NE) and Majority Leader Trent Lott (R-MS) declared the Kyoto Protocol "dead on arrival."[71] The Administration conceded that the treaty had failed to garner the meaningful participation of developing countries, and it elected to withhold the treaty from Senate consideration until at least late 1998. At that time the treaty signatories would reconvene in Buenos Aires, Argentina, and it might be possible to secure additional commitments from such countries as China, India, and Brazil.

Will there be an eventual battle royal between the Clinton-Gore administration and the U.S. Senate? Kyoto has set the stage. Even without treaty ratification, it is likely that the Administration will try to implement some of its Kyoto commitments by issuing regulations and executive orders and increasing public spending.

The NGO Strategy: Good Cop, Bad Cop

How much influence did environmental pressure groups have on the final outcome of the climate negotiations? It is hard to overstate their impact. Yet sometimes it is difficult to understand how NGOs apply pressure precisely because they act both as inside players and outside agitators. They can be the friendliest of critics and the harshest of supporters.

The World Wide Fund for Nature (WWF) had proposed that industrial countries cut their emissions by at least five percent below 1990 levels by 2007.[72] The Kyoto treaty comes remarkably close in calling for a five percent cut by 2012. The treaty also supports the position of the developing countries that they should not have to commit themselves to emission reductions. What might have been a potentially destructive rift between the environmental lobby and the Third World has been avoided for the moment. But it remains to be seen whether Third World countries can be cajoled into accepting emissions cuts at the next Conference of the

Parties (COP-4) to be held in Buenos Aires.

It is noteworthy that the success of the global warming lobby did not stop it from condemning the treaty negotiators. For instance, the World Wide Fund for Nature attacked the accord. A WWF statement read: "The treaty will fail to properly reduce the threat of climate change because key players - in particular the U.S. and Japan - have refused to set realistic targets for emission reductions."[73]

Other NGOs criticized the treaty just as harshly. Greenpeace attacked the Kyoto Protocol as "a tragedy and a farce" with too many "loopholes." "This deal provides absolutely no protection from the increasing environmental and economic damage that the burning of coal and oil will continue to unleash on the world." Friends of the Earth International denigrated the accord, too, saying that a five percent emissions reduction is "far below the 15 percent reduction proposed by the European Union."[74] The Sierra Club's Daniel F. Becker managed to say two things at once. He applauded the treaty as cause for celebration because it helped alter lifestyles in the industrialized world. But he also observed that the Kyoto Protocol was "too weak, and the loopholes too large, to protect our families."[75]

Despite public statements of dismay, many environmentalists were privately jubilant. National Environmental Trust (NET) president Philip Clapp proclaimed, "This is more than the environmental community has done on any single issue in 10 years."[76] NET executive vice president Tom Wathen crowed, "We believe the environmental community scored a monumental victory."

Many environmentalists think NET is a front organization preparing for the Gore for President campaign in 2000. Founded in 1994 with $10 million in foundation grants, most notably from the Pew Charitable Trusts, NET used to be called the Environmental Information Center. Clapp, its president, was a top aide to former Sen. Tim Wirth and his political resume includes Environmentalists for Clinton-Gore.[77]

NET executive vice president Tom Wathen prepared a particularly revealing December 11, 1997 memorandum, "Climate Change Victories at Kyoto," for distribution to the organization's supporters. This remarkable document explains the communications strategy NET used to push the global warming agenda into the mass media.

The memo notes that NET coordinated daily conference calls with as many as fifty reporters from national media outlets. It placed opinion-editorials on global warming for Enron Corporation chairman Kenneth Lay in the *Houston Chronicle, Austin American Statesman, Salt Lake City Tribune and Omaha World Herald* and for former British

Environment Minister John Gummer in the *Washington Post, Denver Post, Tampa Tribune, Pittsburgh Post-Gazette, and Milwaukee Journal Sentinel.*[78] NET conducted eight "town meetings" around the country, which generated much television, radio and print coverage. Wathen also claims NET mailings and briefings with editorial boards generated over 100 favorable editorials in major newspapers across the country. He says they helped change the tone of media stories which "no longer presented global warming as just a theory over which reasonable scientists could differ."

Concerned that television news producers were forced to rely on stock footage of parched fields to show the effect of global warming, NET designed special computer animations that television news programs could use. They depicted how global warming would cause the flooding of fifteen American cities. ABC, NBC, CBS, and CNN used this animation, and it also was routed to local stations via satellite.

NET also took credit for temporarily suspending its opponents' television advertising campaign on the Cable News Network (CNN). On October 2, 1997 CNN announced that it would not show television commercials prepared by the Global Climate Information Project (GCIP) that criticized the Clinton administration position on the proposed treaty. GCIP is a coalition of automakers, farmers, steel mills, petroleum refiners, electricity producers and coal mining unions. It argued that treaty proposals unfairly hurt the American economy by raising U.S. energy costs while exempting developing countries from compliance. The industry group's pithy slogan was: "It's not global, and it won't work."

CNN is a division of media conglomerate Time-Warner, Inc. and the creation of Ted Turner, a major donor to environmental groups. CNN explained that the Environmental Information Center (NET's name at the time) had demonstrated to its satisfaction that the commercials were inaccurate and misleading.[79]

This decision provoked an outcry from treaty opponents who suspected Turner's involvement. Senator Chuck Hagel called for a congressional inquiry,[80] and, in a full-page *Wall Street Journal* ad, GCIP warned Time Warner chairman and CEO Gerald Levin against actions that would make it "a party to censorship."[81] Indeed, the decision coincided with Turner's announcement that he would donate $1 billion to the United Nations. (CNN eventually reversed its decision, but the disruption upset the strategy of global warming opponents.)

Of course, one can be somewhat skeptical of a memo that congratulates itself on the genius of its own communications strategy. But the NET memo reveals the energy and cleverness that goes into good public relations. And the memo reveals something more. It makes clear that environmental pressure groups have developed an effective dual strategy of reward and punishment.

NET takes credit for orchestrating a lobbying campaign that it says enabled President Clinton to select "the most ambitious proposal" from a range of options. NET's Wathen claims that the president did so, "in part because of the substantial amount of national and local media, grassroots activity, and polling information on climate change generated by NET and its campaign partners."

But at the same time Wathen describes how NET delivered a letter to the White House "expressing outrage with the weakness of the Clinton-Gore proposal." A NET "rapid response team" funneled inside information on the climate talks from Kyoto back to environmental activists in the U.S., who then sent hundreds of letters to the Vice President making specific demands. Ultimately, NET credits this strategy with breaking a deadlock by getting Gore to intervene and instruct the State Department to toughen its negotiating position. Initially calling for cutting emissions to 1990 levels by 2010, the Administration agreed to a seven percent reduction below 1990 levels by 2012.

Voices for Freedom and Enterprise

At times there were so many environmental NGOs in Kyoto that they seemed to offer the only alternative to government agencies. But NGO status was not solely their preserve. Nonprofit groups supporting free markets also took advantage of UN procedures for accrediting NGOs, and they too went to Kyoto. Competitive Enterprise Institute president Fred Smith was there along with this writer. Other participants included David Rothbard's Committee for a Constructive Tomorrow, Fred Singer's Science and Environmental Policy Project, Henry Lamb's Sovereignty International, and Phyllis Schlafly's Eagle Forum.

These groups took strong stands against the global warming climate treaty. They were not in Kyoto to represent American corporate interests or the American government. Rather, they were convinced that the exploration, production and use of energy represents a boon to mankind, and they argued that proponents of global warming were fearful of technology and hostile to initiative and enterprise. At Kyoto they formed an ad hoc "contrarian" coalition — named "Friends of Humanity" — and they engaged the Greens in intellectual battles and street theater skirmishes.

Sometimes the name of the game was publicity. For instance, Friends of the Earth International gave a "Scorched Earth Award" — a bowl of burnt soil symbolizing global warming — to representatives of American industry. This led the Friends of Humanity coalition to respond with its own

"Scorched Economy Award" – a bowl filled it with yen coins dramatizing the costs of global energy regulation. The pro-energy coalition announced that the prize went to environmental NGOs and it challenged them to focus on real issues.

These gimmicks make many serious people wince. Yet the prominence of NGO activities in Kyoto demonstrates that public relations is now an essential part of public policy. Demonstrations, op-ed essays, the staged press conference and press release, mastery of the graphic arts, and the bumper sticker slogan are as much a part of the policy process today as speeches and memoranda. International environmental policy-making is no longer a private preserve for diplomats. It is an arena of mass telecommunications, world markets and international public opinion. The Greens understand this, and so must supporters of free markets and free inquiry.

The "Scorched Economy Award" forced Friends of the Earth International and the World Wide Fund for Nature to accept a challenge from the Competitive Enterprise Institute and Committee for a Constructive Tomorrow to formally debate the climate treaty. The "Contrarians vs. Greens" debate permitted serious discussion of the scientific, economic, and ethical implications of global energy restriction. And because it was held in conjunction with a UN conference, it forced delegates to recognize other constituencies critical of the global warming thesis.

Many other nonprofit organizations have produced the papers, books and studies that are affecting what is now a genuine global policy debate. The Cato Institute, the Independent Institute, the Heartland Institute, the Heritage Foundation, Citizens for a Sound Economy, the Center for Security Policy, Consumer Alert, Canada's Fraser Institute, the European Science and Environment Forum, and the Advancement of Sound Science Coalition have published materials critical of the global warming thesis. Their work demonstrates that there is a robust opposition to the climate treaty. Because they reject government funding, the pro-freedom contingent cannot begin to match the resources of the global environmental establishment. Yet their views now have a prominent place at the table of international environmental affairs.

An Inventory of Greenhouse NGOs

Besides the National Environmental Trust and other Green groups already mentioned, here are other prominent proponents of global warming.

Ozone Action. This Washington DC-based group unveiled a "Scientists' Statement on Global Climatic Disruption" at a June 1997 press conference. It secured 2,400 signatures, drawing heavily on members of the Ecological Society of America (ESA), an academic group. "In the broad scientific community," Ozone Action informed the ecologists "there is little debate about whether climate change is happening."[82] Inviting them to "raise awareness" about global warming, Ozone Action asserted, "Our immediate goal is to show scientific solidarity on this issue."[83] Notable signatories include George M. Woodwell, a former ESA president; Jane Lubchenco, ecology professor at Oregon State University; and John P. Holdren, Heinz Professor of Environmental Policy at the John F. Kennedy School of Government.

Redefining Progress. This San Francisco-based think tank garnered 2,000 signatories for the "Economists' Statement on Climate Change." Economists Dale Jorgenson (Harvard), William Nordhaus (Yale) and Nobel laureates Kenneth Arrow (Stanford) and Robert Solow (MIT) organized the effort, encouraging their colleagues to take political action on behalf of the planet: "As economists we believe that global climate change carries with it significant environmental, economic, social, and geopolitical risks, and that preventive steps are justified." The steps include carbon taxes and the auction of permits to reduce carbon dioxide emissions.[84]

Physicians for Social Responsibility (PSR). This coalition of physicians and health professionals founded by activist Dr. Helen Caldicott is a veteran organizer of anti-nuclear demonstrations. An affiliate of the International Physicians for the Prevention of Nuclear War (IPPNW), it petitioned the UN General Assembly to resist global warming, which "would have pervasive adverse impacts on human health and result in significant loss of life." It demanded international policies to increase the efficiency of energy production and use, and accelerated "development and transfer of energy-saving and renewable energy technologies worldwide."[85]

Energy Innovations: A Prosperous Path to a Clean Environment was a study sponsored by another coalition of NGOs. The Alliance to Save Energy, the American Council for an Energy-Efficient Economy, the Natural Resources Defense Council, the Tellus Institute and the Union of Concerned Scientists authorized the study, which claims carbon emissions can be cut to ten percent below 1990 levels without severe damage to the U.S. economy. It also says the economic costs of radical cuts in fossil fuel use can be offset by government policies promoting conservation technology (energy efficient heat pumps, appliances and lighting) and domestic renewable resources (wind, biomass and solar energy). *Energy Innovations* was touted in the Climate Action Network newsletter *Eco*, which was distributed to delegates to the August 1997 climate treaty negotiations in Bonn.[86] Using the study's release to blast American industry,

Alden Meyer of the Union of Concerned Scientists announced: "Now the question is whether the Administration will have the political courage to take on the polluting special interests and protect our children's future."[87]

Environmental Defense Fund. EDF has been particularly active in promoting the climate treaty. Author Philip Shabecoff has called EDF climate scientist Michael Oppenheimer "probably the most influential scientist among those working on climate issues for environmental organizations."[88]

EDF collaborated with the Smithsonian Institution's Museum of Natural History on an exhibition, "Global Warming: Understanding the Forecast." Displayed at the Museum on the Mall in Washington, DC, the exhibition also features an on-line, interactive version for the Internet whose computer simulations and video displays on how energy use overheats the planet predict dire consequences. Donors to the EDF-Smithsonian exhibit included the National Aeronautics and Space Administration, EPA, the National Science Foundation, the Teresa and H. John Heinz III Foundation, the John D. and Catherine T. MacArthur Foundation, the Geraldine R. Dodge Foundation and the W. Alton Jones Foundation. Corporate supporters include Turner Broadcasting System, Enron Corp., and Lehman Brothers.[89]

Climate Action Network. The 160 groups that comprise the global Network made it a powerful lobbying force. Not only did the Network produce the *Eco* newsletter, which proved so valuable to conference delegates, but with 117 registered U.S. participants (see box), it was the major American NGO presence in Kyoto.

Major Environmental NGOs Registered as Official Participants in the Kyoto Climate Negotiations (number of registered participants)	
Center for International Environmental Law	4
Climate Action Network	117
[includes National Environment Trust, IUCN, Sierra Club]	
Environmental Defense Fund	12
Friends of the Earth International	37
Greenpeace International	45
International Center for Local Environmental Initiatives	112
Nature Conservancy	7
Natural Resources Defense Council	6
Redefining Progress	1
Ozone Action	3
Union of Concerned Scientists	4
World Resources Institute	11
World Wide Fund for Nature	36
Source: *UN Framework Convention on Climate Change Secretariat*	

"Business NGOs"

In its quest to secure a binding climate treaty, the Clinton Administration has cultivated the business community. Knowing that industry firmly opposed the 1992 Rio climate convention, the White House has pursued a divide-and-conquer strategy. According to Alden Meyer of the Union of Concerned Scientists, "the Administration has to have some major industry groups behind it to have a chance of building the 67 votes they'll need to ratify a treaty in the Senate."[90] These are the most important business coalitions in or around the global warming camp.

International Climate Change Partnership. The ICCP plays a critical role in U.S. policymaking. A coalition composed of prominent chemical companies, trade associations, and industrial giants, it takes a "moderate" position on global warming. Prominent members include Dow Chemical Co., 3M, General Electric, AT&T, Boeing, United Technologies, and DuPont. The coalition, which had twenty lobbyists registered in Kyoto, does not attack the Clinton administration's stated positions on global warming.[91] Its announced core beliefs are that "climate change is an important global environmental issue that requires participation of all nations," and that global warming is "most effectively addressed at the global level."[92] The ICCP is directed by industry lobbyist Kevin J. Fay. Fay previously represented CFC producers in the Alliance for Responsible CFC Policy during the ozone treaty negotiations. His tactics helped ease the way for the phase-out of his clients' products under the Montreal Protocol.

The ICCP lobbies Clinton administration officials, members of Congress, as well as foreign countries. ICCP staff has represented the coalition's views at all major meetings of the Framework Convention on Climate Change. According to the ICCP, "Attendance at these meetings provided the ICCP staff and membership with personal contact to U.S. delegation members and delegates from other nations, an understanding of the issues as they were being negotiated, and an opportunity to influence the position of the United States as well as the outcome of the international negotiations."[93]

British Petroleum, the world's third largest oil company, is a prominent member of the ICCP, which has formally embraced the theory that global warming is human-induced. BP entered into a partnership with the Environmental Defense Fund to test approaches to carbon emission reductions and to develop alternative fuels such as solar power.[94]

Members of the ICCP resign themselves to the eventuality of global regulation. They hope to influence treaty provisions to protect their economic position and shift burdens to competitors. A Clinton administration proposal to give U.S. multinational companies credits for curbing greenhouse gas emissions in other countries is one of their particular interests. In June 1997 the group organized an International Conference on Climate Change and Technologies Exhibition to demonstrate how business interests could benefit from a climate treaty. The conference was co-sponsored by the EPA and the Departments of State, Commerce and Energy.

The Business Council for Sustainable Energy (BCSE). The most obvious business beneficiaries of global warming mandates are solar energy and wind power providers that can claim to offer an alternative to carbon-based fuel. They stand to reap billions of dollars in renewable energy subsidies from the federal government. Some natural gas producers also support the climate treaty because they think they can gain a competitive advantage at the expense of coal and oil producers, whose products are more carbon-intensive. The BCSE includes the American Gas Association, American Standard Companies, American Wind Energy Association, Enron Corporation, Honeywell, and the Solar Energy Industries Association. The Council is an active participant in the climate treaty talks. Its environmental advisory committee includes the American Council for an Energy Efficient Economy, Environment and Energy Study Institute, Environmental Defense Fund, Natural Resources Defense Council, Union of Concerned Scientists, World Resources Institute, and the Worldwatch Institute. The BCSE had 27 lobbyists registered in Kyoto.

Environmental NGOs have welcomed statements of concern over global warming by the insurance industry. Greenpeace favorably cites remarks by Franklin Nutter, President of the Reinsurance Association of America: "The insurance business is first in line to be affected by climate change. . . it could bankrupt the industry."[95] The phrase "first in line" also may refer indirectly to a possible government bailout. Certainly if the insurance industry's massive financial losses from recent weather-related disasters can be blamed on global warming, then insurers may see the benefit of global cost-sharing remedies. That could be a preferable alternative to the unpleasant option of raising insurance premiums or reducing market exposure in flood zones and coastal real estate areas.

The President's Council on Sustainable Development (PCSD). This group of government officials, industry representatives, and environmental groups was formed after Rio to advise the President about global warming and other issues that could claim a "sustainable development" pedigree. Environmental NGOs on the PCSD include the usual suspects: Environmental Defense Fund, National Wildlife Federation, Natural Resources Defense Council, The Nature Conservancy, Sierra Club, and the World Resources Institute. Corporate representatives include executives from Dow Chemical, Chevron, Enron, Pacific Gas and Electric, and General Motors. The President's Council is not "non-governmental." It includes EPA administrator Carol Browner, Interior Secretary Bruce Babbitt and Agriculture Secretary Dan Glickman.

The first set of recommendations from the PCSD was presented in February 1996. It said nothing specific about the climate treaty, but observed: "If the risks of warming are judged to be too great, then nothing less than a drastic reduction in the burning of coal, oil, and natural gas would be necessary."[96] The PCSD is based on the suspect "stakeholder" concept of representation: the public's representatives do not speak for individual citizens but rely on the assent of groups from a spectrum of special interests demanding a place at the table.

Quasi-official advisory groups like the PCSD are forums that let government agencies and nonprofits debate issues. More importantly, they let Administration officials decide which groups are on their side. The results can be mutually advantageous. EPA, for instance, gives millions of dollars in federal grants to NGOs to advocate the goverment's global warming policies. Whether or not the advocacy persuades others, one thing is certain: the grants win the support of the NGOs for the government's positions.

EPA grant-making reveals the symbiotic relationship between government bureaucrats and NGOs, each of which benefits from environmental policy advocacy. Legions of environmental pressure groups, business lobbyists and tax-exempt research institutes have been put on the global environment dole. In return for Washington's largesse, this vast special interest constituency lobbies government to give itself stronger regulatory powers. This is the illogic by which NGOs consider themselves "non-governmental."

APPENDIX
RECENT SELECTED EPA GRANTS TO NON-PROFIT ORGANIZATIONS

Alliance for Responsible Atmospheric Policy
$103,000*
12/30/98**
Facilitate effective global communication regarding climate change initiatives

American Council for an Energy Efficient Economy
$70,000*
5/18/98**
Assess Climate Wise program for reducing industrial greenhouse gas emissions

American Council for an Energy Efficient Economy
$333,726*
9/30/95**
Promote reduced greenhouse gas emissions in China

American Council for an Energy Efficient Economy
$50,000*
10/31/98**
Disseminate information on energy efficient technologies to industry, government and NGOs

Brookings Institution
$495,367*
9/17/98**
Assess international trade impacts of global warming policies

Center for Clean Air Policy
$250,000*
9/22/98**
Study implementation and management of domestic greenhouse gas emissions trading system

Center for Clean Air Policy
$414,064*
2/13/97**
Provide opportunities for international negotiators and U.S. and foreign officials to "exchange ideas" on Joint Implementation of greenhouse gas reduction projects

Center for International Environmental Law
$80,000*
9/30/97**
Analyze natural resource sector environmental issues with international implications

Climate Institute
$251,336*
8/31/99**
Assist countries in creating action plans to implement an energy management program

Climate Institute
$690,458*
9/19/97**
Green Buildings Initiative to reduce "global warming gases" in municipal buildings

Climate Institute
$469,199*
9/30/99**
"Promote awareness of climate change and air pollution resulting from fossil fuel use"

Climate Institute
$258,000*
4/30/97
Educate "millions of Americans" about global warming

Community Nutrition Institute
$20,000*
9/30/99**
Maintain a dialogue between environmental organizations and industry on trade and environmental issues

Global Environment and Trade Study (GETS)
$105,000*
12/31/96**
Analyze key issues underlying trade and environment debate

International Institute for Energy Conservation
$490,000*
9/1/99**
Assist countries in developing national climate change action plans

Local Environmental Initiatives-USA
$1,383,524*
9/30/99**
"Municipal collaboration" to champion the climate change issue

Local Environmental Initiatives-USA
$104,553
9/30/99
"Local Agenda 21-USA" to promote sustainable development planning at the local level

Natural Resources Defense Council
$729,251*
8/31/98**
Encourage the purchase of energy efficient equipment

*Amount   **Project End Date

continued on next page

contintued from page 59

Natural Resources Defense Council
$113,419*
9/30/98**
Develop regional energy-efficiency code for Russia

The Nature Conservancy
$569,022*
9/30/99**
Develop sustainable development and ecosystem strategies

The Nature Conservancy
$101,246*
9/30/98**
Assess ecological threats to tropical reefs in the Bahamas

The Nature Conservancy
$150,000*
9/30/96**
Study "spatial biodiversity data" for use in environmental planning

The Nature Conservancy
$569,022*
9/30/99**
Develop sustainable development and ecosystem strategies

Pacific Institute for Studies in Development, Environment, and Security
$190,000*
6/30/99**
"Getting the World Out: dissemination of objective information regarding climate change issues through the publication of Global Change magazine"

Resources for the Future
$437,597*
9/30/98**
Research the vulnerability of low income households to the hydrologic effects of climate change

Resources for the Future
$75,000*
6/30/00**
Theoretical and empirical economic research on global warming policies

Resources for the Future
$774,103*
9/14/01**
Climate change economics and policy research

Resources for the Future
$80,000*
9/30/00**
Research technological innovation and reduction in carbon emissions

Resources for the Future
$195,000*
9/30/98**
Assess and propose improvements to international environmental management practices

World Resources Institute
$70,000*
9/30/99**
Examine competitive impact of environmental regulations for business and environmental regulators

World Resources Institute
$20,000
9/30/99
Environmental Governance Initiative to disseminate information on Local Environmental Action Programs to Eastern Europe

World Resources Institute
$1,410,485*
9/30/99**
Environmental statistics and indicators

World Resources Institute
$150,000*
1/31/00**
Assess public health consequences of fossil fuel combustion, show that global warming policy actions can have beneficial effects

World Resources Institute
$389,409*
11/30/98**
Build business support for climate treaty

World Wildlife Fund
$1,130,540*
9/30/96**
Assessment of global marine contamination

World Wildlife Fund
$39,850*
7/14/97**
Train educators "by using biodiversity as an organizing theme"

World Wildlife Fund
$90,000*
5/31/99**
Facilitate participation by NGOs in international chemicals policy-making

TOTAL $12,283,149

Source: *EPA Grants Information and Control System*

*Amount   **Project End Date

NOTES

1. Douglas Colligan, "Brace Yourself for Another Ice Age," *Science Digest*, February 1973.
2. John N. Maclean, "Scientists Predict Catastrophes on Growing Global Heat Wave," *Chicago Tribune*, June 11, 1986.
3. Linda Werfelman, "Study: Adjusting to Global Warming Will Cost Billions," *United Press International*, July 19, 1986.
4. Stanley N. Wellborn "The Skeptics Retreat: Earth's Temperature is Indeed Rising — and With it the Sea; Facing Life in a Greenhouse," *U.S. News & World Report,* September 29, 1986.
5. Timothy Aeppel, "Greenhouse Effect; Group Uses Computer Models to Forecast Global Climate," *Christian Science Monitor*, April 13, 1987.
6. Essma ben Hamida, "Environment: The Hamburger Eating into the Last Forest," *Inter Press Service*, February 26, 1988.
7. Comments by Dan Becker, Sierra Club, in "The Great Global Warming Debate," Pace Energy Project, Pace University School of Law, "Global Warming Central" web site, http://www.law.pace.edu/env/energy/globalwarming.html.
8. Dr. Janine Bloomfield and Sherry Showell, "Global Warming: Our Nation's Capital at Risk," Environmental Defense Fund, May 1997, http://www.edf.org/pubs/Reports/WashingtonGW.
9. http://www.nrdc.org/bkgrd/gwcons.html
10. Dr. Janine Bloomfield and Sherry Showell, "Global Warming: Our Nation's Capital at Risk," Environmental Defense Fund, May 1997, http://www.edf.org/pubs/Reports/WashingtonGW.
11. http://www.eic.org/globimpact.html. The Environmental Information Center has changed its name to National Environment Trust.
12. http://www.nrdc.org/bkgrd/gwcons.html
13. Report on WWF web site, http://www.panda.org/climate/parks/pi_na_final.htm.
14. Christopher Flavin, *State of the World 1990* (New York: W.W. Norton & Co., 1990), p. 20.
15. Frances B. Smith, *The Global Warming Treaty: For U.S. Consumers — All Pain, No Gain,* (Dallas: National Center for Policy Analysis, Brief Analysis No. 238, August 20, 1997).
16. "The Climate Time Bomb," Greenpeace International Climate Campaign, http://www.greenpeace.org/~climate/
17. "What would it take to stop climate change," Ozone Action web site,

http://www.essential.org/orgs/Ozone_Action/stopcc.html.

[18] Ibid.

[19] Mary H. Novak, WEFA Inc., "Global Climate Change, U.S. Living Standards, and Environmental Quality: The Impact on Consumers" *Climate Change Policy, Economic Growth, and Environmental Quality,* symposium of the American Council for Capital Formation, September 24, 1997.

[20] Richard Schmalensee, Massachusetts Institute of Technology, speech to American Council on Capital Formation Program on Climate Change Policy, Risk Prioritization, and U. S. Economic Growth. Washington, D.C., Sept. 11, 1996.

[21] Gareth Porter and Janet Welsh Brown, *Global Environmental Politics,* (Boulder, CO: Westview Press, 1996) p.72.

[22] Richard Elliot Benedick, *Ozone Diplomacy,* (Cambridge, MA: Harvard University Press, 1991) p. 42.

[23] Benedick, p. 46.

[24] Environmental Defense Fund, "Time for Action to Protect Ozone," *EDF Letter,* Vol. XVII, No. 4, October 1986.

[25] Benedick, pp. 31-32.

[26] Edward A. Parson and Owen Greene, "The Complex Chemistry of the International Ozone Agreements," *Environment,* March 1995, pp. 19-20.

[27] Hilary F. French, *State of the World 1997,* (New York: W.W. Norton & Co.,1997), p. 171.

[28] Porter and Brown, p. 94.

[29] Peter H. Sand, "Innovations in International Environmental Governance," *Environment,* November 1990, p. 19.

[30] "Weekend Edition," National Public Radio, May 30, 1992.

[31] President William J. Clinton, Vice President Albert Gore, Jr., *The Climate Change Action Plan,* October 1993.

[32] Daniel Lashof, *The Gap: Climate Plan Faces Major Shortfall,* (Washington, DC: Natural Resources Defense Council, April 19, 1994).

[33] Climate Action Network, "Independent NGO Evaluations of National Plans for Climate Change Mitigation: OECD Countries," Third Review, January 1995.

[34] *Earth Negotiations Bulletin,* Vol. 12, No. 12, (Winnipeg: International Institute for Sustainable Development, March 28, 1995).

[35] *Earth Negotiations Bulletin,* Vol. 12, No. 13, (March 29, 1995).

[36] *Earth Negotiations Bulletin,* Vol. 12, No. 15, (March 30, 1995).

[37] *Earth Negotiations Bulletin,* Vol. 12, No. 21, (April 10, 1995).

[38] *Eco* has been funded by the Environment Ministries of Germany and the Netherlands.

[39] Elaine Dewar, *Cloak of Green: Business, Government and the Environmental Movement,* (Toronto: James Lorimer & Co., 1995) pp. 387-394.

[40] *Eco* NGO Newsletter, Bonn, Climate Action Network, March 4, 1997.

[41] *Eco* NGO Newsletter, Berlin, Climate Action Network, April 7, 1995.

[42] Frederick Seitz, "A Major Deception on 'Global Warming,'" *Wall Street Journal,* June 12, 1996.

[43] Jessica Mathews, "Forging Consensus on Climate Change," *Washington Post,* July 8, 1996.

[44] "EDF Lauds IPCC Report," Environmental Defense Fund news release, December 15, 1995.

[45] Peter H. Stone, "The Heat's On," *National Journal,* July 26, 1997.

[46] "Climate Change Town Meeting in CA Ponders Local Risks," *Greenwire,* October 15, 1996.

[47] "Clinton Meets with Environmentalists in Advance of White House Conference," Bureau of National Affairs, *BNA Daily Environmental Report,* September 16, 1997.

[48] John H. Cushman, Jr., "Intense Lobbying Against Global Warming Treaty," *New York Times,* December 7, 1997.

[49] Flyer from the Energy Conservation Center, Japan, distributed to all Kyoto conference participants.

[50] S. Fred Singer, "The Week That Was," December 7-13, 1997, http://www.sepp.org/weekwas/dec7_13.html.

[51] Thomas Gale Moore, Ph.D. "'Smart Life with Energy Saving': WCR Covers Kyoto," *World Climate Report,* Vol. 3 No. 8, January 5, 1998.

[52] S. Fred Singer, "The Week That Was," December 7-13, 1997, http://www.sepp.org/weekwas/dec7_13.html.

[53] Kahori Sakane, "Kyoto Climate Conference Disposes of Tons of Paper," *Daily Yomuiri,* December 6, 1997.

[54] Joseph Coleman, "Global Climate Meeting Attracts Passionate and Powerful With Global Warming," *Associated Press,* December 4, 1997.

[55] Akiko Shiozaki, "Group Makes 3-Week Journey to Bring Message," *Asahi News Service,* December 2, 1997.

[56] "Thirty Conference Participants Stage Protest at Esso Filling Station in Kyoto," *Kyodo News Service,* December 4, 1997; Willis Witter, "Activists Demonstrate at Kyoto Conference," *Washington Times,* December 6, 1997.

[57] Leyla Boulton, "Japan Attacked as Climate Deal Nears," *Financial Times,* December 5, 1997.

[58] One member of the U.S. delegation, the State Department's Rodrigo Prudencio, was a former activist employed by the National Wildlife Federation.

[59] Bonner R. Cohen, "Gore: US Must Show Increased Flexibility in Kyoto," *Earth Times,* December 9, 1997.

[60] S. Fred Singer, "The Week That Was," December 7-13, 1997, http://www.sepp.org/weekwas/dec7_13.html.

[61] Shoichi Nasu, "Critics Divided on Gore Speech," *Daily Yomuiri,* December 9, 1997.

[62] "Gore: US Must Show Increased Flexibility in Kyoto" *Earth Times,* December 9, 1997.

[63] "Friends of the Earth Calls on Gore: Read Your Book Al!" press release, December 8, 1997.

[64] Friends of the Earth, "Greenhouse Effect, Whitehouse Defect."

[65] "Critics Divided on Gore Speech," *Daily Yomuiri,* December 9, 1997.

[66] "Gore: US Must Show Increased Flexibility in Kyoto," *Earth Times,* December 9, 1997.

[67] Thomas Gale Moore, "'Smart Life with Energy Saving': WCR Covers Kyoto," *World Climate Report,* Vol. 3 No. 8, January 5, 1998.

[68] Thomas Gale Moore, "The Yellow Brick Road from Kyoto," *World Climate Report,* Vol. 3 No. 10, February 2, 1998.

[69] Ramesh Jaura, "Global Warming: NGOs Concerned About Fate of Kyoto Treaty" *Inter Press Service,* December 11, 1997.

[70] Bonner R. Cohen, "Battle over Kyoto Protocol Already Under Way," *Earth Times,* December 13, 1997.

[71] Statement by U.S. Senator Chuck Hagel, press release, December 10, 1997.

[72] Shoichi Nasu, "NGOs Blast Latest Gas Cut Proposal," *Daily Yomuiri,* December 9, 1997.

[73] "Non-governmental Organizations Not Satisfied with Protocol," Kyodo News Service, Tokyo, December 11, 1997.

[74] "NGOs Criticize Kyoto Agreement," *Daily Yomuiri,* December 12, 1997.

[75] Jaura, "Global Warming: NGOs Concerned About Fate of Kyoto *Treaty*."

[76] "Intense Lobbying Against Global Warming Treaty," *New York Times*, December 7, 1997.

[77] Mark Boal, "Gore's Greens," *Village Voice*, January 20, 1998.

[78] Memorandum of Tom Wathen, executive vice president, National Environmental Trust, "Climate Change Victories at Kyoto," Washington, DC, December 11, 1997.

[79] David Bauder, "CNN Pulls Ads on Global Warming," *Associated Press*, October 2, 1997.

[80] Ken Foskett, "Treaty Opponents Object as CNN Pulls Global Warming Ads," *Atlanta Journal*, October 4, 1997.

[81] Phil Kloer, "CNN Changes Tune, Will Air Banned Ads," *Atlanta Journal and Constitution*, October 10, 1997, p. 4H; David Bauder, "CNN Reverses Stance on Disputed Ads," *Associated Press*, October 9, 1997.

[82] Ozone Action cover letter, May 14, 1997.

[83] Letter from James H. Brown, Ecological Society of America President, and Mary C. Barber, Acting Executive Director, May 12, 1997.

[84] *Global Change*, Electronic Edition, (Oakland, California: Pacific Institute for Studies in Development, Environment, and Security, February 1997).

[85] International Physicians' Letter on Global Climate Change & Human Health, delivered to Heads of State and Delegates to the United Nations General Assembly, June 23, 1997.

[86] *Eco* (Climate Action Network) August 4, 1997.

[87] Press release, "Groundbreaking Energy Innovations Study Shows Prosperous Path to Global Climate Protection," Washington, DC, June 17, 1997.

[88] Shabecoff, p. 88.

[89] "Global Warming: Understanding the Forecast" on-line exhibit, http://www.envirolink.org/orgs/edf/funders.htm.

[90] Margaret Kriz, "Chilling Out," *National Journal*, May 3, 1997, p. 867.

[91] Kriz, p. 868.

[92] Kevin J. Fay, "Establishment of a Long-Term Focus for Climate Change Policy: the Need for a Realistic Framework," International Climate Change Partnership, June 1996.

[93] International Climate Change Partnership, 1996 Report of Activity and Accomplishments, November 7, 1996.

[94] William K. Stevens, "On Global Warming, Some in Industry Are Now Yielding," *New York Times,* August 5, 1997.

[95] "The Climate Time Bomb," Greenpeace web site, http://www.greenpeace.org/~climate/.

[96] President's Council on Sustainable Development, *Sustainable America: A New Consensus for Prosperity, Opportunity, and a Healthy Environment for the Future,* February 1996, p. 163.

Chapter 3

Trade and Environmentalism

It is almost an article of faith among environmentalists that trade between nations harms the environment. Ecological economist Herman Daly argues that trade accelerates the depletion of natural resources.[1] The earth has ecological limits, and the more the economy expands, the more quickly it will reach those limits. Daly's criticisms of world trade are an application of the "limits to growth" philosophy. Others regard trade as inherently destructive. In *The Myth of Free Trade*, economist Ravi Batra puts this outlook in simple terms: "Since trade pollutes the earth, it is essential that it be kept to the minimum."[2]

Pragmatic Greens do not want to prohibit all trade. They concede that trade is an engine of economic growth and wealth creation, and that it helps pay for environmental amenities. Yet they harbor deep suspicions of commerce, and their natural sympathies are with its critics. They tend to think trade of even the most basic sort accelerates the environmental degradation of the planet. A joint publication of the World Resources Institute and the United Nations complains that when farmers in poor countries produce coffee, cocoa, and bananas for world markets, they benefit at the expense of forests and wetlands.[3] The Worldwatch Institute's Hillary French feels compelled to observe that trade "exacerbates climate change by increasing the energy requirements of goods transported over long distances."[4] In short, the exchange of goods and services across borders may improve lives, but it is probably ecologically irresponsible. "A richer society is not necessarily a better society," concludes Yale University professor and former EPA official Daniel C. Esty.[5]

To promote "sustainable development," the environmental lobby wants what some now call "sustainable trade." Vice President Al Gore advanced this proposition in his 1992 manifesto, *Earth in the Balance*. There he suggested that "weak and ineffectual enforcement of pollution control measures should also be included in the definition of unfair trading practices."[6]

Environmental pressure groups that promote the idea of protecting the environment by regulating trade have made themselves major players in policy and political battles over international trade agreements.[7] However, they cannot be certain that the Clinton administration will always be their ally. And they face opposition from a developing world eager to industrialize. Moreover, the world's trade bureaucracies contain far fewer environmental ideologues than are employed by the EPA or the

United Nations. Still, the environmental lobby has seized the initiative by arguing that the "global environment" is affected by trade and by demanding a role in trade negotiations. Green groups have lobbied tenaciously for limits on the North American Free Trade Agreement (NAFTA) and the World Trade Organization, demonstrating that even in inhospitable territory they can influence policy and the wealth of nations.

Tuna and Trade

The 1987 Brundtland Report first identified the international trading system as a target for environmental group activism. In its statement of principles, the World Commission on Environment and Development announced that, "Long term sustainable growth will require far-reaching changes to produce trade, capital, and technology flows that are more equitable and better synchronized to environmental imperatives."[8] The Commission, headed by Norway's Gro Harlem Brundtland, concluded that the purposes of the General Agreement on Tariffs and Trade (GATT) "should include sustainable development." GATT, the international treaty created in 1948 to liberalize trade policies, would need to "reflect concern with the impacts of trading patterns on the environment;" and this, said the Commission, would require "more effective instruments to integrate environment and development concerns into international trading arrangements."[9]

These warnings would grow more insistent, but in the late 1980s most environmental groups focused on other priorities. That changed in 1991 when a GATT tribunal unintentionally highlighted the issue by ruling against a U.S. trade embargo of Mexican tuna imports. Environmental groups earlier had filed suit to force the Bush administration to move against Mexico for failing to protect dolphins entrapped by the tuna nets of Mexican fishing vessels.[10] Citing the 1972 Marine Mammal Protection Act, the Earth Island Institute claimed that U.S. trade sanctions should be imposed against Mexico for failing to enact dolphin protection measures. The GATT tribunal, however, found that a U.S. embargo on Mexican tuna violated GATT rules, which prohibited enforcement of a nation's trade regulations outside its own jurisdiction.

The "tuna-dolphin case" infuriated environmental groups, and they spent $50,000 on full-page ads in major newspapers across the country to assail the GATT. Environmental, labor, and liberal farm organizations opposed to unrestricted trade coalesced under the Citizens Trade Campaign, which spent $400,000. The coalition included Ralph Nader's Public Citizen, Friends of the Earth, Greenpeace, National Farmers Union, National Family Farm Coalition, the International Union of Electricians, the Amalgamated Clothing and Textile Workers Union and the International Ladies Garment Workers Union. Public Citizen plastered Washington, D.C. sidewalks with posters of "GATTzilla," a Godzilla-like monster with the earth in its jaws, crushing a dolphin in one hand, pouring out a barrel of DDT with the other, and kicking over the U.S. Capitol building. "GATT is Coming," the signs warned, "What You Don't Know Will Hurt You."

The unexpected furor guaranteed that the environmental lobby would become a force in American trade policy debates. Environmental pressure groups began trying to affect other U.S. trade policies. The National Wildlife Federation (NWF) held briefings urging Congress to tie environmental issues to its re-authorization of "fast-track" legislation, the renewal of presidential authority to expedite the implementation of trade agreements. Under fast-track authority, Congress cannot amend treaties the president has signed and the requirement for treaty ratification is lowered from a two-thirds Senate supermajority to a simple majority of both houses of Congress. NWF convinced legislators like House Majority Leader Richard Gephardt (D-MO), Ways and Means Committee Chairman Dan Rostenkowski (D-IL), and Senate Finance Committee Chairman Lloyd Bentsen (D-TX) that Congress should give President Bush "fast track" authority only on condition that he create a presidential action plan on environmental issues and appoint environmentalists to important trade advisory committees."[11]

Environmental groups also lobbied delegates to put restrictions on the GATT at the 1992 Earth Summit in Rio. *Agenda 21*, the Summit's ecological planning convention, called on governments to "[p]romote sustainable development through trade liberalization" and to make "trade and environment mutually supportive."[12] It specifically supported trade sanctions "to enhance the effectiveness of environmental regulations."[13] Similarly, the Rio Declaration's Principle 12 called for linking trade to environment in "a supportive and open international economic system."[14]

Green groups, however, discovered that developing countries at the Rio conference were distrustful of their ideas. India and South Korea, in particular, worried that developed countries would cite environmental failings to justify protectionist trade barriers against their exports. The Indian and Korean delegations insisted that Principle 12 contain a statement that unilateral sanctions — like the U.S. tuna embargo — "should be avoided."[15]

The American delegation caved in on the language of Principle 12. But EPA officials and others in the U.S. delegation then attached an interpretive statement to Principle 12: it said trade sanctions might be an "effective and appropriate means" to protect the global environment in some circumstances.[16] The U.S. maneuver aroused overseas suspicions of "green protectionism," but it confirmed the influence of environmental NGOs on trade policy.

NAFTA: Linking Trade to Environmentalism

The trade-environment nexus became firmly established during the 1992-93 debate over ratification of the North American Free Trade Agreement (NAFTA). The United States, Canada and Mexico had agreed to form a trade bloc like the European Community. After two years of negotiations and on the eve of the 1992 presidential election, the NAFTA treaty awaited U.S. Senate ratification.

Green groups wanted to change the treaty, and they did their homework. While George Bush and Bill Clinton were campaigning, a group of environment and trade policy experts began meeting to develop a bipartisan environmental agenda for NAFTA and GATT. They wanted to find areas of compromise and agreement so that environmental restrictions could be added to NAFTA. Michael Aho, economic studies director for the Council on Foreign Relations (CFR), and C. Ford Runge, professor of agriculture and applied economics at the University of Minnesota, organized what they called the Study Group on Trade and the Environment. It was funded by grants from CFR, the Cargill Foundation,

THE STUDY GROUP ON TRADE AND THE ENVIRONMENT, COUNCIL ON FOREIGN RELATIONS	
ENVIRONMENTAL GROUPS	GOVERNMENT AGENCIES
Environmental Defense Fund	U.S. Trade Representative
Sierra Club	State Department
World Resources Institute	Department of Commerce
Institute for Agriculture and Trade Policy	Environmental Protection Agency
Natural Resources Defense Council	Agency for International Development
Center for International Environmental Law	Office of Technology Assessment
National Wildlife Federation	World Bank
Environmental and Energy Study Institute	

and the Northwest Area Foundation of Minneapolis and St. Paul. Under CFR auspices the group held eight meetings in New York, Minneapolis, Austin, and Seattle between June 1992 and May 1993. Michael B. Smith, a former GATT ambassador, chaired the meetings, which eventually involved 138 individuals, including participants from the Environmental Defense Fund, National Wildlife Federation, Natural Resources Defense Council, and the Sierra Club. Members of the Bush Administration like Daniel Esty, the chief NAFTA negotiator for the EPA, and Sanford Gaines, of the U.S. Trade Representative's office, also attended the meetings.[17]

At first the environmental activists simply exchanged views with the government bureaucrats. But after the election, they lobbied the new Clinton administration to add environmental restraints to the NAFTA agreement that the Bush administration had already negotiated. Candidate Bill Clinton, who had criticized President Bush for failing to fight for more environmental and labor provisions, was prepared to deliver on his campaign promises.

However, the prospects of success threw confusion into the ranks of the victors. The environmental lobby was divided on NAFTA. Some groups like the National Wildlife Federation and Environmental Defense Fund had no fundamental objections to trade. They were prepared to accept NAFTA now and pursue environmental restrictions later. But anti-trade groups like Public Citizen and the Sierra Club would just as soon see NAFTA defeated. Unless heavy environmental restrictions were added to the treaty, they threatened to work with organized labor to defeat it. With the two strategies in conflict, the Green groups seemed to fall into "good cop-bad cop" roles. One coalition pressured Congress to reject NAFTA, while the other used the threat of opposition as leverage to obtain a seat at the NAFTA negotiating table.

The Clinton Administration walked a fine political line. To hold on to its business supporters, the Clinton-Gore campaign had promised before the election not to scuttle the NAFTA treaty. After the election, Clinton campaign manager Mickey Kantor was appointed as a cabinet-level trade negotiator and put in charge of NAFTA. Kantor sided with the "moderate" environmentalists and opened negotiations with Mexico and Canada to add an environmental side agreement to the accord.[18] An ex-labor rights advocate, Kantor saw green trade rules as a way to protect workers from foreign competition.

Kantor made sure that the Administration's environmentalist supporters received key appointments to the NAFTA negotiating team. Officials from EPA, the Department of Interior, the Food and Drug Administration, and the National Oceanic and Atmospheric

Administration were drawn into the NAFTA negotiations. Daniel Magraw, an EPA associate general counsel for international activities reported that the EPA and FDA co-chaired two of the three teams negotiating standards for the main NAFTA treaty. EPA and the State Department also co-chaired the U.S. negotiating team for NAFTA's environmental side agreements.[19] The greening of NAFTA became a tremendous opportunity to expand EPA's bureaucratic turf.[20]

Environmental groups benefited from the favor of Vice President Al Gore and Undersecretary of State Tim Wirth.[21] Greens were invited to submit their recommendations, participate in public hearings, were appointed to administration advisory posts, and were briefed on the NAFTA negotiations by the office of the U.S. Trade Representative and sometimes by Ambassador Kantor himself. Some even got diplomatic security clearances so they could advise U.S. officials directly during negotiations with Mexico and Canada.[22]

Environmental groups submitted detailed proposals to revise NAFTA so that it addressed their concerns. For instance, how would Mexico revise its economic regulations if they were in conflict with American rules? Stewart J. Hudson and Rodrigo J. Prudencio of the National Wildlife Federation authored one report that urged the NAFTA treaty to force countries to harmonize their environmental standards.[23] Justin Ward of the Natural Resources Defense Council also testified for regulatory harmonization.[24] So did Gary Hufbauer and Jeffrey Schott of the Institute for International Economics, an important Washington, D.C. trade policy think tank.[25]

Kantor publicly acknowledged the input of environmental lobby groups as he testified before a hearing of the Senate Committee on Environment and Public Works chaired by Senator Max Baucus, (D-MT):

> *Our environmental nongovernmental organizations are also another source of help. Just to name a few, on Friday I met with representatives of the Environmental Defense Fund. Along with the Natural Resources Defense Council, they presented some excellent recommendations for crafting an environmental commission. I've also received significant contributions from the National Wildlife Federation and the Sierra Club.*[26]

In his testimony, Kantor revealed that the purpose of NAFTA harmonization was more than environmental protection: it was trade protection. Trade regulations could restrict market access to foreign products under the guise of environmental, health and worker safety concerns. For Kantor, the environmental side agreements were a way to prevent certain kinds of import competition from Mexico:

> *The question for us, I think, in looking at the NAFTA and these supplemental agreements [is]: can we harmonize up standards to lessen [Mexico's] trade advantages as well as to help the environment and worker standards ... in order to ensure the fact that we don't adversely affect U.S. workers and U.S. visitors to the extent they're being affected now?*

The World Wildlife Fund employed trade lawyer Kenneth Berlin, a personal friend of top Clinton administration officials, to help the "good cop" Greens devise strategy for the NAFTA side agreements.[27] Berlin, a partner in the prestigious Washington, D.C. law firm of Winthrop, Stimson, had excellent connections. He was a law partner with Ira Shapiro, the top trade lawyer in the office of U.S. Trade Representative Kantor; he served on the board of directors of Defenders of Wildlife; and he once worked full time on environmental issues for the National Audubon Society.[28] He also participated in the Council on Foreign Relations' Study Group and was intimately familiar with the green trade agenda.[29]

Berlin helped draft the detailed proposal for a NAFTA environmental side accord that a coalition of environmental groups adopted in May 1993. The coalition included the National Wildlife Federation, Defenders of Wildlife, National Audubon Society, World Wildlife Fund, Environmental Defense Fund, the Nature Conservancy, and the Natural Resources Defense Council.[30] The coalition's major proposals called for:

- creation of a North American environmental commission with enforcement powers, including trade sanctions;
- substantial spending on environmental concerns along the U.S.-Mexico border;
- a guarantee that environmental groups would participate in future NAFTA policymaking;
- definition of "production and process methods" so that products like tuna from Mexico would be subject to labor and environmental regulation.

In August 1993, Mexico, Canada, and the U.S. agreed to an environmental accord that was incorporated into NAFTA. A report from the U.S. Trade Representative indicated that the Administration had followed many of the environmental lobby's recommendations.[31] The treaty did establish a Commission on Environmental Cooperation that was authorized to implement NAFTA provisions on the environment, monitor compliance, and promote harmonization of environment regulations among the NAFTA parties. It also created a separate North American Development Bank (NADBANK), NAFTA's version of the World Bank, to finance roughly $8 billion in public works projects and environmental spending in the border region, an area the environmentalists said was particularly degraded by trade.

At a September 1993 press conference, the leaders of six environmental pressure groups – flanked by Vice President Al Gore and EPA administrator Carol Browner – publicly endorsed NAFTA. Jay Hair (National Wildlife Federation), Peter Berle (National Audubon Society), Kathryn Fuller (World Wildlife Fund), Fred Krupp (Environmental Defense Fund), Russell Mittermeier (Conservation International), and John Adams (Natural Resources Defense Council) called on Congress to ratify the treaty and the side agreements.[32] Trade lawyer Berlin's legal analysis of the side agreements concluded that they conformed to the pressure groups' demands. In one case, Berlin found that the accord's "sanctions and penalty provisions are arguably stronger than the penalty provisions proposed [by the environmentalist coalition]."[33]

The "good cop" groups defended NAFTA, whose environment provisions they had helped develop in collaboration with Clinton officials, many of them former colleagues. To a treaty that was supposed to promote free trade, they had managed to add green protectionism, supranational government agencies, and U.S. foreign aid spending. The National Wildlife Federation's Stewart J. Hudson testified before the Senate Foreign Relations Committee:

> *Our decision to support the NAFTA and its environmental agreements is the result of thousands of hours of work, and intense pressure from our members and the Congress to assure that NAFTA would include a strong environmental component. It is part of our overall efforts to promote sustainable development, both globally and at a local, state, and federal level within the United States.*

Peter Berle, president of the National Audubon Society, explained that he supported NAFTA in part because the administration had given him assurances that it would add a migratory bird treaty to NAFTA's environmental accords.[34] Other NAFTA supporters thought the accords set precedents they could exploit elsewhere. As Senator Baucus remarked, "NAFTA sets a new standard for incorporating environmental concerns into other trade agreements."[35] For some this also meant "greening" the GATT.

The "bad cop" environmental groups continued to oppose

NAFTA. They had not participated in the hundreds of meetings at which NAFTA's environmental provisions were drafted. Unmoved by the side agreements, the Sierra Club, Friends of the Earth, and Greenpeace denounced the accord, saying it would only enrich giant corporations at the environment's expense. They joined the emerging animal rights movement, labor unions, and "public interest" groups founded by Ralph Nader to lobby against NAFTA.

The rift in the American environmental movement was serious. Rebuking the pragmatic Greens as corporate collaborators, one anti-NAFTA newspaper advertisement asked "Why are some 'green' groups so quick to sell off the North American environment? Maybe they are too cozy with their corporate funders." Jay D. Hair, then head of NWF, countercharged that anti-NAFTA environmentalists were "putting their protectionist polemics ahead of concern for the environment."[36]

The anti-NAFTA groups were not angered by their exclusion from the hundreds of meetings in which the other Greens took part. They refused to participate because they were hostile to international trade and to all things corporate. Their opposition was ideological, their suspicions visceral and conspiratorial. They refused to trust the Clinton administration's promises. This put them at odds with groups that figured they could restrain multinational corporations by playing trade politics with the Administration.[37]

The anti-NAFTA groups fought for liberal votes in a Democrat-controlled Congress. But they and their labor union allies could not overcome the Administration, which pointed with pride to its support from pro-NAFTA environmental groups and held out military and domestic pork barrel spending for members' districts. The House of Representatives narrowly passed NAFTA 234-200 on November 17, 1993. The Senate followed suit three days later by a larger 61-38 margin.

To Green the GATT

At the end of its first year in office the Clinton administration began negotiating the General Agreement on Tariffs and Trade. This was another exceedingly difficult set of international trade negotiations whose complexity was reduced by politicians and the press to an acronym — GATT. For seven years, negotiators worked to expand the provisions of GATT so that it would cover more world trade in goods and services. GATT was meant to be an interim arrangement when it was founded in 1948. But its supporters never were able to transform it into a genuine world trade bureaucracy. The Uruguay Round Agreements (named after the country where negotiations began) was supposed to replace the GATT with a permanent World Trade Organization (WTO), which together with the International Monetary Fund and the World Bank would manage world trade, monetary and employment matters as parts of a global economic system. This system was begun at a United Nations economic planning conference held in 1947 in Bretton Woods, New Hampshire.[38]

Following NAFTA's ratification, the Clinton administration confronted a December 15, 1993 deadline when its "fast-track" negotiating authority would expire. Clinton's Republican predecessors had tried unsuccessfully to complete the world trade talks. Now the Administration intended to wrap up the marathon negotiations once and for all. The happy results, it claimed, would be a World Trade Organization, a globalized American economy and more American jobs.

Despite their differences, the environmental groups recognized that NAFTA had helped them make inroads in international economic policymaking. "Environmentalists are in the trade arena to stay," declared Jay Hair, president of the National Wildlife Federation. "The environmental dynamic NAFTA set in motion now needs to be extended to the [GATT], rapidly."[39] Friends of the Earth president Brent Blackwelder predicted early on that "unlike NAFTA, I think you'll see a very unified environmental community objecting to GATT."[40] Yet even the most optimistic knew that progress would be difficult. NAFTA involved only three countries; the GATT had 118 member nations.

The Clinton administration began to equivocate. European officials were shaken, when in a March 1993 address in Brussels, Ambassador Mickey Kantor, the President's new trade representative, proposed adding global environmental regulations to the Uruguay Round trade agreement. The Europeans predicted that the commercial parts of the agreement would unravel if developing countries had to accept U.S.-style environmental standards. Kantor backtracked and assured them that the Administration would not demand environmental or labor side agreements until after the agreement was completed.[41]

This led environmental organizations like the National Wildlife Federation, Greenpeace and World Wildlife Fund to announce their opposition to the GATT talks. But at the same time they lobbied the Administration to negotiate treaty revisions they could support.[42] Between NAFTA's November 20, 1993 ratification and GATT's December 15, 1993 negotiating deadline, environmental groups sent Kantor urgent letters detailing their proposed reforms.[43]

- allow countries to set environmental standards higher than GATT-approved standards, without violating GATT;
- authorize environmental groups as NGOs to participate in trade

disputes: let them file amicus-like briefs and add them to GATT dispute settlement panels as expert consultants;
- establish an environmental mandate for the GATT: make preparations for a "Green Round" of global trade negotiations where more elaborate environmental standards could be developed.

Hair's pro-NAFTA National Wildlife Federation sent the first letter. A similar proposal was subsequently submitted jointly by the Natural Resources Defense Council (pro-NAFTA), Friends of the Earth (anti-NAFTA), Defenders of Wildlife (neutral), Center for International Environmental Law (neutral), Environmental Defense Fund (pro), and the Audubon Society (pro). They warned that unless final GATT language was changed, "We believe that virtually the entire environmental community would have to oppose [GATT] actively."[44]

The threats succeeded. Kantor and EPA administrator Carol Browner met with environmental groups in the closing days of the GATT negotiations. Though time was running out — comprehensive revisions stood little chance of adoption — the Greens won an Administration promise to accommodate green protectionism as much as possible in the negotiations' final days.[45]

Green Audacity Yields Results

The belated lobbying produced several victories. According to *The GATT Uruguay Round Agreements: A Report on Environmental Issues,* prepared by the U.S. Trade Representative, the Administration acknowledged the influence of green groups and did press for revisions to the negotiating text.[46] When the negotiations were completed on December 15, 1993, the final treaty text showed many signs of their influence:

- Breaking with the existing GATT, the treaty preamble established "sustainable development" as an objective of the world trade treaty.
- The Clinton administration won new language tightening environmental standards. Under the old GATT, such rules had to be "least trade-restrictive," meaning they had to hinder trade as little as possible. Under a new World Trade Organization (WTO), this no longer pertained.
- The United States won the right to share summaries of trade disputes with NGOs and to provide them with the full text of all U.S. government submissions to the new WTO.
- The Administration also won the right to provide subsidies to private industry if they promoted environmentalist goals.

- A Committee on Trade and the Environment (CTE) was created in the WTO as a forum to consider additional environmental rules.

The Clinton administration had made environmentalism a trade priority. Addressing the European Commission in January 1994, the President proposed a "Green Round" of trade negotiations: "As we bring others into the orbit of global trade...we must ensure that their policies benefit the interests of their workers and our common interest in enhancing environmental protection throughout the globe. That is exactly what we tried to do with the North American Free Trade Association [sic] and, in the coming months, I look forward to continuing discussions on these issues with our EU partners."[47]

Some environmental groups welcomed the World Trade Organization, which they anticipated could become the forum for more environmental regulation of a new system of world trade. The National Wildlife Federation's Jay D. Hair mused openly that in a WTO, unlike the GATT, "distinct issues could evolve without opening the entire contract to renegotiation."[48] Jessica Mathews, then vice president of the World Resources Institute, exulted that "because the WTO is a standing organization, it finally, finally gives us the institutional setting to address the social and environmental issues."[49]

Still, environmental groups were by no means confident that the Clinton administration could increase the authority of international organizations over the world economy. They wanted a total overhaul of world trade rules, and they were realistic enough to conclude that this was more than the Administration could deliver.

There was one other anxiety. Green groups worried that a stronger WTO could be used against them. Other countries might use a world trade bureaucracy to overturn stringent American trade regulations and sanctions for which they had lobbied successfully. The European Union, for instance, had tried unsuccessfully to get GATT to overturn a U.S. fuel-efficiency standard for imported autos. What if the U.S. lost future WTO fights as it had in the GATT tuna-dolphin case?

These second thoughts were quick to surface. For instance, in late January 1994, a small group of environmental NGOs met with U.S. and European trade and environment officials in The Hague.[50] They were led by the Geneva-based World Wide Fund for Nature, the international counterpart to the U.S.-based World Wildlife Fund. The environmentalists were trying to influence the program of the new WTO Committee on Trade and Environment, which was supposed to develop additional environmental rules. The Committee's agenda was to be finalized when the

WTO treaty was signed in Marrakesh, Morocco on April 15, 1994.

After the meeting, forty environmental groups released a joint NGO statement of demands for the WTO.[51] American groups in the coalition included Friends of the Earth, Greenpeace, Institute for Agriculture and Trade Policy, the Citizens Network for Sustainable Development (a coalition body), and the World Wildlife Fund. They urged WTO to:

- support trade curbs on "process and production methods" (i.e. regulate domestic environmental and labor conditions)
- permit national trade sanctions to discourage "eco-dumping" (i.e. prohibit imports of goods that are not governed by U.S.-style environmental rules).[52]

The National Wildlife Federation and Friends of the Earth separately released similar detailed recommendations.[53]

The Developing World Fights Back

The environmental groups issued their green protectionist demands with the sinking feeling that the WTO would never accept them. Green protectionism was a lost cause at the WTO because the developing countries were on red alert to stop it. Third World leaders were keenly aware that the Green agenda would prevent poor countries from using world trade to expand their economies. Indian Prime Minister P.V. Narasimha Rao rallied the Group of 15 (G-15), a consultative forum for developing countries, against what he called "attempts to introduce new protectionist agendas."[54] Rao warned developing countries to "guard against new trade-restricting tendencies in the developed countries using the pretext of social and environmental concerns."[55] The G-15 — which included Brazil, Egypt, India, Indonesia, Malaysia, Nigeria, and Chile — drafted a common strategy opposing trade-restrictive amendments to the WTO.

"We should not countenance any moves to put social and environmental concerns on the trade agenda, with thinly veiled intentions to nullify the comparative advantage of developing countries," Rao said in a subsequent UN meeting.[56] Hong Kong, South Korea, Bangladesh, and China echoed his position.[57] Malaysia's Prime Minister Mahathir Mohamad said that rich-country trade curbs were designed to deprive the Third World of its only trade advantages — raw materials and lower labor costs. Almost the entire Third World opposed attempts to add an environmental component to the WTO. A G-15 communiqué denounced the Clinton administration's environmental proposals as "the very antithesis of the principles of free markets and comparative advantage;" it said they would "create further distortion and inefficiency and undermine growth."[58]

Still, the U.S. pushed green protectionism hard. At the April 1994 Marrakesh signing ceremony, Vice President Al Gore lectured Third World delegates that workers' rights and the environment had to be top priorities for the trading system. But representatives of the developing world were just as adamant in opposing the U.S. agenda. Charging that international environmental rules would curtail trade and growth opportunities, their speeches openly attacked NGO-sponsored efforts. India, Brazil, and Singapore accused the West of using the vocabulary of environmentalism to disguise trade protectionism, shelter uncompetitive jobs, and rob poorer nations of legitimate trading opportunities.[59] The G-15 declined to accept an ambitious Green agenda for the WTO's Committee on Trade and the Environment.

Even as Vice President Gore was pleading with the developing world, other members of the Clinton administration were courting the environmental lobby groups and urging them to support congressional ratification of the GATT/WTO treaty. The Republican victory in the November 1994 elections further complicated the administration's strategy. Caught between opposing international and domestic forces, the Administration's efforts floundered.

Fearing that Republicans might reject the treaty, the President was forced to convene an unusual lame-duck session of the Democrat-controlled 103rd Congress to ratify the WTO. The environmental lobby actively opposed the WTO treaty, but it could not muster enough opposition at the hurried session. The treaty passed the House (288-146) on November 29 and the Senate (76-24) on December 1, 1994.

The situation abroad was no better for the Greens. The Third World would not relent in opposing U.S. initiatives, and it increasingly suspected that international supporters of environmental practices were controlled by U.S. pressure groups. When the Clinton administration proposed that environmental groups be allowed to participate in the WTO as NGO observers, India's GATT delegation objected that this would needlessly politicize the organization.[60] To date, environmental organizations have not been permitted to influence WTO deliberations as they do in the United Nations, even though they do have NGO status.

The Rewards of Green Protectionism

The "good cops" and the "bad cops" of the environmental lobby have won and lost trade policy battles, but all have been paid handsomely for their handiwork. In the period 1991-1994, environmental groups received almost $1.5 million from philanthropic foundations to pursue a Green protectionist agenda. According to one estimate, $860,000 was distributed to the pro-NAFTA groups, while $613,000 went to anti-NAFTA groups. Whatever the ideological incentives to join the trade-environment debate, the availability of foundation funding created others.[61]

GOVERNMENT APPOINTMENTS AND FOUNDATION GRANTS (1991 – 1994)		
Organization	**Advisory committee**	**Foundation support**
World Wildlife Fund	ACTPN, JPAC, NAC	$300,000
Environmental Defense Fund	ACTPN, JPAC, TEPAC, BECC	$0
National Wildlife Federation	ACTPN, JPAC, NAC, TEPAC	$350,000
National Audubon Society	JPAC	$85,000
Natural Resources Defense Council	ACTPN, JPAC, TEPAC	$125,000
Sierra Club	TEPAC	$163,000
Friends of the Earth	TEPAC	$95,000
Public Citizen	None	$355,000
		Total: $1,473,000

Source: *John J. Audley, Green Politics and Global Trade.*
Acronyms: *U.S. Government: ACTPN (Advisory Committee on Trade Policy and Negotiations), TEPAC (Trade and Environment Policy Advisory Committee). NAFTA – JPAC (Joint Public Advisory Committee), NAC (National Advisory Committee), BECC (Border Environment Cooperation Commission).*

Environmental lobbyists also coveted the power and prestige of presidential appointments to high-level advisory panels. Officials of the pro-NAFTA National Wildlife Federation, World Wildlife Fund, Environmental Defense Fund and Natural Resources Defense Council were appointed to the Advisory Committee on Trade Policy and Negotiations (ACTPN). The Clinton administration also gave NWF, WWF, EDF, NRDC, and the National Audubon Society international appointments to the Joint Public Advisory Committee, which advises the three-nation Secretariat of the NAFTA environmental commission. NWF, WWF and Audubon also received spots on the National Advisory Committee, which advises the EPA Administrator on the implementation of the NAFTA environmental agencies.[62] Finally, appointees from the anti-NAFTA Friends of the Earth and the Humane Society of the United States joined pro-NAFTA appointees on the Trade and Environment Policy Advisory Committee (TEPAC). The TEPAC consists of major environment, labor, business, and consumer organization executives. It advises the U.S. Trade Representative and the EPA Administrator on all trade policy matters.[63]

These government panel appointments are rewards for political loyalty to the Administration. Far fewer appointments went to groups opposing the Administration on NAFTA. Whatever their claims, the "non-governmental" organizations are not truly independent of government. They are special interests who travel the corridors of power seeking access to government officials. Ultimately, their standing and influence depends on whether they are effective in lobbying for expanded government power.

MEMBERSHIP
TRADE AND ENVIRONMENT POLICY ADVISORY COMMITTEE

John Adams,
Natural Resources Defense Council

George Becker,
United Steelworkers of America

Brent Blackwelder,
Friends of the Earth

Joseph G. Block,
Venable, Baetjer, Howard, and Civiletti

Lee Botts,
Lake Michigan Federation

Roger Carrick, *Preston,*
Gates and Ellis

Dan Esty, *Yale School of Forestry and Environmental Studies*

Kathy Fletcher,
People for Puget Sound

Hon. James Florio,
Rutgers University

Sally V. Fox,
Natural Cotton Colours, Inc.

Kathryn Fuller,
World Wildlife Fund

Heidi Heitkamp,
State of North Dakota

William Howard,
National Wildlife Federation

Paul Irwin,
Humane Society of the U.S.

Edwin L. Johnson,
Technology Sciences Group, Inc.

Ron Judd,
King County Labor Council of Washington

Rhoda Karpatkin,
Consumers Union

Abe Katz,
U.S. Council for International Business

James Lindsay,
Ag Processing Inc.

Frank Loy,
Environmental Defense Fund

Gareth Porter,
Environmental consultant

Mark Ritchie,
Institute for Agriculture and Trade Policy

Michael Rue,
Cattlett Warehouse

Robert Shapiro,
Monsanto Co.

Arden Sims,
Globe Metallurgical, Inc.

Lee Thomas,
Georgia Pacific Corp.

Lee Weddig,
National Fisheries Institute

Lyuba Zarsky,
Nautilus Pacific Research

Tussle over Tuna, Part II

In 1996, the tuna-dolphin issue returned. To live within the new structure of trade institutions that it had worked so hard to create, the Clinton administration had to revise its trade restrictions on "dolphin unsafe" tuna. American law had to be brought into line with the requirements of GATT and the World Trade Organization, which prohibited nations from erecting trade barriers like the U.S. tuna embargo against Mexico. The Clinton administration responded with "the Panama Declaration," a twelve-nation deal struck with governments in Latin America.

The "tuna treaty," which was crafted with the help of environmental groups, created a legally binding international regulatory regime governing tuna fishing. Trade sanctions against Mexico would be lifted. But in its place the tuna treaty would regulate imports from twelve countries, and it would cap accidental Pacific Ocean dolphin deaths at five thousand per year. Under the accord, the Inter-American Tropical Tuna Commission, funded by U.S. taxpayers, would supervise the fishing vessels of each signatory nation. A Tuna Commission agent would be posted on each tuna vessel to certify that no dolphins died in tuna nets. The agent also would approve tuna for sale in the U.S. In effect, the tuna treaty extended U.S. regulatory controls into the international waters of the Pacific Ocean.

The treaty produced another acrimonious split in the environmental lobby. NWF, WWF, EDF, the Center for Marine Conservation and Greenpeace endorsed the Clinton administration-negotiated Panama Declaration. Like the NAFTA side agreements, they had helped write the new tuna treaty. The usually radical Greenpeace, for example, used its affiliates in Mexico, Chile, Brazil, Guatemala and Argentina to help negotiate the treaty.[64] Pro-treaty groups said the international tuna regime would not only safeguard ecosystems for dolphins, but also for turtles, sharks, juvenile tuna and other sea life. Under the tuna treaty, dolphin deaths eventually would be ratcheted down from five thousand annually to zero. Latin American countries would be hit with trade sanctions if their fishermen failed to comply with the new rules, and by signing the treaty each country forfeited its right to complain to the WTO. Some Green activists claimed the treaty was more restrictive than the original U.S. tuna embargo against Mexico.

But more radical activists at the Sierra Club, Public Citizen, the Humane Society of the U.S., and Earth Island Institute denounced the Panama Declaration, labeling it the "dolphin death act."[65] The Green pressure groups and animal rights lobbyists found unacceptable the allowance of five thousand dolphin deaths per year. Indeed, allowing any marine mammals to be "traumatized" by tuna fishing vessels was immoral. They preferred to ban all trade in tuna between nations. By lifting the embargo so U.S. law would conform to WTO rules, the hard-liners said the pact violated U.S. sovereignty over its own environmental laws and sacrificed dolphins to the ideology of "free trade."[66] Eventually, they proposed a compromise. The U.S. could lift the embargo to satisfy WTO rules, but it should retain the U.S. eco-label definition of "dolphin-safe," i.e., no dolphins were encircled by tuna fishing nets or threatened in any way.

The Panama Declaration is an example of green protectionism. It ends the outright ban on all Mexican tuna, but it does block trade in tuna that fails to comply with U.S. environmental standards. Under the guise of environmental concern, it restricts access to the U.S. market by forcing foreign countries to impose U.S.-inspired rules on their fishing fleets. As for the dolphin: even before the treaty went into effect, fewer than five thousand were killed annually from a Pacific Ocean population of ten million. The species is not endangered or near extinction. However, international tuna regulations do threaten foreign fishermen. The rules benefit large corporate tuna canneries at the expense of Third World tuna fishermen, who bear the burden of scrutiny by the international Tuna Commission.

Legislation implementing the Panama Declaration sailed through the House of Representatives, 316-108, on July 31, 1996. The Senate approved similar legislation several months later. The pro-treaty environmental groups prevailed not only by working with the Clinton administration, but by winning over many Republicans in Congress. Eager to be seen as both "pro-environment" and "pro-trade," the GOP saw the tuna treaty as a way to increase environmental regulation without violating the WTO. Here was another object lesson in the contentious coalition politics of international environmentalism.

The Trade Puzzle

Only in America are environmental organizations able to wield such great influence over trade policy. The Clinton administration, which aims to please Green groups, gives them regular briefings, consults them on the status of trade negotiations and appoints their leaders to official advisory bodies. At the same time, however, it courts the business community with promises of more international business.[67] Such slick tactics have divided the environmental lobby on trade questions.

Ironically, this division has become one of the movement's strengths. On political tactics environmental groups may diverge, but their overall strategy is quite focused. All want more government regulation of trade. The "good-cop, bad-cop" division of labor has often helped advance green trade policy objectives.

By contrast, advocates of consumer-friendly open trade policies have no coherent political strategy, especially in the Republican Congress. In 1995, the business community tried to challenge the environmental lobby over "fast-track" trade-negotiating authority. But now the tables were turned. The Clinton administration and the "good cop" environmental groups wanted "fast-track" because they wanted to add unamendable environmental and labor policy conditions to the trade deals they negotiated. Business groups urged Republicans to narrow the Administration's negotiating authority. As Republicans in Congress and Clinton bickered, organized labor worked on the Democrats in Congress and they altogether denied the Administration's hope for fast-track authority. There is a further twist. It appears that the strongest and most determined pro-trade opponents of environmental pressure groups are neither in Congress nor in corporate America. They are the leaders of the developing nations of the world.

The Clinton-Gore administration and the environmental lobby have a love-hate relationship on trade policy. Yet they depend on one another, and their actions demonstrate that they share common goals more often than not. Despite disagreements over NAFTA, the WTO and the international tuna treaty, the dynamics of the treaty-making process leave environmentalists well-positioned to affect future international trade policy.

NOTES

[1] Herman Daly and John B. Cobb, Jr., *For the Common Good: Redirecting the Economy Toward Community, the Environment, and a Sustainable Future*, (Boston: Beacon Press, 1989); Herman E. Daly, "The Perils of Free Trade," *Scientific American*, November 1993.

[2] Ravi Batra, *The Myth of Free Trade*, (New York: Macmillan, 1993) p. 245.

[3] World Resources Institute, United Nations Environment Programme, United Nations Development Programme, *World Resources 1992-93*, (New York: Oxford University Press 1992) p. 135.

[4] Hillary French, *Costly Tradeoffs: Reconciling Trade and the Environment*, (Washington DC: Worldwatch Institute, 1993) p. 5.

[5] Daniel C. Esty, *Greening the GATT: Trade Environment and the Future*, (Washington, DC: Institute for International Economics, 1994) p. 62.

[6] Al Gore, *Earth in the Balance*, 1992.

[7] Robert Costanza, John Audley, Richard Borden, Paul Elkins, Carl Folke, Silvio O. Funtowicz, and Jonathan Harris, "Sustainable Trade: A New Paradigm for World Welfare," *Environment*, June 1995.

[8] World Commission on Environment and Development, *Our Common Future*, p. 365.

[9] *Our Common Future*, p. 84.

[10] Gareth Porter and Janet Welsh Brown, *Global Environmental Politics*, (Boulder: Westview Press, 1996) p. 131.

[11] Pierre Marc Johnson and Andre Beaulieu, *The Environment and NAFTA: Understanding and Implementing the New Continental Law*, (Washington, DC: Island Press, 1996) pp. 26-28.

[12] United Nations, *Agenda 21: Programme of Action for Sustainable Development*, final text of agreements negotiated by Governments at the United Nations Conference on Environment and Development (UNCED) 3-14 June, 1992, Rio de Janeiro, Brazil, p. 19.

[13] *Agenda 21*, p. 22.

[14] Principle 12, *Rio Declaration on Environment and Development*, final text of agreements negotiated by Governments at the United Nations Conference on Environment and Development (UNCED) 3-14 June, 1992, Rio de Janeiro, Brazil.

[15] Principle 12, *Rio Declaration on Environment and Development*.

[16] Porter and Brown, *Global Environmental Politics*, p. 131.

[17] C. Ford Runge, *Freer Trade, Protected Environment*, (New York: Council on Foreign Relations, 1994) pp. vii-xii, 118-122.

[18] Johnson and Beaulieu, *The Environment and NAFTA: Understanding the New Continental Law*, pp. 31-32.

[19] Daniel Magraw, "NAFTA's Repercussions: Is Green Trade Possible?" *Environment*, March 1994, p. 18. (Magraw was associate general counsel for international activities at the Environmental Protection Agency during NAFTA negotiations.)

[20] John J. Audley, *Green Politics and Global Trade: NAFTA and the Future of Environmental Politics*, (Washington, DC: Georgetown University Press, 1997) p. 53. "According to staff officials, [EPA Administrator William] Reilly saw linking environmental issues to trade policy as a prime opportunity to increase the political authority of the EPA."

[21] Wren Wirth, wife of the Undersecretary, served on the Environmental Defense Fund board of directors. Ibid., p. 161.

[22] Magraw, "NAFTA's Repercussions: Is Green Trade Possible?"

[23] Stewart J. Hudson and Rodrigo J. Prudencio, National Wildlife Federation, Washington, DC, "The North American Commission on Environment and Other Supplemental Environmental Agreements: Part Two of the NAFTA Package," February 4, 1993.

[24] Justin Ward and S. Jacob Scherr, "Environmental Elements of the Nafta Package," Testimony of the Natural Resources Defense Council before the Committee on Environment and Public Works, U.S. Senate, March 16, 1993.

[25] Gary Clyde Hufbauer and Jeffrey J. Schott, *NAFTA: An Assessment*, (Washington, DC: Institute for International Economics, 1993). This study was funded by David Rockefeller and the Tinker Foundation. The Institute for International Economics is supported by the German Marshall Fund, the Ford Foundation, the William and Flora Hewitt Foundation, the William M. Keck, Jr. Foundation, the C.V. Starr Foundation, and the United States-Japan Foundation.

[26] U.S. Trade Representative Mickey Kantor, "Side Agreements to the North American Free Trade Agreement," Senate Environment and Public Works Committee hearing, Reuter Transcript Report, March 16, 1993.

[27] Audley, *Green Politics and Global Trade: NAFTA and the Future of Environmental Politics,* pp. 89 and 162.

[28] Ibid., p. 95

[29] Runge, *Freer Trade, Protected Environment*, pp. 118, 120.

[30] Press release, "Environmental Organizations Outline Proposal for NAFTA Side Agreements," May 4, 1993.

[31] Office of the U.S. Trade Representative, "The NAFTA: Report on Environmental Issues," *North American Free Trade Agreement Supplemental Agreements and Additional Documents,* (Washington, DC: Government Printing Office, November 1993) p. 14.

[32] Peter Behr, "For Environmental Groups, Biggest NAFTA Fight is Intramural," *Washington Post,* September 16, 1993, p. D 10.

[33] Kenneth Berlin and Jeffrey Lang, "The NAFTA Environmental Agreements," Winthrop, Stimson, Putnam and Roberts, Washington, DC, undated, p. 3. Lang was also a participant in the Council on Foreign Relations' Study Group on Trade and the Environment.

[34] Keith Bradsher, "Side Agreements to Trade Accord Vary in Ambition," *New York Times,* September 19, 1993, p. A1.

[35] Behr, *Washington Post,* September 16, 1993.

[36] Keith Schneider. "Environmental Groups Are Split on Support for Free-Trade Pact," *New York Times*, September 16, 1993.

[37] Behr, *Washington Post,* September 16, 1993.

[38] William Drozdiak, "Poor Nations Resist Tougher Trade Rules," *Washington Post,* April 14, 1994.

[39] Jay D. Hair, "GATT and the Environment," *Journal of Commerce,* December 8, 1993.

[40] David R. Sands, "NAFTA Foes Now Take Aim at GATT," *Washington Times,* December 4, 1993.

[41] Keith M. Rockwell and Bruce Barnard, "Kantor: Major Changes Needed in Draft of Uruguay Round Accord," *Journal of Commerce,* March 31, 1993.

[42] Timothy Noah, "Environmental Groups Say Deal Poses Threats," *Wall Street Journal,* December 16, 1993.

[43] "Split Among Environmentalists on NAFTA Healed in United Support for GATT Reforms," *BNA International Environment Daily,* December 7, 1993.

[44] Ibid.

[45] Noah, *Wall Street Journal,* December 16, 1993.

[46] U.S. Trade Representative, *The GATT Uruguay Round Agreements: Report on Environmental Issues,* August 1994, pp. ES-2, 35-40. This report was prepared with the assistance of several cabinet-level agencies participating in the interagency Environmental and Natural Resources Subcommittee of the Trade Policy Staff Committee, the Environmental Protection Agency and the Council on Environmental Quality. The final phase of Uruguay Round negotiations began in late 1992.

[47] "Clinton Pushes Environment for World Trade Talks Agenda," Reuter *European Community Report,* January 11, 1994.

[48] Jay D. Hair, "GATT and the Environment," *Journal of Commerce,* December 8, 1993.

[49] Jessica Tuchman Mathews, McNeil-Lehrer Newshour, "Trading Points," November 29, 1994.

[50] Frances Williams, "WWF Calls for Green GATT Plan," *Financial Times,* February 2, 1994.

[51] "The GATT Trade and Environment Work Programme: A Joint NGO Statement," February 9, 1994.

[52] Frances Williams, "First Steps to 'Green the GATT,'" *Financial Times,* February 22, 1994.

[53] National Wildlife Federation, "The Road to Marrakech: An Interim Report on Environmental Reform of the GATT and the International Trade System," (Washington, DC, January 1994); Friends of the Earth-

International, "Environmental Reform of World Trade: Towards a Green and Democratic GATT," (Washington, DC, April 1994).

[54] N. Vasuki Rao, "G-15 Leaders Blast Non-Economic Trade Curbs in West," *Journal of Commerce*, March 29, 1994.

[55] N. Vasuki Rao, "Developing States to Map Opposition to Trade Curbs," *Journal of Commerce*, March 31, 1994.

[56] Neelam Jain, "ESCAP meet in India to discuss GATT," *United Press International*, April 5, 1994.

[57] "Fears of U.S. Trade Protectionism Dominating UN Meeting," *Agence France Presse*, April 7, 1994.

[58] Rao, *Journal of Commerce*, March 31, 1994.

[59] Drozdiak, *Washington Post*, April 14, 1994.

[60] John Zarocostas, "Environmental Proposal for WTO Met Coolly," *Journal of Commerce*, September 19, 1994.

[61] Audley, *Green Politics and Global Trade: NAFTA and the Future of Environmental Politics.* See appendix. My figures differ from Audley's.

[62] Audley, p. 131.

[63] Office of the U.S. Trade Representative, Joint Statement by U.S. Trade Representative Mickey Kantor and E.P.A. Administrator Carol Browner, November 4, 1994.

[64] "A Dolphin-Safe Label that Really Means It," Greenpeace USA Fisheries Campaign, www.greenpeace.org/~usa/campaigns/biodiversity/tuna.html.

[65] Gary Lee, "Tuna Fishing Bill Divides Environmental Activists," *Washington Post*, July 8, 1996.

[66] WTO rules require the U.S. to end unilateral trade sanctions and impose trade embargoes through international environmental agreements. Faye Fiore, "House Alters 'Dolphin-Safe' Tuna Standard," *Los Angeles Times*, August 1, 1996.

[67] Andrea C. Durbin, "Trade and Environment: the North-South Divide," *Environment*, September 1995, p. 38.

Chapter 4
Building "Sustainable" Cities

On June 3-14, 1996 the Second United Nations Conference on Human Settlements was held in Istanbul, Turkey. "Habitat II," or the "City Summit" as it was also known, focused on questions of housing and urbanization. It was the world body's response to widespread predictions that two-thirds of the world's population would live in cities by the year 2025. Governments feared that cities were spreading out of control. They hoped that by coordinating urban land-use planning they could prevent the breakdown of social institutions threatened by rapid demographic change. Environmentalist NGOs played on these fears. Abetted by UN officials and the Clinton administration, they urged planning on a global level lest urban chaos cause incalculable damage to the world's ecology. City planning became the next target for advocates of "sustainable development."

Habitat II was the culmination of a five-year cycle of UN summits that began at the 1992 Earth Summit in Rio de Janeiro. After Rio there were conferences in Vienna on human rights (1993), in Cairo on population (1994), in Copenhagen on poverty (1995), and in Beijing on women's issues (1995). Habitat II (Habitat I was a related 1976 summit in Vancouver) was supposed to focus on housing and transportation problems. But these issues were redefined to incorporate prevailing UN initiatives on the environment, population, gender, and economic development. The Istanbul meeting became another showcase for the dominant NGO philosophy of central economic planning, mandated restrictions on consumption and energy use, and government population control.

Habitat II was a forum for negotiations among 3,000 official delegates representing over 150 national governments and international agencies. But the conference also attracted some 6,000 NGO representatives.[1] Organizers allowed each accredited national NGO to send two participants to the conference and each international NGO to send five. These representatives — environmentalists, feminist leaders, and population control advocates — arrived in Istanbul well in advance of the official conference delegates. They comprised the international movement for a new urban agenda.

American NGO participants were organized under an umbrella group called the U.S. Network for Habitat II. This organization evolved out of the Citizens Network for Sustainable Development (CitNet), a collaboration of the Women's Environment and Development Organization (WEDO), World Resources Institute, and the United Nations Association-

USA.[2] CitNet called for sustainable communities, social and environmental justice, and rural/urban revitalization. It also was concerned with metropolitan planning and land-use, women's access to credit, population growth and homosexual rights advocacy. Indeed, when participants met at one early Washington, D.C. forum to prepare for Habitat II, their interests were so diverse that some feared their policy recommendations failed to include enough language on housing.[3]

WEDO was very prominent in the preparations for Istanbul. Its self-proclaimed mission was to advocate the "gender dimensions" of shelter and housing issues. Founded and co-chaired by former New York City congresswoman Bella Abzug, a political militant well known for her anti-war activism in the 1970s, WEDO previously had coordinated "Women's Caucuses" at the Rio Earth Summit and other UN conferences.

Other prominent members of the U.S. Network for Habitat II included Habitat for Humanity, the National Wildlife Federation, the Humane Society of the U.S., People-Centered Development Forum, Sierra Club, United Nations Association-USA, World Resources Institute, Global Commission to Fund the UN, and Zero Population Growth. These interlocking groups formed the backbone of NGO advocacy in Istanbul.

Habitat II: How NGOs Planned Their Strategy

The NGOs took conference participation very seriously. Istanbul was not an overseas junket to an exotic locale; it was the culmination of a planned effort that was begun months earlier to promote the concept of sustainable development to American city-dwellers. The success of Habitat II would not be measured in terms of whether the conference planning was orderly or the Turkish site logistics agreeable. (Most UN conferences are logistical nightmares.) Instead, it would be judged by whether NGOs could influence the American political process so that U.S. urban policy was aligned more closely to UN international objectives.

The NGOs tried to make it appear as if American citizens across the country and from all walks of life were enthusiastic supporters of Habitat II. In fact, the only people who cared about the conference were the leaders of a small number of professional non-governmental organizations who were involved in its planning. Even their web site revealed their top-down orientation: "The US Network for Habitat II, the Citizens Network for Sustainable Development and President's Council on Sustainable Development bring Habitat II back home to Main Street USA."[4]

The U.S. Network staged a number of "Town Meetings" that were intended to create the impression that Habitat II was buoyed by a broad base of public support. These meetings were supposed to let ordinary Americans voice their community worries and place them within a global context. This, in turn, would sensitize the delegates in Istanbul to citizen needs in Brownsville, Texas and Oakland, California. Yet turnout was sparse. Only four hundred people attended a meeting in Chicago and as few as seventy showed up for an event in Ames, Iowa, home of Iowa State University. Some meetings, like one in Cleveland, had so few participants that no attendance figure was reported.[5]

Sympathetic local government officials seeded the meetings with NGO activists, who claimed to be "stakeholders" in the local community. But they mainly promoted their own agenda of issues, hoping to include them in the Clinton administration's submission to the Istanbul conference, a document called the "U.S. National Report for Habitat II." The town meetings were also the basis for the "Statement of U.S. Civil Society for Habitat II," the document that the U.S. Network would submit to the conference.

The town meetings were held over a fifteen-month period. They were paid for by grants from the U.S. Department of Housing and Urban Development, the Agency for International Development, the Fannie Mae Foundation and NationsBank. Zero Population Growth (ZPG) and the United Nations Association-USA provided additional in-kind support.[6]

U.S. Network's first Habitat "Issues Forum" was held on September 22, 1995 at the Johns Hopkins School of Advanced International Studies in Washington, D.C. The forum's title, "Why US Citizens Should Care About Habitat II," suggested the extent of Americans' indifference.

The forum panelists were hardly ordinary citizens. They were NGO activists and government officials, leaders in the international environmental movement. The first forum featured Dr. Wally N'Dow, Secretary General of the Habitat II conference and a former veterinarian in Gambia's agriculture ministry; Dianne Dillon Ridgley, president of Zero Population Growth, and Don Edwards, director of the US Network for Habitat II.[7] Edwards' NGO experience included service on the President's Council on Sustainable Development, where he was co-chair of the Environmental Justice Working Group on the Sustainable Communities Task Force. Edwards was also treasurer of the Global Tomorrow Coalition of environmental organizations, and he had helped establish the U.S. Citizens Network on UNCED (the 1992 Rio Summit) and the U.S. Network for Cairo '94 (the UN Summit on Population).[8]

It was clear that it was only an NGO elite who wanted more international oversight of American cities. They had appointed themselves representatives of public opinion, and during the winter and spring of 1995-96, they were putting forward an ambitious policy agenda at forums across America. Another Washington, D.C. forum held at the headquarters of the National Wildlife Federation in December 1995 offered the following set of recommendations. They are the epitome of the NGO mindset.[9]

- *To build a sustainable future, all levels of society (e.g. national governments, local authorities, regional and international organizations, the private sector and business groups, research and academic institutions, religious communities, and especially the NGO community) must be challenged and must act. The search for answers must extend to every hamlet, house, village, town, and to every entity of civil society. It must involve every one of us, not just the UN. Everyone must join in.*

- *Conferences need to be more inclusive of the diverse communities within countries which NGOs and CBOs represent. Concerns raised by these groups at micro levels can help elevate the debate so that more people can be reached.*

- *Micro level components must become integral to macro level decisions. Open paths of communication between macro level groups and community sectors are needed to open the diplomatic process.*

- *Create a network of peoples and organizations in the US concerned with the need for sustainable communities. This can help bring together a set of unique responses and solutions in order to find comprehensive solutions to very complex problems. Business/industry leaders must be included in the debate in order to achieve pragmatic polities which inject the concept and practice of sustainability into economic and political processes.*

- *The idea of 'a global commons' must be translated into concrete political actions where local-level efforts and community-driven strategies can be a source of inspiration at a time when there exists disillusionment in government and international events. Emphasis should be then placed on operationalization at local and individual levels.*

- *NGOs themselves need to be more than just 'friends' of conferences. New conference structures (e.g. partners' forum) in Istanbul should ensure that NGO voices are heard. NGO participation is vital to emphasize how NGOs represent the grassroots and the interests of individuals.*

Of course, the NGOs that organized the Habitat II public forums did not represent "the grassroots and the interests of individuals." They did not represent the Americans who had just given Republicans control of the U.S. Congress. The fifth Issues Forum in Washington, DC acknowledged this: "The 1994 elections and the succeeding political maneuvers and ramifications have had a profound, negative effect for the progressive community and the sustainability movement in general."[10]

U.S. Network's final report, "A Call for a Just and Sustainable United States: A Statement of US Civil Society for Habitat II," reflected international environmentalism at its most expansive. Signed by most NGO meeting participants, it called for reductions in industrial and natural resource use, multi-racial and multicultural decision-making, and zero emissions and waste: "sustainable livelihoods in an atmosphere of social, economic, and environmental justice."[11]

ORGANIZATIONS SIGNING THE "STATEMENT OF U.S. CIVIL SOCIETY" (PARTIAL LISTING)

Bread for the World

Center of Concern

Citizens Network for Sustainable Development

Coalition for a Strong United Nations

Friends of the Earth

Habitat for Humanity

Int'l Gay and Lesbian Human Rights Commission

National Wildlife Federation

Population Action International

Sierra Club

U.S. Network for Habitat II

Women's Environment and Development Organization

Zero Population Growth

> ### A CALENDAR OF NGO TOWN MEETINGS
>
> **BALTIMORE, MARYLAND: JANUARY 20, 1996**
> - NGO participants: Baltimore Housing Roundtable, U.S. Network for Habitat II, Cooperative Housing Foundation, Baltimore Fannie Mae Partnership, Association for Women in Development
>
> **LOS ANGELES, CALIFORNIA: JANUARY 27, 1996**
> - NGO participants: United Nations Association-USA, Southern California District Council of Laborers, U.S. Network for Habitat II, Joint Council of Teamsters, Southern California Council on Environment and Development, Southern California Nuclear Freeze Foundation
>
> **CHICAGO, ILLINOIS: MARCH 2, 1996**
> - NGO participants: Leadership Council of Metropolitan Open Communities, U.S. Network for Habitat II, League of Women Voters, Chicago, United Nations Association-USA
>
> *Sponsors: Bank of America, John D. and Catherine T. MacArthur Foundation*
>
> **BROWNSVILLE, TEXAS: MARCH 16, 1996**
> - NGO participants: Border Information and Solutions Network, U.S. Network for Habitat II, Valley Proud Environmental Council
>
> *Sponsors: Texas Commerce Bank*
>
> **ATLANTA, GEORGIA: MARCH 23, 1996**
> - NGO participants: Physicians for Social Responsibility, U.S. Network for Habitat II, Georgia Environmental Organization, Habitat for Humanity, United Nations Association-USA
>
> *Atlanta Bahai' Chorale performs "Cantata for One Earth"*

The Clinton Administration's Strategy

Like the NGOs, the Clinton administration made extensive preparations for Habitat II. Ostensibly, it also attempted to build public support for the Istanbul conference. But the Administration actually aimed to enlist major constituency and interest groups into its process of consensus-building around the issues of sustainable development. The U.S. Department of Housing and Urban Development (HUD) was the lead federal agency, and HUD Secretary Henry Cisneros appointed a National Preparatory Committee (NPC) comprised of public, private, and nonprofit representatives.

> ### ORGANIZATIONS REPRESENTED ON HUD'S NATIONAL PREPARATORY COMMITTEE (PARTIAL LISTING)
>
> Fannie Mae
> National League of Cities
> AFL-CIO Housing Investment Trust
> National Low-Income Housing Coalition
> Ford Foundation
> U.S. Network for Habitat II
> Progress and Freedom Foundation
> National Law Center on Homelessness and Poverty
> Habitat for Humanity International
> President's Council on Sustainable Development
> National Council of Churches

AMES, IOWA: MARCH 30, 1996
- NGO participants: U.S. Network for Habitat II, United Nations Association-USA, Citizens Network for Sustainable Development, Stanley Foundation

OAKLAND, CALIFORNIA: APRIL 13, 1996
- NGO participants: Earth Island Institute, U.S. Network for Habitat II, International Gay and Lesbian Human Rights Commission

DENVER, COLORADO: APRIL 20, 1996
- NGO participants: U.S. Network for Habitat II, Northeast Denver Housing Center

SARASOTA, FLORIDA: APRIL 27, 1996
- NGO participants: U.S. Network for Habitat II, United Nations Association-USA

"Crystal Dwellings" exhibit

SEATTLE, WASHINGTON: MAY 4, 1996
- NGO participants: U.S. Network for Habitat II, Collaborating Movements Towards Sustainability, Bahai's of Seattle, Seattle Network for Habitat II, Sustainable Seattle, United Nations Association, World Affairs Council, Zero Population Growth

Features "Four Directions" purification ritual

BOSTON, MASSACHUSETTS: MAY 11, 1996
- NGO participants: Architects Forum, U.S. Network for Habitat II

CLEVELAND, OHIO: MAY 18, 1996
- NGO participants: U.S. Network for Habitat II

HUD prepared its own report for submission to Habitat II. It was based in part on an earlier report from the President's Council on Sustainable Development (PCSD), which had also held its own series of White House-sponsored "town meetings" seeded with NGO activists. The members of the President's Council included the power elite of the international environmental movement. NGO members of the PCSD included:

- John Adams, Executive Director, Natural Resources Defense Council
- Jay D. Hair, President, IUCN - World Conservation Union
- Dianne Dillon-Ridgley, President, Zero Population Growth
- Fred Krupp, Executive Director, Environmental Defense Fund
- Jonathan Lash (Co-Chair), President, World Resources Institute
- Michelle Perrault, International Vice President, Sierra Club
- John C. Sawhill, President, The Nature Conservancy

In one major respect the HUD report was different. Unlike the NGOs of the U.S. Network, the Clinton administration wanted to downplay controversial social and political issues. Some officials even denied that central government should play the key role in making cities sustainable. "Our own struggle with centralized intervention in cities has been a history of profound failures," said Melinda Kimble, Deputy Assistant

Secretary of State. "We are increasingly learning that people, not governments solve problems."[12] Still, the American recommendations for Habitat II depended on government intervention in urban affairs. HUD's National Report, "Beyond Shelter: Building Communities of Opportunity," lays out a wide-ranging strategy for land-use planning by federal, state, and local governments.[13] Its recommendations assume that urban variety and opportunity necessarily requires planning and oversight:

• *"promote community design that uses land efficiently, encourages mixed-use and mixed-income development, retains public open space, and provides diverse transportation options";*

• *"create community partnerships to develop regional open space networks and urban growth boundaries as part of a regional framework to discourage sprawl development that threatens a region's environmental carrying capacity";*

• *"[promote] improved design tools [to] help conserve energy and minimize the emission of pollutants;*

• *"create eco-industrial parks that cluster business in the same area to create industrial efficiency, cooperation, and environmental efficiency."*

The May 1996 HUD report brands U.S. cities as "the main causes of ecological contamination and decline," and sternly declares that "our urban areas use the most fuel, generate the most waste and air pollutants, and consume too much agricultural land and wetlands due to poor land use management." The report, which represents official U.S. policy, outlines elaborate programs of sustainable development for America's cities. Yet it also suggests that current federal programs already implement Habitat II goals. In other words, it seems to warn activists against expecting more expensive government programs.

The HUD report counts these federal programs as representatives of the Habitat II agenda:

• "Empowerment zones." The report notes that Vice President Al Gore has program oversight for these economic stimulus areas, and observes that they have received $2.5 billion in tax incentives and $1.3 billion in grants.

• Federal fair housing and discrimination laws. It claims these are more strictly enforced and that HUD is increasing community acceptance of subsidized housing;

• $155 billion in federal transportation spending. Environmental factors from highway design to bike paths are said to be part of the grant and planning process.

• Job programs and increased lending to racial minorities and the poor. While more needs to be done, the Departments of Education and Labor are lauded for their accomplishments.[14]

It is noteworthy that the HUD report does not state that housing is a basic human right. This claim is much in favor among many foreign and UN officials (in proportion to their inability to realize it in practice). But Administration officials rejected any language that might create a new international obligation to subsidize housing.[15]

The Meeting in Istanbul (June 1996)

At Istanbul, the UN bestowed on NGOs an unprecedented status. This was the first UN conference to give NGOs a direct policymaking role in shaping the conference agenda. Earlier conferences included NGO deliberations in the final compilation of documents that were adopted, but NGO statements and recommendations were kept separate. However, NGOs in Istanbul participated in all the negotiating sessions that produced the conference Global Plan of Action. (Press reports, for instance, observed that the Women's Caucus, dominated by WEDO's Bella Abzug, "took advantage of the committee chairman's absence to take the floor.")[16] The primary conference document, the "Habitat Agenda," set out international policy guidelines that had been agreed to by all participant nations and NGOs.[17] Now if their goals were slighted or ignored by public officials or the private sector, the NGOs were entitled to appeal to the international standards they had helped formulate.

Many NGOs hoped the Habitat II conference would propose a concept of "sustainable" urbanization that could be used to strengthen the United Nations and diminish national sovereignty. They wanted to encourage cities to adopt new political and economic identities to set themselves apart from the nations of which they were a part. The city of Seattle, observed Habitat II Secretary General Wally N'Dow, illustrated this point:

> *"Seattle is no longer just an American city. It belongs to Canada. It also belongs to the Pacific Rim. It belongs to Asia in ways that are real — in economic, financial ways, in commerce and the diplomacy of commerce."*[18]

N'Dow would have the UN bypass nation-states and form direct links with cities. The conference blandly set as a top priority "to promote ways to achieve good governance at all levels of society, from the local to the global."[19] But the ambitious Habitat II plan aimed to show cities how to create earth-friendly urban communities through a series of "action plans."

The Habitat model of "sustainable development" envisioned

cities that limited the consumption of food, energy and natural resources. NGOs and their allies — UN officials and like-minded supporters in the U.S., Canadian, and European governments — tied these ideas to aggressive programs of international population control and declarations of a universal "right" to housing. These concepts and programs were developed in the "Habitat Agenda" and proclaimed in the "Istanbul Declaration."

What kind of city life did supporters of UN urban policies want? Laurel McLeod, a member of the conservative group Concerned Women for America, observed that that the NGO movement used its influence "to push a radical social agenda alien to the traditional values of most Americans."[20] Ironically, those who wanted to limit consumption, opposed "over-development," and rejected Western social values were themselves primarily from Western industrial nations. Yet they seemed alienated from it. McLeod observed that NGO participants were fond of dancing, clapping, and candle-burning to attract notice to their causes. One NGO display booth featured videos and posters on transcendental meditation, telepathy and hypnosis. Others promoted "post-industrial" music as an answer to urban housing woes. One NGO submitted a $100 million proposal to construct environment-friendly villages — "eco-villages" — around the world. The houses in these villages would be built with straw bales, making them "recyclable and earthquake resistant."[21]

By contrast, those most threatened by these ideas were its intended beneficiaries — the developing countries of the Third World. They had no interest in earthquake resistant straw houses. Nor were they attracted to the bohemian life-styles and social policies promoted by sustainable development's advocates. Some conference participants began building a coalition of resistance when they discovered what sustainable development had to offer. At various times this shifting coalition included the Vatican, governments in Roman Catholic Latin America and Muslim nations in Africa and Asia. The coalition was all the more striking because it occurred in Istanbul, an ancient city whose poignant history divides the worlds of Christianity and Islam.

Sexual Morality

Disputes that might have seemed peripheral to 21st century city planning suddenly exploded into controversy. Unexpectedly, issues of sexual morality threatened to undermine the consensus that the organizers of Habitat II were trying to achieve. For instance, delegates from developed countries tried to insert into drafts of the final Habitat document language that related to abortion and homosexuality. The Canadian delegation proposed to expand the definition of "family" to include gay and lesbian relationships. And the United States was pitted against the Vatican on the issue of abortion.

After much wrangling, the Vatican and Islamic and Catholic countries managed to remove from the Habitat documents a U.S.-inspired paragraph that would have allowed children to have abortions without parental consent. Despite this defeat, the U.S. persisted in trying to introduce references to "sexual health and reproductive rights" into the Habitat declarations. "This kind of discussion has nothing to do with Habitat," charged Joaquin Navarro-Valls, who led the Vatican delegation.[22]

Many delegates thought the U.S.-inspired terminology was an attempt to impose contraception, abortion, and sterilization on their countries. Shafgat Kakakhel, high commissioner for Pakistan, termed modern sexual practices "the normal western approach," which was unacceptable in Islamic and Catholic parts of the world.[23] Other delegates feared that the U.S. wanted to create an international right to abortion. The U.S. government delegation was afraid that the conference would impose upon governments a universal right to housing, but it seemed to have no reservations about a universal right to abortion.

The procedures for the Istanbul conference required all participant countries to approve in full the final text of the Habitat Agenda. However, delegations could introduce reservations for particular paragraphs of the text. When the U.S. and Canada insisted on document language referring to "reproductive health," the Vatican and Pakistan prepared reservations, foiling any chance of real unanimity. U.S. officials responded that they were defending concepts to which previous UN conferences had already agreed.[24]

Supporters of the UN conference process regretted this lack of consensus, but others celebrated their defense of the traditional family. Mercedes Arzu Wilson of Guatemala declared victory for the Group of 77, a coalition of developing nations. She argued that the Group of 77 had turned back efforts by developed countries to promote sexual orientation language and same-sex marriage. According to Wilson, the western countries said, "If you [G-77 countries] don't agree to a package, there will be no agreement. And the G-77 said 'so be it.'"[25]

Economic Growth and Foreign Aid

The altercations over population control, abortion, and sexual morality reflected a deepening North-South conflict over economic growth. NGOs and developed countries treated Habitat II as an occasion to warn poor countries against "unsustainable" urbanization, economic development, and population growth. But governments of the developing world answered that they could not create wealth if already wealthy countries put international restraints on their resource production and consumption. Instead of "sustainable development," they wanted to speak about "sustained economic growth."[26]

The developing countries made no secret of their suspicions: the language of sustainable development was a form of "Green imperialism." A Malaysian delegate complained that developing countries would have to "starve the present generation for the unborn future generations if they were to embrace sustainable development."[27] Pakistan also voiced its unease. "Developing countries are getting a bit disenchanted with too much stress on sustainable development," declared Pakistan's Kakakhel. He said it was "blatantly unfair" to privilege future generations by sacrificing people now alive.[28]

Rhetoric aside, much of the dispute seemed to be about money. North-South differences emerged over foreign aid and the role of UN agencies. Developing nations wanted Western aid channeled through the UN, and they repeatedly demanded that developed countries meet a UN international assistance target of 0.7 percent of GDP. Developed nations, which had spent prodigious sums in loans and economic aid, argued that UN agencies needed reform first. Many were cynical about poor nations' attacks on sustainable development because they were accompanied by demands for more foreign aid. They suspected that if foreign aid was increased, Third World governments would stop complaining and endorse the controls and regulations that the international agencies wanted to impose on their struggling populations.

Fidel Castro took advantage of North – South tensions. In a speech to the conference, he accused rich nations of exploiting the poor: "They have accumulated a lot of wealth at the expense of the rest of the world, and now they are very powerful. They have monopolized technology."[29] Secretary General Wally N'Dow was captive to Castro's revolutionary spirit. He warned that the division between First World rich and Third World poor "may become the dominant characteristic of the new global urban world order, with consequences at least as dangerous as the period of East-West rivalry."[30] Still, the Cuban model of economic development seemed more an example of sustainable development than an alternative to it. It did not inspire the delegates.

Challenging the UN Message

Increasing urbanization should be neither feared nor prevented. David Rothbard and Craig Rucker attended Habitat II as representatives of an accredited NGO, the conservative Washington, D.C.-based Committee for A Constructive Tomorrow. After comparing the speeches they heard to what they know, Rothbard and Rucker concluded, "Data about rates of urbanization, poverty and environmental impact reveal this doom and gloom rhetoric to be little more than big city hype."[31]

The Habitat II thesis that unregulated urbanization produces environmental and social devastation may give sustainable development's supporters a satisfying vision of apocalypse. But there is much data to refute it. Unfortunately, the UN conference organizers resisted any careful presentation of the facts. They did not make clear that countries grow more urban as they become less poor. In rich industrial countries, 75 percent of the population is urban. In poor countries, only 37 percent live in cities. They did not note that urbanization in Africa and Asia is generally a sign of increasing economic prosperity. Egypt and South Africa are Africa's most urban nations and its most prosperous; Niger and Rwanda are rural and poor. Japan, Taiwan, and Singapore are highly urban and wealthy; India, China, and Nepal are more rural and relatively poor. Developing nations can read these statistics, and it is why they resisted the sustainable development policies promoted by Habitat II organizers.

The American public did not resist Habitat II. They ignored it. The environmental lobby and the Clinton administration worked hard to build media interest and public support, yet few Americans were aware of the summit in Istanbul. The Habitat Agenda promulgated new restrictions on urban growth, designed new standards for land use, and committed governments to energy and population controls. These are measures the American public never would have tolerated - had it been aware of them.

But Habitat II was not accountable to the American people. Instead, the summit participants were accountable to the lobbying and advocacy organizations that wrote its agenda. Regrettably, the victims of the agenda are the peoples of the Third World. If they are required to accept population controls, limits on consumption, restrictions on land use, and violations of their religious beliefs, it will be because yet another global plan is now in place to justify the management of their lives.

NOTES

[1] "NGOs and Local Authorities Shape Goals of Habitat II," *Deutsche Presse-Agentur*, June 4, 1996. Habitat II was plagued by financial troubles from the start. To pay conference expenses Habitat II Secretary General Wally N'Dow of Gambia borrowed $1.4 million from the Nairobi-based Habitat Foundation, a special fund that was established to assist housing projects in developing countries. The unusual loan

aroused suspicion and led the U.S. and other Western governments to demand an audit by the UN inspector general. See Barbara Crossette, "U.N. Meeting on Urban Crises Draws Criticism on Financing," *New York Times,* February 11, 1996, p.16.

[2] The CitNet was once called the US Citizens Network on UNCED, and it had helped NGOs prepare for the original 1992 Earth Summit. It was a project of the Tides Foundation, a San-Francisco-based philanthropy that provides a tax-exempt umbrella for nonprofit projects.

[3] "Policy in Perspective: How Habitat II Will Effect U.S. Communities," Policy Recommendations from the Third Habitat II Issues Forum, December 15, 1995.

[4] http://www.odsnet.com/habitat/home.html

[5] "Town Meeting on Creating Sustainable Communities," http://www.odsnet.com/habitat/twn_rpt.html.

[6] Report from U.S. Town Meetings, "Town Meetings on Creating Sustainable Communities," U.S. Network for Habitat II. http://www.odsnet.com/habitat/twn_rpt.html.

[7] "From Rio to Istanbul: Why US Citizens Should Care About Habitat II", Policy Recommendations from The First Habitat II Issues Forum, September 22, 1995.

[8] Biography of Mencer Donahue Edwards, http://www.odsnet.com/habitat/edwards.html.

[9] "Policy in Perspective: How Habitat II will Affect U.S. Communities," Policy Recommendations from the Third Habitat II Issues Forum December 15, 1995.

[10] "Political Action For Sustainable Communities," Policy Recommendations from the Fifth Habitat II Issues Forum, U.S. Network for Habitat II, April 18, 1996.

[11] "A Call for a Just and Sustainable United States: A Statement of US Civil Society for Habitat II," U.S. Network for Habitat II.

[12] Barbara Crossette, "Hope, and Pragmatism, for UN Cities Conference," *New York Times,* June 3, 1996.

[13] Ibid.

[14] "Beyond Shelter: Building Communities of Opportunity," The United States Report for Habitat II, U.S. Department of Housing and Urban Development, May 1996.

[15] Karen Gellen, "Istanbul Prepares for a World Conference," *Earth Times,* January 31-February 14, 1996, p. 9.

[16] Barbara Lewis, "Istanbul Documents Nearly Ready as Sexual Rights Row Ends" *Agence France Presse,* June 13, 1996.

[17] *Earth Negotiations Bulletin* Vol. 11, No. 37, International Institute for Sustainable Development, 1996.

[18] Barbara Crossette, "The Return of the City-State," *New York Times,* June 2, 1996, p. 4.

[19] "Governance, Participation and Partnerships," UN Department of Public Information Press Kit for Habitat II.

[20] James M. Sheehan, "Clinton Embraces Radical Agenda at UN City Summit," *Human Events,* July 19, 1996, p. 6.

[21] Suna Erdem, "Aid Activists Meditate, Dance at UN Conference," *Reuters World Service,* June 11, 1996.

[22] Suna Erdem, "Wrangling Drags out UN Cities Conference," *Reuters World Service,* June 14, 1996.

[23] Barbara Lewis, "Deadlock at UN Summit as Vatican Opposes Sexual Rights," *Agence France Presse,* June 12, 1996.

[24] Barbara Lewis, "Sexual Rights Row Blocks Habitat Agenda," *Agence France Presse,* June 13, 1996.

[25] Daniel J. Shephard, "Not a Smooth Finish for Habitat," *Earth Times,* June 16, 1996.

[26] Daniel J. Shephard, "Habitat II," May 29-June 15, 1996, *Earth Times,* p. 7.

[27] Yue Pang Hin, "North-South Divide Over Issues Unavoidable," *New Straits Times Press* (Malaysia) June 12, 1996.

[28] Daren Butler, "North-South Divide Holds Up UN Conference Agenda," *Reuters World Service,* June 11, 1996.

[29] "Sexual rights row blocks Habitat Agenda," *Agence France Presse,* June 13, 1996.

[30] Kelly Couturier, "In Teeming Istanbul, UN Opens Conference on Crush of Mega-Cities," *Washington Post,* June 4, 1996.

[31] David Rothbard and Craig Rucker, "Habitat II Teeming with Hype," *Washington Times,* Jun 1, 1996.

Chapter 5
Food Fight: NGO Conflict Over Population Control and Biotechnology

On November 13-17, 1996 the UN's World Food Summit convened in Rome, Italy to plan national and international food policies for the next century. Sponsored by the UN Food and Agriculture Organization (FAO), the summit was supposed to improve the prospects of 840 million people thought to be suffering from chronic malnutrition. A "Declaration on World Food Security" and "Plan of Action" pledged to reduce by half the number of the world's hungry by the year 2015.

The conference dealt with many questions that delegates from around the world considered crucial to global "food security" — agriculture, food marketing and distribution, foreign aid, humanitarian assistance and world trade. But NGO representatives wanted the conference to be organized around the concept of sustainable development. The newspaper headlines might emphasize the distress of the world's hungry, but environment and population control advocacy groups were thinking instead about how to control resource production and consumption. Rather than reduce the number of the world's hungry, their bottom line was controlling the world's population. Mankind's survival was apparently threatened most by life itself – the threat of "overpopulation."

The United Nations estimates that by the year 2030 the world's population will increase by three billion people, and it frets that there is no way for food production to keep pace. The neo-Malthusians who lobbied delegates to the World Food Summit demanded international action. Regrettably, the FAO sided with them. Officials of the UN agency, which conducts agricultural monitoring and research, forecast that world food production must rise 75 percent by 2030 just to keep up with the expected increase in population.

The Rome Declaration on Food Security declared, "The problems of hunger and food insecurity have global dimensions and are likely to persist, and even increase dramatically in some regions, unless urgent, determined and concerted action is taken, given the anticipated increase in the world's population and the stress on natural resources."[1] Without the ability to control birthrates, the FAO claimed that governments could not increase agricultural productivity to handle the expanding hunger crisis. Representatives of the Worldwatch Institute, a think tank NGO participating in the conference, even went so far as to question the relevance of parts of the Summit Plan of Action if they were not directly linked to population control measures. [2]

Market-based solutions to the problem of hunger were given short shrift. U.N. Development Program (UNDP) administrator James Gustave Speth argued that economic liberalization and private initiative could not deal with the crisis. Speth, a former president of the World Resources Institute and one-time head of President Carter's Council on Environmental Quality, was responsible for re-orienting UNDP towards sustainable development. He argued that the crisis in food and population required more foreign aid from industrial nations. Said Speth: "The idea that the private sector can replace development cooperation is a myth."[3] But for Speth, the most important form of development assistance was preventing Third World people from having children. "Population stabilization" reducing the rate of human population increase, would be the developed world's greatest gift to developing countries.

Was it a sign of hard times that the meeting cost for the hunger summit was a meager $1.2 million? The FAO, like other UN agencies, was under severe financial constraints during the 1990s. And though the agency had a staff of 2,000 and a biennial budget of $650 million,[4] it was hard-pressed to put on a show equal to the Rio or Beijing summits. The FAO's organizers were forced to cut costs by using other UN employees to help with conference preparations, and they decided to stage the proceedings at their Rome headquarters rather than relocate to a distant city. Some international agencies could still host grand gatherings; the World Bank's annual bash in Washington, D.C. cost $11 million. But a lavish hunger summit might be in bad taste.[5]

Despite organizers' best efforts to mount a cut-rate policy spectacular, the World Food Summit had less public impact than the other UN conferences of the decade. Few heads of state bothered to attend and worldwide news coverage was perfunctory. Fidel Castro, perhaps the biggest available attraction, launched fiery accusations against rich capitalists for causing world hunger.[6]

As at most UN conferences, bold statements by conference organizers disguised widely divergent agendas. The conference's final "Declaration on World Food Security" affirmed a "fundamental human right to be free from hunger and malnutrition."[7] And its "Plan of Action" – crafted in language purporting to offer the conference's strategic vision – defined food security as access to sufficient amounts of basic food, "based on healthy and culturally adequate food habits."[8] This curious definition accommodated a wide range of nutrition concerns. For instance, the U.S. national food security plan identified high-fat diets, lack of exercise and obesity as significant food problems.[9] The plan was developed by the U.S. Department of Agriculture several weeks prior to the conference and it devoted several paragraphs to the problem of over-eating — a strange use of bureaucratic energy for a hunger conference.

Or perhaps, not so strange. The Summit's Plan of Action made clear that food security was simply another aspect of sustainable development. Hence it was related to the special needs of women (the principal issue at the Beijing confence) and population stabilization (Cairo). It could also relate to the issue of over-consumption by the rich, which sustainable development wants to end. The Plan of Action made it clear that food — whether too little or too much — was tied more to an ideology of resource limitation than to actual pangs of hunger.

Setting the Stage: The 1994 Cairo Conference

The World Food Summit can only be understood in the context of other UN efforts to limit population. The groundwork for the 1996 Rome conference had been laid by the 1994 International Conference on Population and Development in Cairo, Egypt. One hundred eighty countries attended that UN summit, which was dedicated to holding world population, currently 5.67 billion people, under a target level of 7.27 billion by 2015. Governments were supposed to control their populations by spending $17 billion annually on foreign aid and other programs.

The Cairo conference was dominated less by environmental NGOs than by population control advocates like the International Planned Parenthood Federation. Some environmentalists even complained that the conference was hijacked by the women's empowerment agenda.[10] The Cairo conference highlighted issues that were considered important in the struggle against overpopulation: women's rights, sex education, reproductive health measures and abortion.

Despite their different emphases, the NGO environmental and population control factions agreed that the world should direct its international agencies and political processes to curtailing childbirths. The environmental movement reasoned that slowing population growth would cut resource use. The Commission on Global Governance, an independent UN advisory group linked to Maurice Strong, doubted "the capacity of the earth to withstand the impact of human consumption as numbers multiply if present trends of rising economic activity and rising consumption continue unchanged."[11] Human beings affect the environment in terms of "what people use and waste," the Commission asserted. "Not only population but also consumption has to be reduced if sustainability is to be achieved." The Commission's report, *Our Global Neighborhood*, estimated that "some 80 percent" of "what is thought of as prosperity" was actually bad for the planet.[12] Despite what those enjoying it might think, the pleasure of prosperity was ecologically unsustainable.

The Cairo conference on population was defined as a conference on population control, and population control was defined in terms of government support for family planning and abortion. This set the stage for international conflict over the foundations of morality. NGO population control proposals — including one proposal to make abortion a basic human right — met fierce resistance in Cairo, not least from Islamic countries. Muslims, who feared the impact of Western immorality on their societies, demonstrated against the conference and urged their leaders to boycott it. And the governments of several Islamic countries — Saudi Arabia, Lebanon, Sudan and Niger — were so offended that they did just that.[13]

The Vatican, joined by delegations from predominantly Roman Catholic countries, also opposed many conference proposals. Pope John Paul II condemned what he called the "culture of death" permeating the policies of many national government programs and UN agencies. That the Vatican entered a de facto coalition with Muslim authorities demonstrated the extent of their common opposition to rising divorce rates, family decline, and deteriorating public mores. U.S. organizations of religious and social conservatives, some of whom attended the conference, also voiced opposition to its population control measures. They included Focus on the Family, National Association of Evangelicals, Family Research Council, the Rockford Institute, Catholic Campaign for America, Family of the Americas Foundation, Population Research Institute, and Human Life International.[14]

Journalist J. Michael Waller noticed the predominance in Cairo of NGOs favoring abortion as a method of population control. The United Nations Population Fund, International Planned Parenthood Federation (IPPF), Women's Environment and Development Organization (WEDO), and allied abortion activists tightly controlled many conference events. And New York's Bella Abzug was a galvanizing force behind the powerful "Women's Caucus." The UN attempted to portray the Cairo Conference as the culmination of an open process welcome to NGOs of many backgrounds. But a number of NGOs - including the IPPF, the Center for Reproductive Law and Policy, and Catholics for a Free Choice – mounted an unsuccessful effort to strip the Vatican of its UN observer status.[15] Waller also describes an incident in which a journalist was removed from a conference event and almost deported by armed UN police after a member of the National Organization for Women accused him of being a pro-life activist.[16]

Planned Parenthood, an organization whose revenues depend on the availability of legal abortion, played an almost oppressive role in the Cairo proceedings. Supported by corporate manufacturers of contraceptive devices and drugs like Norplant, it exercised an influence over at least 26 delegations from poor countries like Peru and Bolivia. Planned Parenthood offered to pay for IPPF staff and UN employees to represent countries too poor to send delegates to Cairo. IPPF had over 200 organizers and lobbyists in Cairo. The U.S. Agency for International Development sent a contingent of 122. The leader of the U.S. delegation, former Colorado senator Tim Wirth, the Under Secretary of State for Global Affairs, was supportive of Planned Parenthood goals; he was once on the board of directors of a Colorado Planned Parenthood affiliate.

By contrast, the Vatican sent a delegation of only seventeen.[17] It tried to counter IPPF tactics in Latin America by asking governments there to put pro-life NGOs on their delegations. But of 1,200 NGOs in Cairo, only two dozen were from Catholic and pro-life organizations.[18]

Some NGOs from developing countries resented the claim that large families were responsible for poverty. "The countries of the South reject the main assumption prevailing throughout the [Cairo] document that population growth in the South is the reason behind poverty and underdevelopment," their statement said. "We argue the opposite ... The poor will continue to have more children as long they have high infant mortality, lack education, social and health security, and need children for labor to support the family." Instead of government aid for birth control, the group urged that aid be re-directed to combat poverty.[19]

Other groups from developing countries argued that population control demands were racist. Elida Solorzano, head of the Nicaraguan delegation, said Western population controllers "don't want any more dark people multiplying, we know that." Third World community workers complained that UN-supplied health centers in their countries lacked antibiotics, but were plentiful in condoms, pills, and intra-uterine devices. Kenyan pediatrician Margaret Ologa explained, "We are running out of vaccine. We have no syringes, no needles, no sulfa drugs, no penicillin. Yet our Family Welfare Centers never lack birth-control supplies."[20] Health workers from the Philippines and Tanzania said they were not warned that contraceptives like Depo Provera had dangerous side effects which could cause hemorrhaging, permanent sterility and other injuries to women.[21]

The 1994 Cairo conference gave population controllers the conference document they wanted – the "Plan of Action." Rumors had circulated among Third World country delegations that U.S. State Department officials were threatening to cut off foreign aid funding unless they voted for the Plan of Action.[22] The Vatican and Islamic countries were forced to accept watered-down language on "reproductive rights," which could be interpreted to suit the UN and its IPPF allies.

NGOs Call the Shots

The 1996 World Food Summit gave population and environment NGOs another chance to organize their forces. The Clinton administration worked closely with them, as State Department Undersecretary Wirth and his deputy Melinda Kimble made sure that even the radical fringe of the movement was intimately involved in crafting U.S. policy. The Administration relied heavily on the opinions of Dianne Dillon-Ridgley, president of Zero Population Growth (ZPG), and appointed her to the U.S. delegation to Rome.[23] It also took its signals from Lester Brown, founder of the Worldwatch Institute and another prominent Administration adviser. Wirth publicly commended Brown for helping craft the federal government's policy positions.[24] (In late 1997 Wirth left State to manage media mogul Ted Turner's $1 billion foundation, which will fund UN environment and population initiatives.)

The NGO outlook figured prominently in the U.S. Position Paper that the Agriculture Department prepared for the World Food Summit. This lengthy document surveys recent scholarly projections of future world food supply and demand. Yet it takes seriously the predictions contained in the Worldwatch volume *Full House: Reassessing the Earth's Population Carrying Capacity* (1994) by Brown and Hal Kane. Brown and Kane say that in the food sector, "human demands are colliding with some of the earth's limits." Ecological constraints are starting to slow the growth of food production, such that "food security will replace military security as the principal preoccupation of national governments." They also repeat earlier predictions of doom that never materialized: "Over the next 40 years, the world will face massive grain deficits in Africa, the Indian subcontinent, and China."[25] The U.S. government position paper side-steps the truth of the statements and credits the authors by advising that "regardless of their validity ... Brown's analyses offer an important warning against becoming complacent about the future food situation."[26]

While official delegates to the Summit were meeting, NGO representatives conducted a separate forum courtesy of the Italian Foreign Affairs Ministry, which provided $320,000 in funding.[27] This gave the over 1,500 NGO participants somewhat less power than they enjoyed at the Habitat II conference in Istanbul, where NGO delegates directly participated in official negotiations. Yet it afforded participants an opportunity "to do some strategic planning for campaigns we are working on," in the words of Susan Davis, executive director of WEDO.[28]

The Path to Rome

Direct NGO involvement in World Food Summit deliberations was limited to input provided at five earlier regional conferences. Held in Morocco, Burkina Faso, Israel, Thailand, and Paraguay and sponsored by the FAO, they allowed NGOs to give vent to their passions.[29] Groups like Oxfam, Christian Aid, and Action Aid used the meetings to inject their views into the process that would produce the final text of the Summit's key documents, the Rome Declaration and Plan of Action. They insisted on more foreign assistance for population control – and offered themselves as administrative conduits.

Just before the Summit, the FAO invited more than 200 NGOs to Rome on September 19-21, 1996 for yet another "consultation session." This meeting became a rallying point for proponents of sustainable agriculture, representatives of peasants and indigenous peoples, advocates for consumers, the urban poor, children's rights and fair trade, and feminists and AIDS activists.[30] The NGOs used the session as a platform to criticize the free market system. They declared the market economy "generates exclusion and poverty, and is not conducive to attaining equitable and sustainable development, social justice and gender equality."[31]

In sweeping statements that would end advances in science, industry and commerce, the NGOs spelled out alternative measures to guarantee sustainable human development and food security:[32]

• Organizations of farmers, especially women farmers, rural workers and peasants, should be involved in food system decision-making at all levels.

• "Indigenous and traditional knowledge" of food production practices should be disseminated widely. This preference for traditional agriculture practices is an indirect criticism of biotechnology.

• Women must be given rights to land and resources.

• World Bank and IMF structural adjustment policies should be reconsidered and renegotiated.

• National governments should impose food price regulations

• Breastfeeding should be emphasized and breast milk should be considered an important natural resource.

• Developing countries should become self-sufficient in the production of basic food staples.

- Governments should directly support farmers and "fisherfolk" (a politically correct term for fishermen).

- Governments and NGOs should jointly design "food security policies."

- Governments should provide the urban poor with land, credit, social services and jobs.

- All women should have access to "reproductive health care" and "family planning services."

- All developed countries should comply with UN foreign aid targets of 0.7 percent of gross national product.

- The paradigm of science that currently supports innovation and diffusion of technology is destructive of nature. It should be replaced by what is called the "sustainable agriculture rural development paradigm," or SARD.

- Appropriating genetic resources, such as seed varieties, for private corporate profit threatens the conservation of agricultural biodiversity.

- It is wrong to treat food as a commodity that can be freely traded in the open market to produce foreign exchange earnings. Unregulated trade in food threatens global food security and degrades the environment.

- The external debts of developing countries should be canceled

- Transnational corporations should be regulated; but farmers should be subsidized.

- Governments should negotiate and implement a "global convention on food security" that will fully engage civil society organizations and NGOs.

- Governments, international organizations, and multilateral institutions should empower all relevant stakeholders. "Stakeholder" is a new term for interest groups that demand special representation and accommodation for their views.

- Food security is a "human right."

NGO and Government Paths Diverge

The NGOs at the earlier consultation session were in no mood to temporize when they arrived at the Food Summit. Delegates said a draft of the Plan of Action did not go far enough. The Plan implied that hunger was a fault of governments' unwillingness to guarantee human rights, but it carefully declined to endorse an explicit "right to food," not wanting to impose a legal obligation on governments.

The debate over the "right to food" was reminiscent of the Habitat II dispute over the "right to housing." Fearing a new right would give U.S. citizens legal standing to sue the federal government, the U.S. delegation filed a reservation so that "right to food" claims could not be legally binding. The United States announced that it accepted the Rome Declaration, but delegates noted that it would not lead to "any change in the current state of conventional or customary international law."[33] Administration officials carefully explained that no right to food was in the U.S. Constitution, and they took exception to the UN proposal that Western governments target 0.7 percent of their national wealth for foreign aid. They did promise that the U.S. would strive to guarantee freedom from hunger through "empowerment" programs.

The NGOs were displeased. More than 1,200 agrarian and development aid groups from 80 countries complained that the Rome Plan of Action was inadequate. Their list of alternatives included demands for higher subsidies to small farmers and the promotion of ecological farming practices.[34] On the last day of the Summit, NGO protesters shouted "farce" and heckled the UN's FAO director-general Jacques Diouf of Senegal.[35]

Clash Over Population Control

If the United States was the most powerful and outspoken government advocate for population control, its primary opponent was the Roman Catholic Church. As at Cairo, the Vatican refuted claims that overpopulation was the major cause of world hunger. In an address to the conference, Pope John Paul II declared, "Populations on their own don't imply food shortages, and we must do away with the sophistry that if we are numerous then we are condemned to be poor." The Pontiff appealed to the delegates: "Arbitrary stabilization, or even reduction, of population will not solve the problem of hunger."[36] Eleven Islamic countries joined the Vatican in filing reservations to the Summit Plan of Action. (A country declares provisions non-binding when it files a reservation.) They objected to language on sexual and reproductive rights and family planning, terms they regarded as favorable to abortion.

But the NGOs rejected these countries' message and left little doubt about their own agenda. "Although scientifically, there is no proof that we cannot feed all the people in the world, in reality it just will not happen," said Ingar Brueggemann, Secretary General of the International Planned Parenthood Foundation (IPPF).[37] The pro-abortion NGOs fell back on the mantra-like assertion: countries must not "re-open" questions that were settled in Cairo. The 1994 population conference documents are virtually etched in stone, and countries ought not to upset the continuity of subsequent UN summits.

In a report on the Summit, the pro-life group Human Life International (HLI) accused IPPF and the U.N. Fund for Population Activities of "spread[ing] misery throughout the world, especially in unsuspecting developing nations in the guise of 'family planning.'"[38] HLI, Concerned Women for America and other pro-life organizations were shut out of the UN proceedings even though they had obtained "NGO status," which ought to have afforded them access to the plenary session and enabled them to speak with delegates. But the UN revoked their NGO privileges at the last minute. Eleven women from pro-life groups in six nations protested this exclusion at a press conference.[39]

Gathering Clouds

Despite their massive presence in Rome, the NGOs were troubled by the direction of the Food Summit. The agenda sometimes seemed outside their control, and they suspected that multinational corporations had hijacked it. Official summit delegates appeared not to focus solely on population and gender equality, but also discussed the Uruguay Round trade agreement in favorable terms. WEDO's Davis concluded, "This summit became a food trade summit rather than a food security summit as the trade negotiators were almost all the same people who were going to Singapore [for the World Trade Organization meeting in December]."[40]

The NGOs feared that Third World agriculture was vulnerable to the logic of the marketplace. They insisted that poverty is caused by the unequal distribution of wealth, inequitable trade between developed and developing countries, and flawed macroeconomic policies. They urged developed countries to meet the U.N. foreign aid goal of 0.7 percent of gross domestic product (GDP).[41] They called for "sustainable agriculture," the term for farming without the chemicals, pesticides, and fertilizers that increase crop yields on fewer acres.[42] They denounced any expression of interest in biotechnology and accused Western corporations of exploiting and polluting the genetic resources of developing countries. Corporations that tried to increase agricultural productivity by manipulating plant genes stood accused of tampering with nature for profit.[43] Instead, the NGOs championed "farmers' rights" and supported subsidies and other benefits for ecologically sound farming by members of local indigenous communities.

In Rome five protesters — including three naked women with anti-American slogans painted across their bodies — disrupted a news conference by U.S. Agriculture Secretary Dan Glickman to publicize their opposition to biotechnology. They accused U.S. agribusiness of employing seed hybrids, undermining local competition in Europe, and devastating European farm interests.[44] The protesters thought seed hybrids dangerous, although government agencies in the U.S. and Europe have declared them safe.

The Campaign Against Biotechnology

The Green attacks on biotechnology have accelerated since the World Food Summit and are part of its crusade against genetic engineering. Jeremy Rifkin, founder of the Foundation on Economic Trends and the guru of the anti-technology movement, frets that biotechnology will produce "a form of annihilation every bit as deadly as nuclear holocaust." [45]

The issue has become particularly volatile in Europe, where Greenpeace is at the forefront of a campaign against technologically improved foods.[46] Switzerland's Ciba-Geigy, for instance, has developed a new variety of corn that is resistant to a pest known as the corn borer. But environmental groups have concentrated their attacks on the possibility that bacteria could latch on to the pest-resistant gene, which might then become resistant to antibiotics. Instead of hailing a private industry innovation that reduces the need for pesticides, the Greens speculate wildly that technology can release biological forces and unleash untold horrors.

Monsanto is attacked for engineering a soybean that resists one of the company's own herbicides. The innovation will enable farmers to plant the new soybean without fear that use of a weed-killer can damage the crop. But in November 1996 five Greenpeace protesters were arrested in Louisiana for disrupting a Cargill grain-loading terminal where Monsanto soybeans were being transported by ship. Using inflatable rafts, the Greenpeace activists posted yellow signs on two ships that read "X-Genetic Experiment." Other Greenpeace protesters, wearing white hats and blue overalls labeled "Genetic Experiment," chained themselves to gates and grain barges at the Archer Daniels Midland grain terminal in Louisiana, protesting exports of genetically modified soybeans.[47] Greenpeace also blockaded ports in Antwerp and Ghent, Belgium that were receiving soybean imports from Cargill.[48] And it has targeted food companies, including Unilever, Danone and Nestle, in nine European countries to prevent the sale of foods enhanced by biotechnology.

The business community recognizes the seriousness of the activist anti-biotech campaign, fearing it will mislead the public. "The commercial interests in the business, particularly in Germany, are nervous about the effects Greenpeace and their small band of activists can have on the oilseed markets," reports Jim Hershey of the American Soybean Association.[49]

The biodiversity treaty, which was negotiated at the 1992 Rio summit, is one device that the environmental movement intends to use to exploit fears of biotechnology. "A Trojan Horse" is what policy expert Henry I. Miller of Stanford's Hoover Institution calls the treaty. For instance, the treaty contains a Biosafety Protocol that proposes the development of international biotechnology regulations. Says Miller, "No one anywhere would be allowed to grow and test a biotechnology derived crop or garden plant - even on a plot as small as one-tenth of an acre – without prior approval from the U.N. bio-police."[50]

The biotech scares are false. Advances in biotechnology promise to capitalize on the "Green Revolution" in agricultural production and deliver even more benefits in high-yielding crop varieties, pest-resistant hybrids and other genetic innovations. In the Third World, six million square miles of cropland today feed twice as many people as was possible in 1960. Because of agricultural productivity there are no signs of imminent world famine, despite environmentalist predictions. Where famine does occur, the cause is not a failure in productivity, but one of political will and judgment.[51]

Unfortunately, international environmentalism's hostility to new technology has had consequences for developing nations. "Extremist environmentalists" opposed to chemical fertilizers and biotechnology now threaten Africa's ability to grow more food. That is the recent warning of Dr. Norman Borlaug, winner of the 1970 Nobel Peace Prize for the pioneering scientific work that made possible the "Green Revolution" in Third World agriculture. Borlaug warns that opponents of biotechnology actually increase the likelihood of environmental degradation. By preventing the use of fertizers and pesticides to increase crop yield, they will force farmers to convert forest and mountain lands to cropland of marginal productivity.[52]

"The trend toward harvesting more from fewer acres ... is perhaps the most environmentally favorable development of the modern age," writes Gregg Easterbrook, an environmental journalist. Yet when Borlaug tried to bring the latest agricultural technologies to Africa in the 1980s, the environmental movement "became determined to stop him," pressuring the World Bank and the Ford Foundation not to fund high-yield farming methods, fertilizer and pesticide use. They said modern farming techniques would destroy the environment and argued that more food sustains human population growth which, said Easterbrook, "they see as antithetical to the natural world."[53]

Despite the influence of the Malthusian environmental lobby, most Third World countries appear to be rejecting gloom and doom messages. Compared with earlier UN conferences, the NGOs participating in the Rome World Food Summit lost ground. The official delegates focused their attention on a wider range of issues than grim warnings about sustainability. Perhaps that's because Third World governments know that their economic futures depend on freer trade and modern agriculture, not cultural isolation and ecologically restricted farming. The important role of religion in the developing world also suggests that governments will hesitate to impose population and farming restrictions on their people. Surely they have higher aspirations than the diversion of public resources to these ends.

Population growth is an overblown concern. Rising population has been no obstacle to economic development in the West or in Japan and Korea. Moreover, the rate of Third World population growth has been decreasing for nearly thirty years, and it's likely that the cause has been rising prosperity not government population controls. If there is ever any breakdown in mankind's ability to feed itself, the cause will be politics not overpopulation. Human society is resourceful; we can solve the problems of putting food on the table. And technology will make that task easier, not more difficult.

NOTES

[1] Rome Declaration on Food Security, World Food Summit, 13-17 November, 1996.

[2] Paul Holmes, "FAO Chief Defends Food Summit as Critics Weigh In," *Reuters North American Wire*, November 12, 1996.

[3] Mahesh Uniyal, "Food Summit: Pay Up Or Else..." *Inter Press Service*, November 13, 1996.

[4] Ashali Varma, "The Organization: Food, Agriculture, and Distribution," *Earth Times*, November 16-30, 1996.

[5] Kyu-Young Lee, "Rome Gets Ready to Play Host to Thousands," *Earth Times*, November 16-30, 1996.

[6] Paul Holmes, "UN Food Summit Ends Under Shadow of Disagreements," *Reuters North American Wire*, November 17, 1996.

[7] Rome Declaration on World Food Security, World Food Summit, 13-17 November 1996.

[8] World Food Summit Plan of Action, 13-17 November 1996.

[9] "The U.S. Contribution to World Food Security: The U.S. Position Paper Prepared for the World Food Summit," U.S. Department of Agriculture, July 1996.

[10] Philip Shabecoff, *A New Name for Peace*, (Hanover, NH: University Press of New England, 1996) p. 181.

[11] Commission on Global Governance, *Our Global Neighborhood*, (New York: Oxford University Press, 1995) pp . 27-28.

[12] *Our Global Neighborhood,* p. 145.

[13] Eileen Alt Powell, "Singing, Canvassing, and Lobbying for Family Planning," *AP Worldstream*, September 2, 1994.

[14] Cliff Kincaid, *Global Bondage*, (Lafayette, LA: Huntington House Publishers, 1995) p.99.

[15] Thalif Deen, "Population-Religion: NGOs Set Sights on Holy See's UN Status," *Inter Press Service,* September 6, 1994.

[16] John Michael Waller, "Bella's Babies," *American Spectator,* April 1995.

[17] Ibid.

[18] George Moffett, "UN Population Conference Meets Religious Resistance," *Christian Science Monitor,* September 6, 1994.

[19] *Agence France Presse*, "It's Poverty that Causes Population Boom, Not Other Way Round: NGOs," September 12, 1994.

[20] Waller, "Bella's Babies."

[21] *Inter Press Service,* "Population-Contraceptives: Problems of the Poor and Uninformed," September 12, 1994.

[22] Eileen Alt Powell, "Singing, Canvassing, and Lobbying for Family Planning," *AP Worldstream,* September 2, 1994.

[23] Other NGO representatives included C. Payne Lucas, President, Africare; Charles MacCormack, President & CEO, Save the Children; Leland Swenson, President, National Farmers Union. Private Sector Advisors to the U.S. Delegation to the World Food Summit as of 10/15/96.

[24] World Food Summit public briefing, U.S. Department of Agriculture, October 17, 1996 (attended by author).

[25] Lester Brown and Hal Kane, *Full House: Reassessing the Earth's Population Carrying Capacity,* (New York: Norton, 1994).

[26] "The U.S. Contribution to World Food Security: The U.S. Position Paper Prepared for the World Food Summit," U.S. Department of Agriculture,

July 1996.

[27] Ibid.

[28] C. Gerald Fraser, "NGOs: Using the Summit to Organize Campaigns," *Earth Times,* November 16-30, 1996.

[29] Regional conference reports available at http://www.fao.org/wfs/resource/resource.htm.

[30] Committee on World Food Security, Twenty-second Session Rome, 23-27 September 1996, FAO/NGO Consultation on the World Food Summit, (19-21 September 1996): Key Points of the Consultation.

[31] FAO/NGO Consultation on the World Food Summit, (19-21 September 1996).

[32] Ibid.

[33] Michael Adler, "World Food Summit Left Key Issues Unresolved," *Agence France Presse*, November 18, 1996.

[34] *Deutsche Presse-Agentur,* November 17, 1996

[35] Paul Holmes, "UN Food Summit Ends Under Shadow of Disagreements," *Reuters North American Wire,* November 17, 1996.

[36] Dipankar De Sarkar, "Food Summit: Pope Declares Overpopulation Not the Problem," *Inter Press Service*, November 13, 1996.

[37] Dipankar De Sarkar, "Population: NGO Slams Pope's Food Summit Message," *Inter Press Service,* December 2, 1996.

[38] De Sarkar, "Population: NGO Slams Pope's Food Summit Message."

[39] "Pro-Family Group Silenced at FAO Summit," press release, Concerned Women for America, November 15, 1996.

[40] De Sarkar, "Population: NGO Slams Pope's Food Summit Message."

[41] Jorge Pina, "Development: Foreign Debt Question Divides North and South," *Inter Press Service,* September 28, 1996.

[42] Dave Juday, "The U.N's Food Fight," *The Weekly Standard*, November 25, 1996, p. 20.

[43] Dipankar De Sarkar, "Agriculture: Rich-Poor Clash Looms at FAO Conference," *Inter Press Service,* June 17, 1996.

[44] Philip Pullella, "Food Summit Opens with Appeal for Zaire," *Washington Times*, (Reuter), November 14, 1996.

[45] Quoted in Henry I. Miller, "Techno-bashers Distortions Are Hurting Earth Day," *Houston Chronicle*, April 22, 1997.

[46] Control Risks Group Ltd., *No Hiding Place: Business and the Politics of Pressure,* July 1997, pp.23-26.

[47] *Reuters North American Wire,* "Greenpeace Activists Arrested" for Blocking Grain Terminal," November 14, 1996.

[48] *Reuters European Community Report,* "U.S. Greenpeace Activists Arrested in Biotech Soy Protest," November 21, 1996.

[49] *Reuters Financial Report,* "ASA, Monsanto Take Greenpeace Protests Seriously," September 20, 1996.

[50] Henry I. Miller, "Harming the Environment," *Journal of Commerce,* July 31, 1997.

[51] Juday, "The UN's Food Fight."

[52] Gene Kramer, *Associated Press,* "Nobel Laureate Favors Fertilizer," August 4, 1997.

[53] Gregg Easterbrook, "Forgotten Benefactor of Humanity: Agronomist Norman Borlaug," *Atlantic Monthly,* January 1997.

Chapter 6
International Forest Regulation

NGOs have been a driving force behind U.N.-sponsored environment conferences, policy statements and treaty ratifications. So when negotiations on an international environmental convention veer away from the counsel of NGOs, the event bears watching. This is what happened in recent negotiations over the world's forests. Fearing defeat, environmental advocacy groups were forced to oppose a process that they championed and that had usually served them well. Their tactical agility and strategic sense was tested. This time they are far from success.

In June 1997 delegates to a UN General Assembly Special Session (UNGASS) gathered in New York City to review the progress of action taken since the 1992 Rio Earth Summit. Delegates to the "Rio +5" summit faced an unusual demand: More than eighty NGOs announced that they found unacceptable a proposed treaty on use of the world's forests.

It was almost unprecedented for NGOs to call for a treaty's rejection. Declaring the treaty too weak, groups like Greenpeace, Friends of the Earth, and the World Wide Fund for Nature demanded a halt on negotiations over the treaty's provisions. They issued a joint statement: "Our organizations, representing millions of people worldwide, believe that a forest convention negotiated at this time not only will fail to effectively safeguard the world's forests, but could actually threaten them."[1]

The forest treaty agenda demonstrates how environmental advocacy groups can lose control of a UN negotiating process. The NGOs had concluded that they were too weak to force changes to the treaty. But they were still strong enough to postpone negotiations that were apt to go against them. At the close of the UN special session, delegates from member states – encouraged by the Clinton-Gore administration – agreed to postpone consideration of the treaty and to continue forest discussions for what would likely be another two to three years.

The treaty-making process had gone out of control. What started out as an effort to restrict the harvest of timber resources went awry when delegates from participating countries actually sat down at the bargaining table. Governments from both the developed (North) and less-developed (South) areas of the world were favorably disposed toward forest use; many subsidized commercial forestry. They counteracted Green lobbying strategies as private industry groups explained their positions.

The story of the foiled forest agreement underscores how the actions of NGOs undermined their influence and exacerbated the divisions between countries of the "North" and "South."

It Started in Rio

NGOs discovered they had a problem during the 1992 Rio Summit. Developing countries like Malaysia and India had been unwilling to negotiate a forest treaty because they feared they might lose control over their national forest resources. A treaty, they suspected, would let activists meddle in their affairs and postpone or prevent development. The upshot was that all sides could agree to nothing more than a vague nonbinding "Statement of Forest Principles." The Earth Summit produced no call for international export restrictions or regulations on trade in tropical forest products.[2]

From 1995 to 1997 talks continued as the UN Commission on Sustainable Development tried to cobble together a binding treaty. The European Union, Canada, and Russia, member states on the Commission's Intergovernmental Panel on Forests (IPF) favored a loose treaty setting down global principles of forest management. Sensitive to the interests of their own national forestry and paper industries, they proposed uniform forestry practices and conservation measures that industry could live with. But developing countries continued to worry that a treaty could thwart their efforts to hasten development. "Governments have not been very inclined to sign on to something that tells them what to do with their economic policies," commented the Worldwatch Institute's Janet Abramowitz.[3]

The Third World's apprehension was a reaction to the zealotry of the environmental movement. Its aggressive style alienated many developing countries. "Some of these Western environmentalists are dismissed by their developing-country counterparts as "greentroopers," wrote Pranay Gupte, editor of the *Earth Times*.[4]

An outbreak of skirmishes produced uncertainty and confusion. Developing countries feared a forest treaty would be too restrictive; but NGOs thought it was too lax. The NGOs were convinced the treaty would be dominated by timber and trade interests; they accused Northern logging countries of favoring permissive standards to encourage more commercial timber harvesting. Bill Mankin, director of the Global Forest Policy Project, called the proposed treaty "purely an avoidance technique, a form of 'greenwashing' that they can wave around to make them look like they're environmentally sensitive."[5] Greenpeace lambasted the emerging treaty as the "Chainsaw Convention."[6]

Yet the NGO influence on Northern governments was more significant than they acknowledged. *Countdown,* a newsletter of the Winnipeg-based International Institute for Sustainable Development, which monitored the talks, observed, "For the first time in history, NGO representatives were allowed to participate freely in the UNGASS [UN General Assembly Special Session] proceedings alongside heads of state and government."[7] (The NGO voice was not wholly independent; it was funded by the Ministry of Forests of British Columbia, the Canadian Forest Service, and the Canadian Pulp and Paper Associations.)

U.S. delegations to the IPF included many environmental movement leaders who opposed the treaty. For instance, Rafe Pomerance, who was president from 1975 to 1979 of Friends of the Earth, one of the more militant environmental groups, and later worked for the World Resources Institute, was Assistant Secretary of State for Environment and Development in 1997. He would testify before Congress that "having heard the views of a range of domestic forest constituencies, we were convinced that such negotiations would not be helpful to advancing the goal of sustainable forest management at this time." Pomerance concluded, "The U.S. was successful in leading the effort to defeat the treaty."[8] Dr. Patrick Moore offered a more caustic view. Moore, a founding member of Greenpeace who has grown critical of its extremism, said treaty opponents posed an ultimatum: "It would be fine to have an agreement as long as it banned cutting trees."[9]

The Japanese and Australian government delegations also sympathized with the NGO position and helped the U.S. scuttle the treaty. Negotiators then deferred completion of an international convention on forests until at least the year 2000. The discussions that may or may not eventually produce a treaty will be conducted under the auspices of IPF's successor, an Intergovernmental Forum on Forests.

MAJOR NGOS PARTICIPATING IN UN INTERGOVERNMENTAL PANEL ON FORESTS :

Greenpeace International

International Union for the Conservation of Nature (IUCN)

Environmental Investigation Agency

Global Forest Policy Project

(Sierra Club, National Wildlife Federation, Friends of the Earth-US)

Friends of the Earth International

World Wide Fund for Nature

Source: UN Dep't for Policy Coordination and Sustainable Development

Looking for Policy Alternatives

If the forest treaty helped commercial forest harvesting, then the NGOs needed alternative ways to restrict forest use. "We've got a lot of instruments out there," said Bill Mankin, director of the Global Forest Policy Project.[11]

One alternative was the Biodiversity Convention. Signed by 98 nations in Rio in 1992, the treaty was supposed to protect the habitat of species. But NGOs saw that many of its provisions could be focused on forests. The convention had adopted NGO definitions of conservation and sustainable use, and it specified that they were to be integrated into national planning. It also called for the use of environmental impact assessments, set-asides of "protected areas," and restrictions on development. And it granted special rights to "indigenous peoples" and local communities, urged structuring "economically and socially sound" development incentives, and demanded a guarantee of "equitable sharing of benefits" from the use of natural resources.[12]

If the Biodiversity Convention were ratified by the U.S. Senate, these provisions could have serious consequences for American land use. Federal authority to restrict public and private land use would be greatly expanded if forestlands were regulated by the treaty's "ecosystem management" philosophy – a concept implying minimal human interaction with wildlife.

Another possible treaty mechanism to protect forests was a global climate treaty. If forests could be defined as "carbon sinks" able to absorb dangerous greenhouse gases, then it might be argued that too much commercial timber harvesting worsened global warming. Yet a third alternative was to enlarge an existing Central American forest preservation accord. It authorized NGOs, indigenous people, and "stakeholders" to govern forest practices and land use.[13]

Mandated use of "eco-labels" was yet another political measure for controlling forest use. The Canadian government had proposed labeling paper and lumber to certify whether or not it was produced in an "environmentally friendly" manner. However, it soon became apparent that domestic lumber concerns might use labeling to keep out foreign imports. Under those conditions the concept of sustainability would become an anti-competitive trade barrier benefiting domestic forest producers.

Not all policy alternatives require the imposition of international regulations. For instance, the Forest Stewardship Council (FSC), an international organization located in Oaxaca, Mexico, has developed voluntary eco-labels for forest products. Working with environmental groups like the World Wildlife Fund, FSC monitors private timber logging practices and raises funds by requiring the companies it certifies to pay a licensing fee to use the FSC logo. The group also receives grants and contributions from other NGOs, philanthropic foundations, and government sources.

International Law: An Uncertain Application

We do not yet know the outcome to this story. The Clinton administration, other Western governments and their NGO allies effectively suspended discussions of the Intergovernmental Panel of Forests when it seemed that developing nations might thwart or change its recommendations. It is possible that the IPF will curtail forest harvesting as the NGOs desire. However, it is also possible that the negotiations will again produce results discouraging to the environmental advocacy groups.

Federal officials send mixed signals when they are asked whether international treaty processes are binding on their actions. Sometimes they try to deny the influence of NGO-inspired forest agreements. Pomerance claims the recommendations of the Intergovernmental Panel on Forests "are in no way binding on governments." He took the same position on another set of international forest discussions, the Montreal Process Working Group, which had produced a document called the Santiago Declaration. It set forth criteria and indicators for sustainable forest management that NGOs basically approved. Pomerance, however, said it "is not a legal agreement and imposes no legal obligations or other restrictions on the United States."[14]

Yet it cannot be denied that U.S. forest policies and practices are affected by official international forestry discussions in which NGOs play a prominent role. U.S. Forest Service chief Michael Dombeck testified to Congress on September 11, 1997 that his agency is "developing measures that will integrate the seven Montreal Process criteria into current Forest Service strategic planning, information management, and inventory and monitoring activities."[15]

A global economy can increase demand for lumber production and lower costs for wood and wood products. But U.S. government policies that rely on international forest treaty processes accept the influence of NGOs that want resource controls. Moreover, they leave themselves open to the indirect influence of domestic producers who want trade protectionism. Clearly, Forest Service chief Dombeck values his domestic clients more than foreign competitors. He reassured members of Congress that the negotiation of international rules "helps to prevent underpriced timber from being 'dumped' on the world market adversely affecting the U.S. forest product industry."

Understanding Forests and Forest Policy

What is the condition of forests worldwide? Environmental NGOs claim that commercial forestry is responsible for deforestation and species loss: "The world's forests face more acute pressure than during any other period in history," claims the World Wide Fund for Nature (WWF).[16] But international forestry meetings seldom assess carefully the health of forests around the world, and NGO allegations go unexamined in many official discussions. Available data presents a different view. Forest expert Roger Sedjo has explained:[17]

• Commercial forestry is not a major cause of deforestation because it does not permanently convert land to another use. Northern temperate forests provide three fourths of world commercial timber production, but these forests are expanding both in terms of area and forest volume.

• The clearing of land for agriculture is the primary reason for deforestation in the world today. Most deforestation occurs in poorer undeveloped countries, where tropical forest lands are needed to grow crops. But this is the region of the world with the least commercial harvesting of forests.

• Temperate forests in developed countries are being steadily reforested. Improved tree-growing technology, tree plantations, wildfire controls, and the reversion of agricultural lands to forests have reforested the American South and East. Once cleared for agriculture, these lands are converted back to forestland. Today, New England is between 60 and 90 percent forested. Similarly, we can expect reforestation in tropical undeveloped countries like Brazil, India and Malaysia as their economies develop.

• One important reason why Western industrial countries tend to regenerate their forestlands is an enforceable legal framework of land tenure, secure private property rights, and relatively free markets. Undeveloped countries that lack institutions to establish clear land titles create additional incentives for deforestation. Unclear land ownership encourages slash-and-burn style agriculture aiming for short-term harvesting. Government subsidies for land clearing exacerbate this situation.

This analysis is missing in international forums where NGOs exert influence. And the flawed forestry policies that result is evident in countries like Nepal, where a post-colonial nationalization of forests has produced vast open-access commons and a dramatic decline in forest resources that should make environmentalists shudder. The kind of regulatory command-and-control policies favored by environmental activist groups already have put unnecessary constraints on America's forests and subjected them to misconceived management policies and self-interested political controls.

Biological diversity and forest health can be protected only when forest management objectives respect local conditions. The United States, for instance, contains different kinds of forests: plantation forests in the South, the Northeast's managed-hardwood forests, old growth forests in the Pacific Northwest, and aging pine growth forests in the Rockies. A single global standard determined by a politicized international negotiating process cannot begin to satisfy the varying needs and priorities of local landowners and residents. The same is true for governance of the world's forests. Diverse forests and forestland peoples deserve diverse forest management policies, something no UN bureaucracy can ever achieve.

NOTES

[1] Farhan Haq, "NGOs Blast Plans for Forestry Convention as Premature," *Inter Press Service,* February 10, 1997.

[2] Gareth Porter and Janet Welsh Brown, *Global Environmental Politics,* (Boulder: Westview Press, 1996) p. 124-126.

[3] Stevenson Swanson, "Forest Treaty Out on Limb at Earth Summit," *Chicago Tribune,* June 26, 1997.

[4] Pranay Gupte, "Unfashionable Forests," *Newsweek*, October 6, 1997.

[5] Russ Banham, "Green Groups Slam Canada's Pact Proposal," *Journal of Commerce,* March 10, 1997.

[6] Farhan Haq, "NGOs Blast Plans for Forestry Convention as Premature," *Inter Press Service,* February 10, 1997.

[7] *Countdown,* Issue 8, (Winnipeg: Institute for International Sustainable Development, August 1997).

[8] Testimony of Rafe Pomerance, Deputy Assistant Secretary of State for Environment and Development, submitted to the House Subcommittee on Forests and Forest Health, Committee on Resources, U.S. House of Representatives, September 11, 1997.

[9] Dr. Patrick Moore, "Green Bans Won't Save the Forests," *Canberra Times,* July 14, 1997.

[10] Michael Bond, "Forest Grumps," *New Scientist,* July 5, 1997.

[11] Swanson, "Forest Treaty Out on Limb at Earth Summit."

[12] *Countdown,* Issue 8, (Winnipeg: Institute for International Sustainable Development, August 1997). Information is taken from Aarti Gupta,

"Combating Deforestation: The Role of Existing Agreements," UN Development Program/MacArthur Foundation, 1995.

[13] Porter and Brown, *Global Environmental Politics*, p. 126.

[14] Testimony of Rafe Pomerance, Committee on Resources, U.S. House of Representatives, September 11, 1997.

[15] Statement of Mike Dombeck, chief, USDA Forest Service, before the Subcommittee on Forests and Forest Health, Committee on Resources, U.S. House of Representatives, September 11, 1997.

[16] http://www.panda.org/forests4life/forests4life.htm

[17] Roger A. Sedjo, senior fellow, Resources for the Future, "Forests: Conflicting Signals," *The True State of the Planet*, Ronald Bailey, ed., Competitive Enterprise Institute (New York: Free Press, 1995).

Chapter 7
The Yellowstone Controversy: A Question of Sovereignty

Environmental groups, federal agencies, and the international community are discovering that they can use United Nations treaties to block private economic development in the United States. As a demonstration of what can happen when environmental groups and U.S. officials insist on enforcing international treaty law on U.S. citizens, consider the fate of a Montana mining project. In 1995 it found itself out of compliance with the 1972 World Heritage Convention and the UN's Man and the Biosphere program.

In 1978 the United Nations named Yellowstone National Park as a UN "World Heritage Site," a designation authorized by the 1972 World Heritage Convention, which had been convened by UNESCO and signed by President Nixon. In the next decade Yellowstone also would be designated a UN "Biosphere Reserve." What this meant for Americans only began to become clear in 1995.

NGOs Petition the United Nations

The controversy unfolded when a private firm proposed to open a gold mine near Cooke City, Montana, three miles northeast of Yellowstone National Park. Crown Butte Mines, Inc., a U.S. subsidiary of a Canadian company, had been trying since 1989 to get the U.S. Forest Service to approve its request to begin mining at a site to be known as the New World Mine. The company spent several million dollars producing an environmental impact statement (EIS) in compliance with federal rules, and it took additional steps to complete the arduous federal EIS permitting process.

Environmental pressure groups feared that New World Mine would pass government inspection and searched desperately for a way to deny it authorization. Their brainstorm: Invoke the World Heritage Convention. On February 28, 1995 fourteen environmental organizations began a process that would hopelessly entangle the New World Mine in global red tape. The groups petitioned the UN's World Heritage Committee in Paris to investigate the gold mine as an alleged threat to Yellowstone's status as a World Heritage Site. Even though the mining project had not even started, they asked the UN committee to put Yellowstone on its "World Heritage in Danger" list and undertake planning for "corrective measures." The groups also asked to be allowed to participate in the federal government's environmental review process, a proceeding that was unrelated to the World Heritage treaty.[1]

"World Heritage": The Convention, the Committee, the Sites

The World Heritage Convention was established to designate - "inscribe" in UN parlance — sites of natural or cultural significance.[2] The Convention authorizes creation of a World Heritage Committee, which maintains a roster of "World Heritage Sites." The Committee also may place sites on a special "in danger" list if it believes World Heritage values are threatened. The Committee is an affiliate of Paris-based UNESCO, the UN Educational, Scientific, and Cultural Organization. During the Reagan Administration the U.S. left UNESCO because of its record of financial mismanagement. The U.S. has never rejoined UNESCO.

Sites in the United States	Inscribed	Sites in the United States	Inscribed
ALASKA		**MONTANA**	
* Wrangell-St. Elias National Park and Preserve	1979	* Waterton-Glacier International Peace Park	1995
* Glacier Bay National Park and Preserve	1992	**NEW YORK**	
ARIZONA		* Statue of Liberty National Monument	1984
* Grand Canyon National Park	1979	**NEW MEXICO**	
CALIFORNIA		* Carlsbad Caverns National Park	1995
* Redwood National Park	1980	**NORTH CAROLINA/TENNESSEE**	
* Yosemite National Park	1984	* Great Smoky Mountains National Park	1983
COLORADO			
* Mesa Verde National Park	1978	**PENNSYLVANIA**	
FLORIDA		* Independence National Historic Site	1979
* Everglades National Park	1979	**VIRGINIA**	
HAWAII		* Monticello	1987
* Hawaii Volcanoes National Park	1987	**WASHINGTON**	
ILLINOIS		* Olympic National Park	1981
* Cahokia Mounds Satte Historic Site	1982	**WYOMING/MONTANA**	
KENTUCKY		* Yellowstone National Park	1978
* Mammoth Cave National Park	1991	**PUERTO RICO**	
		* La Fortaleza-San Juan National Historic Site	1983

Biosphere Reserves

The purpose of a Biosphere Reserve is to control land use and promote "biological diversity" concepts agreed to at the 1992 Rio "Earth Summit" (United Nations Conference on Environment and Development).[3] Biosphere Reserves are UNESCO land designations defined as "multi-purpose areas...to serve as demonstration areas for cooperation in building harmonious relationships between human activities and the conservation of ecosystems and biological diversity."[4] They are also referred to as "laboratory regions of sustainable development," and as tools for "promoting sustainable development and associated cultural values." Such ambiguous definitions raise more questions than they answer.

Even more mysterious is why the U.S. participates in the UN Biosphere Reserve program. In 1968, UNESCO held its first Biosphere Conference in Paris. In 1983 UNESCO convened the First International Biosphere Reserve Congress in the city of Minsk in the then-Soviet Union. These obscure conferences were held in cooperation with other UN agencies and the IUCN-World Conservation Union, an NGO. The U.S. is no longer a member of UNESCO and no treaty or convention has established the terms of U.S. participation in the program. Nonetheless, the U.S. State Department administers the U.S. Man and the Biosphere program by coordinating 47 U.S. reserves with the UN, in cooperation with the IUCN-World Conservation Union. Man and the Biosphere Committees comprised of government scientists, environmental officials and environmental pressure groups nominated the 47 U.S. sites, which were then approved by UNESCO officials in Paris. Some notable Biosphere reserves are the Grand Canyon, the Florida Everglades, and Rocky Mountain National Park.

According to the Interior Department, the program "is a designation which is basically designed to encourage voluntary associations of stakeholders, local people, to get together and try to do planning for sustainable development."[5] The term "stakeholder" is a term of art that can be applied to anyone who thinks he has a "public interest" in helping decide matters from which he is otherwise excluded. Scholarly experts, environmental pressure groups and other non-governmental organizations may claim that their concerns make them important "stakeholders" in the outcome of decisions in which others have well-defined legal rights. NGO opinions are recognized as important factors in the Biosphere Reserve planning process.

The U.S. National Committee for the Man and the Biosphere Program is a group run by the State Department's Bureau of Oceans, Environment and Science. Chairman Dean Bibles says that a Biosphere Reserve "consists of a core protected area, an area of managed use and an area of cooperation outside of the legally protected areas."[6] In UN terminology, these three areas of spatial distribution are referred to as "Core Area," "Buffer Zone," and "Transition Area."[7]

* Protected/Core Area is reserved for nature and "minimally disturbed ecosystems" and is not for human activity.

* Managed Use Area/Buffer Zone allows some tourism, recreation, and human habitation, but only economic activities compatible with "ecological principles."

* Zone of Cooperation/Transition Area allows some land use and economic development managed by a cooperative process involving government agencies, property owners and environmental advocacy group "stakeholders" (i.e., NGOs).

The Strategic Plan for the U.S. Biosphere Reserve Program says that the program's "framework for cooperation" will "enable stakeholders to plan types, levels, and patterns of protection and human uses [of land]." Areas in the Biosphere Reserve will be "connected by corridors judiciously linking different ecological units."[8] In the so-called "zone of cooperation," government agencies and "stakeholder" environmental activists will presumably plan the human uses of both public lands and private property.

"An immediate investigation is critically needed to help ensure that the potential impact and risks to the national and international values of Yellowstone National Park are broadly understood and averted," read the environmentalists' letter. "Rigorous assessment of the project and its consequences are needed to ensure that corrective or alternative actions which eliminate risks to Yellowstone...are fully explored and adopted."

The "international values" the Green groups referred to quickly became apparent. The activist organizations listed a series of threats to Yellowstone that included not only the proposed mine but other human activities: timber harvesting, oil and gas development, road building, and home building. These activities were said to be "encroaching" on wildlife habitat in areas around the park. The environmental activists threw in everything, even accusing tourists of being an unwelcome nuisance. "Increasing levels of visitation create problems related to over-crowding, including disturbance to wildlife," declared the letter.

The environmentalist letter reminded the World Heritage Committee that its jurisdiction extended beyond Yellowstone Park boundaries. The activists cited language the federal government had used in 1978 when it nominated Yellowstone as a World Heritage Site. The nomination made reference to "buffer zones in the form of National Forests surround Yellowstone for added protection."[9] The environmentalist coalition complained to the Paris-based Committee that existing U.S. law regarding these "buffer zones" was probably not strong enough to stop the New World Mine. The project would operate on adjacent private land, not on government land. It was likely that the owners of Crown Butte would argue that their mining project was protected from outside intervention because they held property rights to land they had leased and to which they were legally entitled.

Still, the environmental lobbyists reasoned that the National Park Service's "Statement for Management" might justify regulating some private property outside Yellowstone boundaries: "The evolution of an ecosystem management approach has been spurred by encroaching civilization ... management of public and private lands within the greater Yellowstone ecosystem is inextricably entangled."[10] Thus, green groups presented a legal argument – based on a philosophy of "ecosystem management" – for government to usurp Crown Butte's private property rights. "The United States has treaty obligations here," said Bob Ekey of the Greater Yellowstone Coalition. "It is our responsibility to keep Yellowstone not just for us but for the world."[11]

> **THE ENVIRONMENTAL GROUPS THAT INVITED THE UN TO YELLOWSTONE**
> National Parks and Conservation Association
> Greater Yellowstone Coalition
> American Rivers
> The Wilderness Society
> Sierra Club
> Trout Unlimited
> National Wildlife Federation
> World Wildlife Fund
> National Audubon Society
> Natural Resources Defense Council
> Mineral Policy Center
> Friends of the Earth
> Beartooth Alliance
> Canadian Parks and Wilderness Society

The Greens' scheme worked. Within weeks, sympathizers at the UN began to act on the appeal. Bernd von Droste, an ecologist and director of the UNESCO World Heritage Center (a UN appendage that coordinates "emergency action" on threatened sites)[12] contacted Clinton Interior Department official George T. Frampton Jr., Assistant Secretary for Fish, Wildlife and Parks. Writing from Paris on March 6, 1995, von Droste informed Frampton that the environmentalist coalition's Yellowstone claim "is sufficient to raise considerable concern about the long-term sustainability of the World Heritage values of this World Heritage site."[13]

Von Droste heaped praise on the activists, advising the Assistant Secretary that the fourteen groups petitioning the World Heritage Committee were "the most prestigious and influential in the field of natural resources conservation," and that Frampton should understand that their concerns warranted UNESCO investigation. Of course, ecologist von Droste was well aware that one of the petitioning groups was the Wilderness Society whose considerable political clout owed much to the fact that its former president was none other than George T. Frampton, Jr.

Von Droste went on to describe in detail the process for a World Heritage Committee investigation. If the Committee decided to place a World Heritage Site on its official "World Heritage in Danger" list, then the IUCN-World Conservation Union, UNESCO's NGO technical advisor, would have to monitor the situation and issue a report. Thus, one international environmental group would evaluate the validity of complaints raised by a coalition of other environmental groups.

Von Droste's letter also spelled out what he said were the U.S. Interior Department's UN treaty obligations. "Article I of the World Heritage Convention obliges [the U.S.] to protect, conserve, present and transmit to future generations World Heritage sites for which they are responsible." UNESCO interpreted this to include property beyond Yellowstone Park. "This obligation extends beyond the boundary of the site," alleged von Droste. "Thus, if proposed developments will damage the integrity of Yellowstone National Park," he concluded, "[the U.S. government] has a responsibility to act beyond the National Park boundary." The UNESCO official went so far as to advise a strengthening of U.S. law enforcement powers. "If enabling legislation is not adequate," von Droste counseled, "new legislation should be considered, as was the case in Australia with respect to the Tasmanian Wilderness World Heritage Site." Frampton was told to submit "a comprehensive report on the situation."[14]

Frampton's June 27, 1995 response mirrored von Droste's sentiments: "The Secretary [Bruce Babbitt] and the National Park Service have clearly expressed strong reservations with the New World Mine proposal," he wrote.[15] Frampton indicated that he agreed with the environmental coalition's assessment that the Park was in danger and the federal government's response must be much tougher. He invited the World Heritage Committee to visit the site and meet with mine opponents, and even offered to have the federal government pay for the trip.[16] UN involvement would in effect bypass U.S. law regarding the approval of mining projects. Frampton seemed to admit the extra-legality of his actions by writing, "It is unclear whether several specific concerns of the Department of the Interior ... and of the conservation community will be taken into account in the EIS process." Further, he agreed to let the IUCN-World Conservation Union assess the ongoing EIS review, an open invitation for the international NGO to meddle in an American legal review process.

Indeed, the Assistant Secretary's response confirmed UNESCO's far-reaching interpretation of the U.S. government's treaty obligations under the World Heritage Convention. "Considering the national and international significance of Yellowstone, and in compliance with the World Heritage Convention, the United States must assume full responsibility for assuring the integrity of World Heritage values is not compromised by adverse environmental actions taken either internal or external to World Heritage Site boundaries."[17] Frampton was invoking the World Heritage treaty to stake the federal government's claim to new powers. Undefined but formidable, these powers would include securing the sustainability of "World Heritage values" on the Yellowstone site as well as on property outside it.

The UN Monitors Montana

The collusion of Frampton, von Droste and the international NGOs did not go unnoticed. Montana's U.S. Senator Conrad Burns contended that American sovereignty was violated by any suggestion that the UN had authority to conduct an inspection of Yellowstone. His worry seemed less far-fetched when Yellowstone Park Superintendent Mike Finley explained to Wyoming's *Casper Star Tribune* newpaper that the World Heritage Convention had the force and statutory authority of federal law and that the accord mandated UN scrutiny of U.S. domestic policies.[18]

The World Heritage Committee took its cue from the Clinton administration. In September 1995, it scheduled a visit to Yellowstone National Park to begin its investigation of the World Heritage Site. The Committee's trip was carefully orchestrated by Clinton administration officials: the National Park Service organized a five-day "public hearing" at Yellowstone Park. Environmental activists packed the forum with boisterous mining opponents, who used the pseudo-legal hearing on the World Heritage site as a platform to publicize their campaign against a gold mine on private property. With the Clinton administration's help, the pressure groups urged the UN panel to help them.

Of course, the World Heritage Committee was already in sympathy and needed no persuasion. The Committee's chairman, Thailand's Adul Wichiencharoen, condemned the U.S. environmental permitting process as a "fragmented approach" that was failing to protect the total environment: "Certainly, the forest areas around Yellowstone belong to the same ecosystem," he told the *Billings Gazette*.[19] Wichiencharoen urged the federal government to manage the ecosystem better by expanding Yellowstone Park's boundaries. He recommended a giant buffer zone that would restrict economic development on an additional 12 million acres of surrounding land.

George Frampton could not have said it better. In 1987, as head of the Wilderness Society, Frampton advocated returning national parks to the wilderness. He complained that Yellowstone had too many roads, campsites, concessions, and airplane fly-overs. To keep people out, he proposed a comprehensive strategy of closing roads and enlarging "buffer zones," including curtailing mineral development on private land.[20]

On December 4-9, 1995 the World Heritage Committee considered the Yellowstone controversy at its annual meeting in Berlin, Germany.

Its verdict: the proposed gold mine violated the World Heritage treaty. According to minutes of the session, the September mission by Committee chairman Wichiencharoen and officials of the IUCN-World Conservation Union (the UN's NGO advisor) had helped it reach a decision: the Park was indeed "in danger." Moreover, the U.S. government apparently gave the Committee a green light to interfere since the Clinton administration would not "consider action by the Committee to be an intervention in domestic law or policy."[21] The UN group added Yellowstone National Park to its international "World Heritage in Danger" list.

Environmentalist groups were jubilant; they had been confident that UN "experts" would take their side. Even before the meeting was over the National Parks and Conservation Association, American Rivers, Beartooth Alliance, and Greater Yellowstone Coalition issued a press release from Berlin with the news: "The World Heritage Committee today voted to add Yellowstone...to the international list of World Heritage in Danger."[22]

Word of UN involvement in the approval process prompted angry protests from Western states residents and legislators. The *Montana Standard* asked, "Will the New World Order sabotage the New World Mine? Clinton administration officials appear to be scheming to bring that about."[23] By inviting the UN to Yellowstone, siding with development opponents, and politicizing the regular review and permitting process, the Administration confirmed Western states' fears that U.S. environmental policy was no longer decided by the give-and-take of domestic politics. Now it was captive to international bureaucracies and the environmental pressure groups that understood their rules and methods. U.S. Senators Alan Simpson and Conrad Burns blasted the Interior Department. "Does [George Frampton] want foreigners to determine our environmental requirements?" asked an incredulous Rep. Barbara Cubin of Wyoming.[24]

With help from allies in Paris and Washington D.C. the environmental pressure groups had scored an impressive triumph over private property owners in Cooke City, Montana. Their international power play successfully derailed the mine. Federal government officials cooperated by using a UN treaty to prolong and confound the federal permit process. Crown Butte mining officials faced a costly and protracted struggle against bureaucrats in the Clinton administration and at the UN who held the upper hand. Crown Butte succumbed in August 1996. It abandoned the project in exchange for an Administration offer of mineral claims elsewhere. The swap gave Crown Butte a $65 million piece of federal land in place of the New World Mine, whose estimated value was $600 million in gold, silver, and copper.[25]

Members of Congress took notice. Rep. Don Young, Republican of Alaska and chairman of the House Resources Committee, sponsored legislation re-asserting Congress' constitutional authority over federal lands. "Land designations under World Heritage and Biosphere Reserve programs have been created with virtually no congressional oversight and no congressional hearings. The public and local governments are rarely consulted," said Rep. Young.[26]

In September 1996 the House Resources Committee held congressional hearings on Young's "Land Sovereignty" legislation. Genuine grassroots witnesses and local government officials testified that no one notified them when a UNESCO land designation was imposed on their communities. They were shocked and surprised to learn that UN World Heritage and Biosphere Reserve designations could be used to suppress economic development and use of private property in their local communities.[27]

For instance, residents in the Catskill mountain region of New York mobilized opposition to a UN Biosphere Reserve designated for their area because they feared it would lead to more land use control. So did Americans living in the Ozarks of Missouri and near New Mexico's Carlsbad Caverns. Some local communities have caught on to the tactics of the global environment lobby, and they don't want the Yellowstone experience replicated in their back yards.

The international process that fourteen environmental lobby organizations set in motion has enormous implications for constitutional government and American liberty. By inviting the World Heritage Committee to investigate Yellowstone National Park, the Clinton administration defeated the New World Mine. But it also exercised executive branch administrative power to internationalize a domestic land use decision. Will the President or a future President use the vague mandate of "World Heritage values" and treaty compliance to justify more restrictions on public and private lands at the behest of environmental pressure groups?

NOTES

[1] Letter to Adul Wichiencharoen, chairman of World Heritage Committee, signed by National Parks and Conservation Association, Greater Yellowstone Coalition, American Rivers, The Wilderness Society, Sierra Club, Trout Unlimited, National Wildlife Federation, World Wildlife Fund, National Audubon Society, Natural Resources Defense Council, Mineral Policy Center, Friends of the Earth, Beartooth Alliance, Canadian Parks and Wilderness Society, Exhibit B,

"Sovereignty Over Public Lands," Hearing Before the Committee on Resources, House of Representatives, 104th Congress, September 12, 1996, U.S. Government Printing Office, Washington DC, pp. 140-149.

[2] The official title is "Convention Concerning Protection of the World Cultural and Natural Heritage."

[3] Biosphere Reserve Directorate, U.S. Man and the Biosphere Program, *Strategic Plan for the U.S. Biosphere Reserve Program*, 1994, p. 3.

[4] "Biosphere Reserves in Action," United States Man and the Biosphere Program, Department of State Publication 10241, Bureau of Oceans, International Environmental and Scientific Affairs, June 1995, p. v.

[5] Statement of George T. Frampton, Jr., Assistant Secretary for Fish and Wildlife and Parks, U.S. Department of the Interior, before the Committee on Resources, U.S. House of Representatives, September 12, 1996.

[6] D. Dean Bibles, chairman of the U.S. National Committee for the Man and the Biosphere Program, testimony before the Committee on Resources, U.S. House of Representatives, September 12, 1996.

[7] *Strategic Plan for the U.S. Biosphere Reserve Program*, p. 4 at note 2; The United States Man and the Biosphere Program, Department of State Publication 10187, Bureau of Oceans and International Environmental and Scientific Affairs, January 1995, pp. 8-9.

[8] Strategic Plan for the U.S. Biosphere Reserve Program, pp. 3-11.

[9] Letter to Adul Wichiencharoen, Sept. 12, 1996.

[10] "Statement for Management, Yellowstone National Park, November 1991, pp. 39-40, Ibid.

[11] Nadia White, "UN to Judge if Park 'in Danger,' Environmentalists seek international review of mine plan," *Casper Star-Tribune*, August 22, 1995.

[12] "The Who's Who of World Heritage," *World Heritage*, UNESCO, June 1996.

[13] Letter from Bernd von Droste, director of World Heritage Center, UNESCO, to George T. Frampton Jr., Assistant Secretary for Fish and Wildlife and Parks, U.S. Department of Interior, March 6, 1995.

[14] Ibid.

[15] Letter from George T. Frampton Jr., Assistant Secretary for Fish and Wildlife and Parks, U.S. Department of Interior, to Bernd von Droste, director of World Heritage Center, UNESCO, June 27, 1995.

[16] The offer was withdrawn after it became public.

[17] Ibid.

[18] Chris Tollefson, "Park Service Defends Decision to Invite Panel," *Casper Star-Tribune,* September 9, 1995.

[19] Michael Milstein, "Panel: Park Needs Buffer Zone," *Billings Gazette,* September 10, 1995.

[20] Fred Thomas, "Crowds, Development Called Threats," *Omaha World Herald,* September 16, 1987.

[21] Minutes of World Heritage Committee, United Nations Educational, Scientific, and Cultural Organization, Nineteenth session, Berlin, Germany, 4-9 December, 1995. WHC-95/CONF.203/16.

[22] National Parks and Conservation Association, American Rivers, Beartooth Alliance, and Greater Yellowstone Coalition, "Yellowstone Declared 'In Danger,' 'Ascertained and Potential' Threats to World's First National Park Cited by International Committee," press release, December 5, 1995.

[23] "New World Sabotage," *Montana Standard*, Butte, Montana, August 27,1995.

[24] Valerie Richardson, "UN 'Intrusion' Stirs Anger at Yellowstone; Environmental Alarm Seen As Meddling," *Washington Times*, February 1,1996.

[25] "Clinton Deals to Stop Gold Mine," *Cable News Network,* August 12, 1996.

[26] Gayle M.B. Hanson, "UN-Sponsored Aliens Land in Yellowstone," *Insight,* October 28, 1996.

[27] "Sovereignty Over Public Lands," Hearing before the Committee on Resources, House of Representatives, September 12, 1996.

Chapter 8
Seeing Green at the World Bank

The World Bank is an international lending institution that finances economic development projects in the Third World. Founded in 1944, it disbursed $20 billion to 241 projects in Latin America, Eastern Europe, Asia, and Africa in 1997. The U. S. government provides roughly one-fifth of the World Bank's funding. Other Western governments and Japan contribute the rest. Environmental advocacy groups are well aware that these funds give the World Bank an enormous influence over the economies of borrower nations. They rightly conclude that it is often more effective for them to lobby the World Bank than to lobby foreign governments.

At one time environmental pressure groups organized picket lines outside the World Bank's Washington, DC headquarters. They were eager to denounce Bank lending projects because they considered them environmentally dangerous. But over the past decade environmental lobbyists have adopted a new role. They have become counselors to the World Bank and conduits for its lending. NGOs remain critical of many World Bank loans, but as they become distributors and beneficiaries of Bank grant-making, they have grown more prudent in their criticisms and more understanding of the Bank's problems.

In 1988 one OECD official offered this positive description of non-governmental organizations: "To us on the official side, the NGO sector represents an educator of our publics, an aspect of our support, the origin of some of our policy, a welcome financial contribution, the source of insights on methodology and a vehicle for administering a portion of our official assistance."[1]

In the past decade those activities have increased and become institutionalized. Senior World Bank managers turn more and more to NGOs. In 1997, NGOs participated in nearly 50 percent of all Bank projects.[2] Often these were so-called "development NGOs" that provide direct services with World Bank funds — private voluntary organizations like Red Cross societies and refugee relief organizations like Oxfam and Save the Children Fund. They were involved in 81 percent of the Bank's agriculture projects, 60 percent of its health and population programs, and 69 percent of other social sector projects.

But environmental advocacy groups are also major participants in Bank projects. Indeed, environmental pressure groups have won an extraordinary influence over Bank lending policies in a short time. Environmental NGOs were active in the twelve Bank environmental sector projects undertaken in 1997. Although only five percent of its projects are in the environmental sector, the Bank's record of lending is impressive. The World Bank has extended $11.6 billion in cumulative loans for environmental projects through 1997, up from 1.89 billion in 1990.[3]

One other point. In 1997, the World Bank spent $832.6 million on its staff, $119.5 million on consultants, and $126 million on travel.[4] It's possible that the transformation of NGOs from fierce Bank critics into sympathetic collaborators may be related to their appreciation of the Bank's capacity for generous spending.

The World Bank's History of Failed Reform

In the early 1980s environmental groups were valuable critics of World Bank operations. Even as Third World governments eagerly lined up for Bank funding, NGOs argued that its loans were too often spent on large and poorly-conceived projects. Often these were massive construction projects that forced the resettlement of tens of thousands of people, destroyed local communities and violated human rights. The NGOs pointed out that Bank financing for economic development was actually perpetuating poverty and environmental despoliation.

NGOs often cite Brazil's Polonoroeste project in regional development and agricultural colonization as a demonstration of how World Bank financing produces ruin. This colossal example of central planning envisioned bringing a vast area of the Amazon rainforest into agricultural cultivation. It also proposed an extensive road building program to connect the project to populated areas of the nation.[5] But NGOs charged that $443 million in World Bank loans produced catastrophic effects. By introducing slash-and-burn agricultural practices, the loans subsidized the rapid deforestation of the Amazon basin. The project even helped spread malaria from the Amazon region to more populous parts of Brazil.

The director of Canada's Probe International, an environmental group, documented the Bank's role in a 1991 book, *Odious Debts*. Patricia Adams condemned the impact of Polonoroeste: "Indian lands are systematically seized, generally without compensation, and Indian economies destroyed," she wrote. "The livelihoods of non-Indian dwellers — mainly rubber tappers who for generations had collected rubber, Brazil nuts and rainforest products – are also threatened."[6]

Bruce Rich, a program officer at the Environmental Defense Fund (EDF), agreed. His book *Mortgaging the Earth* describes Polonoroeste as "an unprecedented ecological and human calamity."[7] Rich also described other unfortunate Bank loans. One $770 million development loan to Indonesia was intended to create enough economic opportunities to prompt two and one-half million impoverished people to migrate to more remote parts of the nation. But the project failed, producing more deforestation than jobs, and generating only more human misery.

Confronting reports of abuses like these, groups like EDF, the Natural Resources Defense Council, the Environmental Policy Institute, National Wildlife Federation and the Sierra Club petitioned Congress for relief. In 1983, environmental groups and Indian tribes testified before a congressional committee against the Bank, which answered with a forty-eight page memo attempting to refute their charges. The Bank assured Congress that it would not repeat its mistakes and warned that the environmentalist testimony "may create the misleading impression that past trends continue."[8]

The World Bank worked hard to neutralize environmental critics. Bank president A.W. Clausen, a former head of Bank of America, met with environmental leaders and asked them not to lobby against Bank funding. He said the Bank was amending its operations manual and would no longer finance projects that degraded the environment or forced human resettlement. The Greens acquiesced and merely lobbied Congress to require the Bank to increase its environmental staff, share information with NGOs, and support smaller, less destructive projects.

Other reforms followed. Congress enacted legislation to require the U.S. executive director of the World Bank to submit internal Bank documents to the Library of Congress. (The Bank has several executive directors, one of whom is always an American appointed by the President.) This act opened Bank finances and project information to public scrutiny. Congress also required the U.S. executive director to vote against any World Bank projects that failed to meet U.S. environmental standards. These oversight measures gave environmental groups serious political clout. Bank officials were forced to pay attention to their objections.[9]

Environmentalist fortunes further improved in 1986 when New York's Barber Conable, a senior Republican member of the House of Representatives, succeeded Clausen. With the world press reporting on the failure of many loan projects, Conable's mission was to restore the Bank's credibility and convince his former colleagues that the institution deserved continued taxpayer support. Shortly after taking office, Conable launched an aggressive Bank reorganization and began soliciting the views of environmental NGOs. Groups like the World Resources Institute submitted lists of complaints and an agenda of reforms.

Within a year, Conable had formed a new environmental department and hired or detailed staff to publish position papers and prepare action plans. A new policy required all Bank loans to be screened for environmental impact and a new class of environmental loans was devised. The Bank also promised to involve the environmental NGOs of both borrower and donor countries in decision-making.[10]

Environmental lobbyists were elated. Gus Speth, then head of the World Resources Institute, rejoiced that Conable's program was "a charter for a new day at the World Bank."[11] The Environmental Defense Fund even took credit for the changes. "At a recent World Bank Board meeting," read an EDF press release, "nine of the Bank's 21 Directors supported aspects of the environmental reforms in international development bank lending policy called for by U.S. legislation proposed and drafted by EDF."[12]

The Conable reforms did not markedly improve Bank performance. A 1992 internal review determined that 37 percent of the Bank's 1991 projects were unsatisfactory. According to the Bank's own criteria, they were failing to produce benefits. The review, conducted by then-Bank vice president Willi Wapenhans, attributed deterioration of the loan portfolio to the Bank's deep-rooted financial problems, including a "systematic and growing bias towards excessive optimistic rate of return expectations at appraisal." Wapenhans described borrower nations' failure to comply with financial loan covenants as "gross and overwhelming."[13] The Conable reforms had no real impact.

Environmentalist frustrations and criticisms mounted. By 1992 the left-wing Friends of the Earth and the NGO Development Group for Alternative Policies (Development GAP) had organized "Fifty Years is Enough." This referred to the upcoming fiftieth anniversary of Bretton Woods, the conference that created the World Bank, the International Monetary Fund (IMF) and the General Agreement on Tariffs and Trade (GATT), the modern institutions of the world economic order. Convinced that the Bank was too eager to lend money for "development" at the expense of the environment, a campaign spokesman flatly declared, "The Bank has done more damage than good."[14]

Anti-Bank NGOs then announced their opposition to continued U.S. funding for the International Development Association (IDA). This was the World Bank's sizable "soft loan window," which provides low-interest subsidized loans for poor countries. The Environmental Defense Fund, Friends of the Earth, Greenpeace, and the Sierra Club announced that the "tenth replenishment" of IDA — the tenth successive appropriation of U.S. tax dollars for the Association — would further degrade the world's environment without alleviating world poverty. Said Lori Udall, an attorney with the Environmental Defense Fund, "At this point in time we don't believe the World Bank can be trusted to use taxpayers' money in a responsible manner which helps the poor and the environment in developing countries. Along with our counterparts in borrower and donor countries, we are launching a worldwide campaign to reduce funding to the World Bank."[15]

The NGO mobilization against "IDA-10" was made more urgent by the drama of the Narmada dam, a World Bank-financed project in India. Environmental and development organizations and human rights activists joined forces against the massive water project. They claimed the dam, also known as the Sardar Sarovar project, would cause the involuntary resettlement of 200,000 people. They also publicized human rights abuses alleged by local villagers protesting the project and World Bank involvement. By 1993, anti-Narmada forces had generated so much unfavorable publicity that the government of India cancelled the project. Jubilant environmentalists saw Narmada as a model for future campaigns and looked forward to a chain reaction of World Bank loan cancellations. "Clearly the World Bank is not an institution that can be trusted to use American taxpayers' money wisely in developing countries," said EDF.[16]

More than fifty organizations, including Oxfam and Greenpeace, joined "Fifty Years is Enough." In 1994, the campaign staged a sit-in at an official press conference in Madrid, Spain for the Bretton Woods fiftieth anniversary celebration. Other protest activities followed. The campaign, said one commentator, caused the Bank and the IMF to suffer "the worst loss of reputation in their history."[17]

This steady drumbeat of NGO pressure yielded further World Bank reform efforts. The Bank established Project Information Documents. These were sets of prepared materials describing Bank activities in every borrowing country. It opened a Public Information Center at its Washington, D.C. headquarters. It established an Independent Inspection Panel which developed a review procedure so NGOs could challenge projects that they believed were failing to adhere to the Bank's own environmental guidelines. The Bank also encouraged staff exchanges with NGOs, and it included NGO representatives on its country missions.[18]

But U.S.-based NGOs contended that the World Bank was incapable of reforming itself. Despite years of lobbying and the promise of reforms initiated by Conable and his successor, Lewis Preston, environmental groups concluded that the Bank's decision-making was driven by an internal bureaucratic imperative to loan billions of dollars. Said Lori Udall in 1994 congressional testimony:

> *"For more than a decade, citizens' groups in the United States, in collaboration with partner organizations in the Third World and Eastern Europe, have lobbied the IMF and the World Bank, as well as the U.S. government, for reforms in [their] operations*

> and policies. *"Despite these efforts and the growing chorus of criticism from the U.S. Congress, governments and UN agencies, the IMF and World Bank continue to resist fundamental and meaningful change."*[19]

Writer John Thibodeau of Canada's Probe International pronounced the Bank reforms "resounding failures." His study, "The World Bank's Persisting Failure to Reform," excoriated management failings over a ten-year period. It claimed the Bank was intent on burying its critics in paper, "adding new policies and practices, producing new handbooks and guidelines for staff, and undertaking review after review, all intended to address the ill-effects of its lending."

The Probe report wondered whether the Bank could be reformed at all. Probe urged donor governments to "halt future appropriations of their constituents' scarce tax dollars to this flawed institution."[20]

Enter Wolfensohn

In 1995 a new president took charge of the World Bank. James Wolfensohn was a prominent Wall Street investment banker and a protégé of Maurice Strong, the UN's top advisor on reform. A champion of wildlife and habitat, Wolfensohn quickly became an outspoken critic of Bank projects that he considered dangerous to the natural environment. Early in his tenure, he canceled the Arun dam, a major $175 million construction project in Nepal.

In June 1995, Wolfensohn asked U.S. and international NGOs to advise him on the Bank's structural adjustment programs. These were loans made on condition that the borrower country reform its macroeconomic policies on trade and industrial development. NGOs argued that most structural adjustment loans imposed on developing countries tax incentive and subsidy policies that were harmful to the poor. Following an exchange of views, the Bank in December 1995 launched a Structural Adjustment Participatory Review Initiative. It pledged to hold public meetings to review structural adjustment lending in ten countries. Significantly, the Bank designated Development GAP, the group that launched the "Fifty Years is Enough" campaign, to serve as the NGO "secretariat" for this consultative process.[21]

Wolfensohn's sheer activism also helped ease NGO pressures on the Bank. He has met frequently with local NGOs on his travels to World Bank borrower nations in Eastern Europe and the Third World. At the World Bank's 1995 annual meeting, Wolfensohn held a joint press conference with three development NGOs – Forum of African Voluntary Development Organizations, Oxfam International, and InterAction –

where he urged the U.S. to increase its Bank funding.[22]

The Bank also has signed a cooperation agreement with the IUCN-World Conservation Union, a global NGO with members in 130 countries. Bank staff meet regularly with the IUCN to evaluate opportunities for NGOs to participate on environmental projects and initiatives. Bank staff serve as well on IUCN commissions and program advisory groups. One result of the Bank-IUCN collaboration is a proposed Critical Ecosystems Partnership Fund, which aims to restrict economic activity around parks and protected areas in developing countries.[23]

In 1997 the Bank began making the first in a series of loans to implement the anticipated Kyoto global warming treaty. Intended to promote development while protecting the environment, the loans are meant to be a model for future World Bank lending. The Bank also is moving to make more loans to small-scale projects considered less harmful to habitats. "My reading is that the Bank is clearly moving in the right direction," says Robert Watson, director of the World Bank's environment department.[24] Watson is himself a token of environmental concern; he is an atmospheric scientist who has worked for years in the federal government promoting the ozone hole and global warming scares.

Yet James Wolfensohn's promises and actions only repeat the tactics of A.W. Clausen, Barber Conable and Lewis Preston. An April 1997 internal Bank review of 150 projects concluded that his reforms were not going well. The Bank's internal culture of rapid loan approval had not been slowed, nor was there any speed-up in the cancellation of non-performing loans. One in-house survey of the Bank's re-organized Africa division found that less than a third of its staff believed the Wolfensohn reforms had improved Bank performance.[25]

The Wolfensohn reforms pursue two incompatible goals. They try to cut red tape, which has plagued Bank projects for years. But they also try to make the Bank's bureaucracy responsive to environmental pressure groups, which urge it to pursue "sustainable development" policies. But the Bank cannot trim its staff while initiating the far-reaching social and environmental reviews demanded by the NGOs. Caught between political crosscurrents, the quality of Bank projects continues to languish. "It's fair to say that the bank has launched some new environmental initiatives," comments Andrea Durbin, director of international programs at Friends of the Earth. However, "the implementation has been slow and sometimes doesn't happen, (and) the over-all portfolio hasn't shifted significantly."[26]

In 1997, most of the anti-World Bank NGOs collaborated with the Center for Strategic and International Studies, a Washington, D.C.

think tank, to evaluate the performance of the World Bank and other multilateral development banks. A task force chaired by former Democratic Senator Bill Bradley and House Budget Committee chairman John Kasich concluded that the Bank had failed to reform its lending processes, overhaul its bureaucratic structure, and achieve transparency and accountability to outside review. Blasting the Bank as "adept at keeping outsiders from differentiating between public relations pronouncements and real changes in bank activities," the task force warned that the Bank risked the loss of U.S. funding.[27]

The Money Tree

Will the NGOs now follow through on their severe criticisms? Will they force reform by lobbying to de-fund multilateral lenders? A few groups like Canada's Probe International will go that far, but most will not. Development NGOs in Europe and the Third World are particularly reluctant to cut U.S. funding. Their food aid and disaster relief programs depend on U.S. government subsidies. But many environmental lobby groups also have a diminishing interest in fighting the World Bank. In 1996, World Bank direct grants to NGOs totalled $36.8 million. The Bank's annual report, however, shows that it made $105.3 million in direct contributions to the Special Grants Program.[28] These grants have given the environmental lobby and other NGOs an enormous incentive to keep quiet whenever it is time for Congress to approve the World Bank budget.

The World Bank provides no public accounting of how much of its lending actually benefits NGOs. Some grant money goes directly to NGOs for studies and consultations. Typically, however, a foreign government will request Bank funding for a project. But the grant is usually administered by one or more NGOs acting on the government's behalf.[29] In theory, the NGOs are paid consultants or contractors to the government receiving the loan. In practice, they often run the show. (See Appendix One.)

Social Funds. In Latin America and Africa, the Bank has apportioned over $1 billion cumulatively to some 30 "social funds" that it has established to pay for particular projects involving NGOs. For instance, the World Bank gave $2.3 million to the Planned Parenthood Association of Ghana to pay for programs to prevent childbearing and population growth.[30] The Bolivian Emergency Social Fund paid NGOs for what it termed "long term development activities."[31] Clearly, NGOs face great temptation to engage in self-dealing. When NGO representatives sit on World Bank social fund boards that decide how monies are distributed; when they serve on social fund committees that design, select and evaluate projects; and when they help borrower governments administer social funds, there will be many opportunities to enhance the NGO role.[32]

Special Grants Program. This World Bank program typically gives NGOs between $200,000 to $2 million per grant. The unclear purpose of this program is to help NGOs participate in the "development process." Funds from the program have been used to cover travel expenses for NGO representatives to attend such UN meetings as the Population Conference in Cairo, the World Summit on Social Development in Copenhagen, and the Women's Conference in Beijing.[33] By subsidizing NGO travel, the World Bank gives UN conferences the appearance of broad public support. In fact, the NGOs receiving travel benefits are selected because they endorse UN objectives. In 1996, NGOs received a total of $5.34 million through this program.

In 1996, NGOs also received $800,000 through the *Safe Motherhood Special Grants Program* for "maternal health advocacy research and interventions,"[34] and $850,000 through the *Population NGOs Special Grants Program* to promote "demand creation" for abortion, contraception and sterilization.[35] Grants programs also supported NGO conferences, seminars and networking activities (e.g., a women's leadership seminar in India, a small business workshop in the Philippines, a conference on environmental problems in the Black Sea.)[36] Another $10 million was budgeted in 1997 for the Project in Support of NGOs in West Bank/Gaza.[37]

Small Grants Program. In 1996, the Bank gave out $600,000 in small grants of between $10,000 and $15,000 to "promote dialogue and dissemination of information about international development." In 1997, $700,000 went to 60 organizations. Program grants support "conferences, seminars, publications, networking activities, and other information-related activities."[38] The program gave $15,000 to a Honduran NGO for a conference to discuss the "initial results" of a Green Manure Technology Kit. It provided $9,000 to Conservation Asia, an NGO in Nepal, to facilitate "networking on environmental issues." The Lorma Community Development Foundation received $13,000 for NGO caucuses to lobby the Philippine government.[39] Another $15,000 went to a Brazilian NGO to participate in the June 1997 Rio+5 conference on the results of the 1992 Earth Summit. The program is a slush fund for NGO planning.[40]

Global Environment Facility. Many World Bank subsidies to NGOs are delivered through programs like the Global Environment Facility. The GEF is a lending agency to support the goals of the Climate Change and Biodiversity conventions, among others. The World Bank and the United Nations jointly run it. By 1994, NGOs had received a cumulative total of $10 million from the GEF to promote the UN's global warming agenda as well as to implement land use controls in the Third World. The U.S. government funds GEF activities even though the U.S. Senate has not ratified the Biodiversity convention. (See Appendix Two.)

Despite harsh criticism of the World Bank by environmentalist NGOs, World Bank grants underwrite NGO activities throughout the Third World.[41] Such grants safeguard the Bank's strategy of institutional adaptation and survival. In her book *Masters of Illusion: The World Bank and the Poverty of Nations,* author Catherine Caufield explains:

> *[The World Bank] is now committed (at least on paper) to helping the private sector, women, and the poor; to working with non-governmental organizations and the people directly affected by its projects; to increasing its lending for education, health, nutrition, and micro-enterprises; to protecting or improving the environment, the rule of law, and equitable income distribution – and to doing it all "sustainably."*[42]

What Do NGOs Want?

When environmental NGOs opposed World Bank lending, they helped stymie the financial and environmental mismanagement of borrower governments, the proximate cause of decades of Third World stagnation. NGO lobbying also reduced the foreign aid burden of American taxpayers.

But environmental NGOs now refuse to take the final step. They oppose attempts in Congress to reduce or end U.S. funding of the World Bank. In 1995, Rep. Tom DeLay (R-TX) offered legislation to eliminate Global Environment Facility funding. In part, he relied on the 1994 criticisms of the agency leveled by EDF director Bruce Rich in *Mortgaging the Earth.* "It is ironic that at the very moment when other forms of hyper-centralized planning and management have collapsed or are in crisis all around the world, the industrialized nations have endorsed just such an approach through the GEF," wrote Rich. "The GEF serves to propagate the profound fallacy that addressing global environmental problems is a matter of industrialized nations contributing an additional few billion dollars for more projects (in this case 'green' ones)."[43]

But when DeLay threatened GEF's funding, EDF and other groups rallied to its defense. "Funding from the GEF is essential to solving critical environmental problems," claimed a coalition of groups including EDF, Center for International Environmental Law, Conservation International, Friends of the Earth, Greenpeace, National Audubon Society, National Wildlife Federation, Natural Resources Defense

Council, Sierra Club, and the World Wildlife Fund.[44] A few months earlier, they had attacked the GEF as "dysfunctional" undemocratic, and unaccountable. Now they rushed to endorse the World Bank contention that the GEF had undergone "a major restructuring" to correct its problems. Were the environmental groups pressured by development NGOs to maintain a united front? What explains the change of heart?[45]

EDF's Bruce Rich, who literally "wrote the book" on the World Bank's environmental devastation, has gone strangely soft. "Cuts in funding will be the greatest spur to reform," he wrote in 1994. "It is the only external pressure that World Bank management appears to take really seriously."[46] Yet one year later, Rich's tone was radically different: "There is clearly a role for such an institution, but [the Bank] must focus on quality rather than quantity in its lending." Rich deemed the Bank's reform efforts credible and criticized as "irresponsible" proposals to zero out federal appropriations.[47] Says Doug Hellinger, executive director of Development Gap, "Wolfensohn is still our last, best hope to bring about change." The group that organized the "Fifty Years is Enough" campaign now acts as a Bank consultant.[48]

Some environmental NGOs go even further. They suggest that the Bank can be the catalyst that replaces a world economy based on free exchange with a new model of "sustainable development" controls on economic growth. In a world order of trade controls and income transfers, the World Bank can be an instrument of global development planning. The Worldwatch Institute, for instance, urges the World Bank to promote the agenda of the 1992 Rio Earth Summit. What are its tasks?

> *Among other things, creating a sustainable society will require stabilizing and ultimately reversing the buildup of carbon dioxide in the atmosphere; preserving the earth's forest cover, soils, and biological diversity; reducing overconsumption of resources in rich countries and population growth in developing countries; decreasing income inequalities between and within nations; and improving the status of women.*[49]

What's going on here? It is clear that environmental NGOs understand that only one aspect of the World Bank's power is the billions of dollars it lends. The Bank is also an enforcer of international economic policy advice. By attaching conditions to its loans, it imposes its recommendations on borrower countries. Despite badly flawed structural adjustment policies that worsen poverty, NGOs do not want to give up the Bank's power to control the trade, industrial and fiscal policies of borrower countries.[50]

Catherine Caufield's study of World Bank reform concludes: "There is much truth in the saying that development – at least in the monopolistic, formulaic, foreign-dominated, arrogant, and failed form that we have known – is largely a matter of poor people in rich countries giving money to rich people in poor countries." But environmental advocacy groups refuse to accept her finding. Seduced by World Bank grants, they seem determined to imagine the Bank as the instrument of their own purposes. Sadly, as they become influential insiders, the environmental NGOs lose interest in reforming a failed institution.

APPENDIX ONE
WORLD BANK FUNDING FOR NGOS (FY 1996)

Special Grants Program	$5.34 million
Safe Motherhood Grants	$800,000
Population NGOs Grants	$850,000
Female Genital Mutilation & Adolescent Reproductive Health Grants	$450,000
Small Grants Program	$600,000
Consultative Group to Assist the Poorest	$3.3 million
Institutional Development Fund	$24 million
Fund for Innovative Approaches in Human and Social Development	$1.5 million
	Total: $36.84 million

Appendix Two
NGOs and the World Bank's Global Environment Facility
(As of 1998)

Major NGO Executing Agencies/

Collaborating Organizations	Country	Project Funding
World Conservation Union-IUCN, World Resources Institute	Global	$745,000
IUCN	Global	$348,000
IUCN, Conservation International, The Nature Conservancy	Global	$4,000,000
World Resources Institute, IUCN	Global	$2,000,000
World Resources Institute, IUCN	Global	$5,000,000
IUCN	Central Africa region	$12,000,000
World Wide Fund for Nature, IUCN	Danube basin region	$3,900,000
IUCN, WWF	Pacific Islands	$2,440,000
IUCN	Indonesia/Malaysia	$2,000,000
IUCN	West Africa region	$7,000,000
Greenpeace, The Nature Conservancy	South Pacific islands	$10,000,000
WWF-US	Bhutan	$10,000,000
WWF-Brazil	Brazil	$20,000,000
WWF-US	Cameroon	$5,960,000
WWF	China	$17,800,000
IUCN	Congo	$10,000,000
WWF	Czech Republic	$2,000,000
Center for Marine Conservation	Dominican Republic	$3,000,000
The Nature Conservancy	Ecuador	$7,200,000
WWF	Georgia	$120,000
Conservation International	Guyana	$6,000,000
WWF-India	India	$20,210,000
WWF-Indonesia, WALHI	Indonesia	$14,400,000
WWF, IUCN	Lao PDR	$5,000,000
IUCN	Lebanon	$2,530,000
Conservation International	Madagascar	$21,300,000
WWF-US	Malawi	$5,000,000
WWF, Conservation International	Mexico	$25,000,000
IUCN	Mozambique	$5,000,000
The Nature Conservancy, WWF	Papua New Guinea	$5,000,000
IUCN, The Nature Conservancy	Peru	$5,000,000
WWF-US, Conservation International	Philippines	$20,000,000
WWF-Germany	Romania	$4,500,000
WWF	Russia	$20,100,000
IUCN, WWF	Seychelles	$186,000
WWF, IUCN	Slovak Republic	$2,300,000
IUCN	Sri Lanka	$5,417,000
IUCN	Sri Lanka	$4,100,000
WWF	Tunisia	$89,000
WWF, IUCN	Uganda	$10,290,000
IUCN	Ukraine	$112,000
WWF	Ukraine	$1,500,000
WWF, IUCN	Vietnam	$3,000,000
	Total	$311,547,000

Source: Global Environment Facility

NOTES

[1] OECD Cooperation Directorate: *Voluntary Aid for Development: The Role of Non-governmental Organisations* (Paris: OECD, 1988) p. 15, cited in Seamus Cleary, "The World Bank and NGOs," in *The Conscience of theWorld,* Peter Willets, ed., (Washington, DC: Brookings Institution, 1996) p. 69.

[2] *World Bank Annual Report 1997,* (Washington D.C.: World Bank, 1997) p. 16.

[3] *World Bank Annual Report 1997,* p. 24.

[4] *World Bank Annual Report 1997,* p. 159.

[5] Patricia Adams, *Odious Debts: Loose Lending, Corruption, and the Third World's Environmental Legacy,* (London: Earthscan 1991) pp. 28-31.

[6] Adams, p. 30.

[7] Bruce Rich, *Mortgaging the Earth: The World Bank, Environmental Impoverishment, and the Crisis of Development*, (Boston: Beacon Press, 1994) p. 27.

[8] World Bank, "Response to Statements of Environmental Organizations, Sent by the U.S. Executive Director" (Washington, DC, World Bank, unpublished, January 11, 1984), p.1, cited in Rich, *Mortgaging the Earth,* p. 337 at note 26.

[9] Rich, *Mortgaging the Earth,* p. 119 and Seamus Cleary, "The World Bank and NGOs," in *The Conscience of the World,* Peter Willets, ed., (Washington, D.C., Brookings Institution, 1996) p. 83.

[10] Rich, *Mortgaging the Earth,* p. 146

[11] Ibid.

[12] Environmental Defense Fund, *EDF News Brief,* Vol. XVIII, No. 1, March 1987.

[13] Portfolio Management Task Force, "Effective Implementation: Key to Development Impact," Report No. 92-195, World Bank, Washington, DC, November 3, 1992.

[14] Clay Chandler, "The Growing Urge to break the Bank," *Washington Post,* June 19, 1994.

[15] Environmental Defense Fund, "EDF Calls For US Funding to World Bank to be Cut Dramatically," *EDF News Release,* October 26, 1992.

[16] Environmental Defense Fund, "World Bank To Cancel Loan To Narmada Dam In India: EDF Calls World Bank Environmental And Social Record Dismal," *EDF News Release,* March 30, 1993.

[17] Cleary, p. 89.

[18] Cleary, p. 90.

[19] Testimony of Lori Udall, Director, International Rivers Network on behalf of the Fifty Years is Enough Campaign, Senate Appropriations Committee, Subcommittee on Foreign Operations, May 17,1994.

[20] John Thibodeaux, "The World Bank's Persisting Failure to Reform," (Toronto, Probe International, May 1995).

[21] World Bank, NGO Group, Social Development Department, "Cooperation Between the World Bank and NGOs," FY96 Progress Report, August 1997, p. 20.

[22] *FY96 Progress Report*, p. 22.

[23] World Bank, *Environment Matters at the World Bank*, Summer 1996, pp. 24-25.

[24] Jeremy Peolfsky, "It's a Small Lender, After All: World Bank Shifts Focus to Leaner, More Ecologically Sound Projects," Bloomberg News, *The Gazette* (Montreal), September 11, 1997, Pg. D5.

[25] Bruce Stokes, "Wolfensohn's World," *National Journal*, Vol. 29, No. 38, September 20, 1997 p. 1846.

[26] Peolfsky.

[27] Abid Aslam "Finance: Development Banks Seen Lagging on Reform, *Inter Press Service*, September 19, 1997.

[28] *World Bank Annual Report 1997*, p. 159.

[29] World Bank, Operations Policy Department, *Working with NGOs; A Practical Guide to Operational Collaboration Between The World Bank and Non-governmental Organizations*, March 1995, p. 47.

[30] Working with NGOs, p. 48.

[31] World Bank, Participation and NGO Group, Poverty and Social Policy Department, *The World Bank's Partnership with Non-governmental Organizations*, (Washington DC: World Bank, May 1996), p.8.

[32] World Bank, NGO Group, Social Development Department, "Cooperation Between the World Bank and NGOs," *FY96 Progress Report*, August 1997, p. 14.

[33] *The World Bank's Partnership with Non-governmental Organizations*, p. 10.

[34] *Working with NGOs*, p. 49.

[35] *FY96 Progress Report*, p. 14.

[36] *The World Bank's Partnership with Non-governmental Organizations*, p.11.

[37] *FY96 Progress Report*, p.15.

[38] *FY96 Progress Report*, p.14.

[39] "The Small Grants Program," World Bank, 1997.
[40] "Small Grants Program," Final Statement of Grant Requests Approved – FY1997, June 30, 1997.
[41] *Working with NGOs*, p. 50.
[42] Catherine Caufield, *Masters of Illusion: The World Bank and the Poverty of Nations*, (New York: Henry Holt, 1996), p. 306.
[43] Rich, *Mortgaging the Earth*, p. 312-313.
[44] Coalition letter to members of Congress, June 22, 1995.
[45] Bill Dawson, "DeLay Targets Global Ecology Facility; Lawmaker Wants to End U.S. Monetary Support," *Houston Chronicle*, June 27, 1995.
[46] Rich, *Mortgaging the Earth*, p. 315.
[47] "World Bank Too Important To Be Left on Auto-Pilot, Says EDF; EDF Calls on Congress and Treasury Department To Strengthen Oversight on World Bank," *EDF News Release,* March 27, 1995.
[48] Bruce Stokes, "Wolfensohn's World," *National Journal*, Vol. 29, No. 38, September 20, 1997 p. 1846.
[49] Hilary F. French, "Rebuilding the World Bank," in *State of the World 1994,* Worldwatch Institute, (New York: W.W. Norton & Co., 1994) p.157.
[50] Doug Bandow and Ian Vasquez, *Perpetuating Poverty,* (Washington: Cato Institute, 1995).
[51] Caufield, *Masters of Illusion,* p. 338.

Chapter 9
The Road Ahead

The international environmental establishment is growing slowly but inexorably. International conferences and their follow-up meetings are developing elaborate timetables to implement the sustainable development agenda and build global bureaucracies. What Green activists sometimes refer to as "the process" is shaping treaty negotiations and international law.

This monograph has focused largely on the work of NGOs. But their involvement with the Clinton-Gore administration, grantmaking foundations, and the UN bureaucracy is integral to the story. All are working to forge a new international environmental order.

In a pivotal speech at Stanford University in April 1996, then-Secretary of State Warren Christopher unveiled the Clinton administration's "Environmental Initiative for the 21st Century." Christopher proposed to integrate international environmental issues into the apparatus of U.S. foreign policy. He said all State Department missions and embassies would take up the challenges of the environment. They would dedicate themselves to the problems of climate change and to combating species loss and deforestation. Proclaimed Christopher, "We are determined to put environmental issues where they belong: in the mainstream of American foreign policy."[1]

Some observers interpreted the Christopher speech as another sign that *Earth in the Balance,* Vice President Gore's manifesto, increasingly guides White House ideas and policies.[2] Christopher's address sets forth the intellectual underpinnings of environmental diplomacy. It emphasizes the importance of public relations. A Green foreign policy will require lots of discussion, education and outreach to quiet any public doubts. Moreover, if the battle over environment is the equivalent of yesterday's Cold War, then environmental pressure groups have a very important public mission: They must support and promote the actions international agencies take to intervene in markets and regulate private decision-making around the world.

On Earth Day 1997, Secretary of State Madeleine Albright announced the fulfillment of Christopher's vision: "Today environmental issues are part of the mainstream of American foreign policy"[3] A year later, Albright's Earth Day address could not have been more emphatic about America's foreign policy priorities. Observed Albright, 'The prosperity of our families will be affected by whether other nations develop in sustainable ways."[4]

Was Albright saying that when environmental problems cause worldwide political unrest and economic dislocation they become national security concerns? That argument will yield environmental groups plenty of EPA grants and foreign aid contracts. NGOs can anticipate a shower of spending from the international family planning programs of the U.S. Agency for International Development and the global warming accounts of the Global Environment Facility.

Private monies are also flowing to the global Green cause. An old ally, Tim Wirth, former Undersecretary of State for Global Affairs, will be generous in distributing Ted Turner's fortune through the new United Nations Foundation. Wirth acknowledges that NGOs will be central players in implementing the UN's sustainable development agenda, which is sustained by Turner's $100 million per year.

Another major foundation funding source is the new Pew Center on Climate Change. It will be directed by Eileen Claussen, former Deputy Assistant Secretary of State for Environmental Affairs in the Clinton administration and a principal negotiator of the global climate treaty. The Pew Charitable Trusts has dedicated $5 million to the center, which will manage a public education and advertising campaign for the global warming treaty. Several corporations, including Enron, British Petroleum, and United Technologies, have lent their names to this effort, and they will likely call on their competitors to share the cost burdens of implementing the treaty. Large foundation-financed efforts like the Pew Center will ensure that climate change remains prominent in public and political debate.

Two directories conclude this volume. The first looks at major environmental advocacy groups and traces their sources of funding. The second reverses the order. It looks at major grantmaking foundations and lists selected grants to environmental groups in 1995, 1996, and for some groups, 1997.

One thing has not changed. Power broker Maurice Strong is again important in UN environmental policymaking. For almost three decades Strong has been a central figure. He launched the 1972 Stockholm conference and directed the 1992 Rio Earth Summit. Most recently, in January 1997, he was appointed special adviser to UN Secretary General Kofi Annan and is charged with coordinating the world body's reform and restructuring efforts. He also has assumed a position on the board of Turner's UN Foundation.

Mounting NGO Frustration

It appears that all the pieces are in place for "global governance." Yet to date the legacy of the 1992 Rio Earth Summit is not what its architects dreamed. The burst of Western financial aid for sustainable development in poor countries has not materialized. Support for the UN is dwindling financially and politically.

In 1996, two irate NGOs issued harsh reports scolding the world's governments for not acting quickly enough. The Worldwatch Institute and the Costa Rica-based Earth Council, chaired by Maurice Strong, excoriated the U.S. and other developed countries for failing to carry out *Agenda 21*. They took the U.S. to task for failing to ratify the biodiversity treaty and for not providing enough foreign aid. The Earth Council lamented, "It seems that nothing has changed for the better since 1992."[5]

NGOs believe political leaders have broken commitments made to them. But the reality is that plans for global sustainable development are unpopular with people. Maurice Strong admits as much when he complained: "Far too few countries, companies, institutions, communities, and citizens have made the choices and changes needed to advance the goals of sustainable development."[6]

In March 1997, five hundred delegates and NGO representatives gathered in Rio to set the tone for a special June 1997 "Rio + 5" UN conference reviewing progress on the *Agenda 21* agreement.[7] Strong explained that the second Earth Summit was "designed to regenerate some of the momentum, which to some degree has faltered."[8] Rio + 5 organizers focused on the commitments of governments and on the "value systems" of their people. An effective environmental agenda "is unlikely to be the result of a single top-down plan," counseled Worldwatch Institute's Christopher Flavin.[9]

Yet top-down planning is precisely what the international environmental establishment demands. Global Greens are unwilling to seek the people's consent or wait for public attitudes to change. Instead, they have achieved what they set out to get – power in the circuit of international agency bureaucracies. Green activists, writes Philip Shabecoff, "have forced their way into the previously closed rooms of international diplomacy." The persistent pressure groups are "placing their position papers on the table and speaking out, not just in the corridors but in the once sacrosanct plenary halls and in the small, out-of-the-way chambers where deals are hammered out in secret meetings."[10]

The Future

Sustainable development has become part of the international vocabulary. UN officials, diplomats and NGO lobbyists now are doing their best to make sure that the language becomes reality. But, as the Rio + 5 meetings demonstrate, the work of the global environment lobby is far from completion.

The current issue on center stage is global warming. The December 1997 Kyoto Protocol proposes to cool the planet by mandating restrictions on the use of energy. Secretary of State Albright has announced "a diplomatic full-court press to encourage meaningful developing country participation in the effort to combat global climate change." [11] The U.S. Senate will not ratify a treaty that imposes economic hardship only on industrialized countries. Yet its position is rejected by developing countries that believe economy-wrecking energy restrictions will prevent their escape from poverty. Global Greens must find areas of compromise. The November 1998 Fourth Conference of Parties, which will be held in Buenos Aires, Argentina, is the next battleground.

In other areas, the international environmental establishment continues to end-run the sovereignty of nation-states. The Clinton-Gore administration seeks U.S. Senate ratification of several outstanding UN treaties with implications for national autonomy and self-rule:

- *The Biodiversity Convention.* Under the pretext of species protection, the federal government could control uses of private land. Plans already exist to extend the convention's restrictions to biotechnology innovation.
- *The Basel Convention.* By defining various metals as "hazardous," this treaty controls trade in waste, scrap and recyclable materials. Greenpeace wants to use the pact to organize an embargo on trade with developing countries, excluding them from global scrap metal markets.
- *The Convention to Combat Desertification.* This pact to prevent land degradation already provides $30 million in foreign aid to African governments. Past aid has perpetuated land mismanagement by promoting centrally planned irrigation projects, subsidized farming and water usage, and inept agro-forestry policies.[12]

Global Greens have an insatiable appetite for funding, and they know that the most impressive treasury belongs to the United States. Ted Turner and other private grantmakers can prime the pump, but only U.S. taxpayers can make it gush. To finance burgeoning bureaucracies, implement expanding treaty commitments, and entice Third World regimes,

Green groups look to the Clinton-Gore administration. They need increased appropriations for agencies like the World Bank, the Global Environment Facility, and the U.S. Agency for International Development. Most of all, they need to strengthen the United Nations system on whose behalf they will urge Congress to make full payment of back "dues."

Their success, however, is not inevitable. Environmental pressure groups have bet heavily on mastering the bureaucratic processes and timetables of international conferences and agencies. Global Greens have put their faith in the "process." They have achieved success even when their ideas have been discredited. What's needed now is the vigilance to detect their maneuverings and the skill to overcome them.

NOTES

[1] Secretary of State Warren Christopher, "American Diplomacy and the Global Environmental Challenges of the 21st Century," Address at Stanford University, Palo Alto, California, Bureau of Public Affairs, U.S. Department of State, April 9, 1996.

[2] Moffet, "'Green' Issues Become Force in Driving US Foreign Policy," *Christian Science Monitor*, April 8, 1996, p. 1.

[3] U.S. Department of State, "Environmental Diplomacy: The Environment and U.S. Foreign Policy," 1997, http://www.state.gov/www/global/oes/envir.html.

[4] Secretary of State Madeleine K. Albright, Remarks on Earth Day 1998 at the National Museum of Natural History, Washington, DC, Federal News Service, April 21, 1998.

[5] Maricel Sequeira, "NGOs to Evaluate Earth Summit," *Inter Press Service*, January 16, 1997.

[6] "Little Progress Since Rio, Says Earth Council," *Europe Environment*, January 14, 1997; David Briscoe, "Worldwatch: World in Bad Shape," *Associated Press*, January 12, 1997.

[7] Daniel J. Shephard, "Ambitious Plans Mark Fifth Anniversary of Rio Parley," *Earth Times,* December 22, 1996.

[8] Colin Macilwain, "Rio Review to Rejuvenate Green Initiatives," *Nature* Vol. 385, January 16, 1997, p. 188.

[9] Vicki Allen, "Earth's Symptoms Worsen Since Rio Summit," *Reuter European Community Report,* January 12, 1997.

[10] Philip Shabecoff, *A New Name for Peace*: *International*

Environmentalism, Sustainable Development, and Democracy, (Hanover, NH: University Press of New England, 1996) p. 76.

[11] Secretary of State Madeleine K. Albright, Remarks on Earth Day 1998 at the National Museum of Natural History, April 21, 1998.

[12] See Julian Morris, *The Political Economy of Land Degradation: Pressure Groups, Foreign Aid and the Myth of Man-Made Deserts,* (London: Institute of Economic Affairs, 1995).

Directory of Environmental Lobby Organizations

Funding for International Advocacy

Center for International Environmental Law
1621 Connecticut Ave NW Suite 300
Washington DC 20009-1052
tel. (202) 785-8700
web: www.econet.apc.org/ciel

Assets[1]: $867,264
Income: $1,265,942

1995 Grants

Wallace Genetic Foundation, Inc.	$60,000
W. Alton Jones Foundation	$50,000

Conservation International
1015 18th St. NW
Washington DC 20036-5203
tel. (202) 429-5660
web: www.conservation.org

Assets: $9,974,510
Income: $18,371,260

1995 Grants

BankAmerica Foundation	$50,000
Compton Foundation, Inc.	$15,000
	$10,000
W. Alton Jones Foundation	$325,000
John D. and Catherine T. MacArthur Foundation (3 yr.)	$150,000
(3 yr.)	$70,000
Moore Family Foundation	$250,000
Pritzker Fioundation	$100,000
Wallace Genetic Foundation, Inc.	$10,000

1996 Grants

David and Lucile Packard Foundation	$114,180
Prospect Hill Foundation	$20,000
San Francisco Foundation	$52,000

Environmental Defense Fund (EDF)
257 Park Ave S
New York NY 10010-7304
tel. (800) 684-3322
web: www.edf.org

Assets: $18,355,422
Income: $27,141,022

1995 Grants

Lynde and Harry Bradley Foundation, Inc.	$111,000
S. H. Cowell Foundation	$25,000
Geraldine R. Dodge Foundation, Inc.	$100,000
	$12,500
Joyce Mertz-Gilmore Foundation	$150,000
Ann and Gordon Getty Foundation	$101,500
Heinz Family Foundation	$100,000
	$50,000
John D. and Catherine T. MacArthur Foundation (2 yr.)	$125,000
	$75,000
Wallace Genetic Foundation, Inc.	$50,000

1996 Grants

Boston Foundation	$10,000
Ford Foundation	$400,000
	$300,000
	$250,000
Joyce Foundation (2 yr.)	$323,000
	$200,000
	$75,000
	$50,000
F.M. Kirby Foundation, Inc.	$30,000
McKnight Foundation	$170,000
Andrew W. Mellon Foundation	$250,000
Charles Stewart Mott Foundation	$125,000
	$120,000
	$100,000
	$30,000
Public Welfare Foundation, Inc.	$125,000
Rockefeller Brothers Fund (2 yr.)	$100,000
	$25,000
Starr Foundation (2 yr.)	$500,000
Surdna Foundation	$100,000
	$50,000

Environmental Information Center/National Environmental Trust
1200 18th Street NE 5th Flr
Washington DC 20002-2002
tel. (202) 887-8800
web: www.eic.org

Assets: $889,525
Income: $2,653,984

1995 Grants
Compton Foundation, Inc.	$25,000
John Merck Fund	$60,000

1996 Grants
Joyce Foundation	$75,000
Rockefeller Brothers Fund	$150,000
Surdna Foundation	$75,000
Weeden Foundation	$15,000
Pew Charitable Trusts	$890,000
	$770,000
	$450,000
	$300,000

Friends of the Earth (FOE)
1025 Vermont Ave NW Ste 300
Washington DC 20005-3516
tel. (202) 783-7400
web: www.foe.org

Assets: $1,109,040
Income: $2,603,277

1995 Grants
Beldon II Fund	$15,000
Nathan Cummings Foundation, Inc.	$40,000
Foundation for Deep Ecology	$25,000
Richard and Rhoda Goldman Fund	$16,500
W. Alton Jones Foundation, Inc.	$200,000
	$50,000
(for FOE-Japan)	$100,000
Scherman Foundation, Inc.	$50,000
Wallace Genetic Foundation, Inc.	$136,000

1996 Grants
Bullitt Foundation	$25,000
Educational Foundation of America	$75,000
Roy A. Hunt Foundation	$10,000

Charles Stewart Mott Foundation (2 yr.)	$150,000
(2 yr. for FOE-Paris)	$204,000
Public Welfare Foundation	$150,000
Surdna Foundation	$100,000

Greenpeace
1436 U St NW
Washington DC 20009-3997
tel. (202) 462-1177
web: www.greenpeace.org

Assets: $14,567,905 (Greenpeace Fund, Inc.)
$2,524,559 (Greenpeace Inc., non tax-exempt)
Income: $9,636,091 (Greenpeace Fund, Inc.)
$21,425,231 (Greenpeace Inc, non tax-exempt)

1995 Grants

Beldon II Fund	$10,000
HKH Foundation	$10,000
Lannan Foundation	$100,000
Wallace Genetic Foundation, Inc.	$15,000

1996 Grants

Joyce Foundation	$60,000
Rockefeller Foundation (for UK)	$20,000

International Institute for Sustainable Development
Winnipeg Manitoba R3BOY4,
CANADA
tel. (204) 958-7700
web: iisd1.iisd.ca

Assets: NA
Income: NA

1995 Grants

John D. and Catherine T. MacArthur Foundation	$35,000
	$15,000

1996 Grants

Rockefeller Foundation	$23,000

International Union for Conservation of Nature and Natural Resources/World Conservation Union (IUCN)
c/o National Museum Of Natural History
1400 16th St NW 5th Flr
Washington DC 20036-2217
tel. (202) 797-5454
web: w3.iprolink.ch/iucnlib

Assets: $492,767
Income: $304,816

1996 Grants
Ford Foundation	$208,000
Charles Stewart Mott Foundation (2 yr.)	$360,000
	$225,000

National Audubon Society
700 Broadway
New York NY 10003-9501
tel. (212) 979-3000
web: www.audubon.org

Assets: $109,601,353
Income: $105,724,261

1995 Grants
S.H. Cowell Foundation (2 yr.)	$100,000
Cleveland H. Dodge Foundation, Inc.	$50,000
Wallace Genetic Foundation, Inc.	$100,000
Florence and John Schumann Foundation	$100,000
	$100,000
Ittleson Foundation, Inc.	$10,000
New York Times Company Foundation, Inc.	$15,000

1996 Grants
Bullitt Foundation	$95,000
	$30,000
	$20,000
	$25,000
David and Lucile Packard Foundation	$4,000,000
	$150,000
Charles Stewart Mott Foundation (2 yr.)	$70,000
Mary Flagler Cary Charitable Trust	$30,000
	$25,000
George Gund Foundation (2 yr.)	$120,000
Liz Claiborne & Art Ortenberg Foundation	$12,200

Penzance Foundation	$20,000
Procter & Gamble Fund	$30,000
Prospect Hill Foundation, Inc.	$20,000
Rockefeller Foundation	$200,000
Pew Charitable Trusts	$500,000
	$300,000

National Wildlife Federation (NWF)
8925 Leesburg Pike
Vienna VA 22182-1742
tel. (703) 790-4000
web: www.nwf.org
or
1400 16th St NW,
Washington, DC 20036-2217
tel. (202) 797-6800

Assets: $69,224,345
$73,003,510 (National Wildlife Federation Endowment Inc.)
Income: $101,950,287
$44,123,591 (National Wildlife Federation Endowment Inc.)

1995 Grants

Compton Foundation, Inc.	$35,000
S.H. Cowell Foundation	$40,000
Wallace Genetic Foundation, Inc.	$15,000
John D. and Catherine T. MacArthur Foundation (2 yr.)	$80,000
W. Alton Jones Foundation	$33,600
	$25,000

1996 Grants

Kenneth T. and Eileen L. Norris Foundation	$10,000
Liz Claiborne & Art Ortenberg Foundation	$16,200

Natural Resources Defense Council (NRDC)
40 W 20th St
New York NY 10011-4211
tel. (212) 727-2700
web: www.nrdc.org

Assets: $39,694,251
Income: $26,475,605

1995 Grants

Beinacke Foundation, Inc.	$350,000
Geraldine R. Dodge Foundation, Inc.	$100,000

David Geffen Foundation	$25,000
HKH Foundation	$15,000
John D. and Catherine T. MacArthur Foundation (1Ω yr.)	$250,000
Richard King Mellon Foundation	$150,000
Wallace Genetic Foundation, Inc.	$25,000
W. Alton Jones Foundation	$300,000
	$75,000
	$75,000
	$50,000

1996 Grants

Bullitt Foundation	$150,000
Columbia Foundation	$18,500
Marion O. & Maximilian Hoffman Foundation	$165,000
Joyce Foundation (2 yr.)	$275,000
Charles Stewart Mott Foundation (2 yr.)	$200,000
Pew Charitable Trusts	$150,000
	$225,000
Public Welfare Foundation, Inc.	$200,000
Starr Foundation	$25,000

1997 Grants

Clark Foundation	$100,000

The Nature Conservancy
1815 N Lynn
Arlington VA 22209
tel. (703) 841-5300
web: www.tnc.org

Assets: $1,358,866,481
Income: $1,112,458,392

1995 Grants

AT&T Foundation	$100,364
Compton Foundation, Inc.	$30,000
John D. and Catherine T. MacArthur Foundation	$49,500
Monsanto Fund	$70,250

1996 Grants

Alcoa Foundation	$20,000
Amoco Foundation	$110,000
	$50,000
Charles Stewart Mott Foundation	$25,000
David and Lucile Packard Foundation	$150,000
Rockwell International Corporation Trust	$25,000

Seaver Institute	$140,000
Shell Oil Company Foundation	$15,000
Surdna Foundation	$125,000
Union Pacific Foundation	$10,000
Wallis Foundation	$25,000

Ozone Action
1636 Connecticut Ave NW Ste 300
Washington DC 20009-1043
tel. (202) 265-6738
web: www.ozone.org

Assets: $138,893
Income: $359,779

1995 Grants
HKH Foundation	$10,000

1996 Grants
Charles Stewart Mott Foundation	$180,000
Rockefeller Brothers Fund	$25,000

Sierra Club
85 Second St 2nd Flr
San Francisco CA 94105-3459
tel. (415) 977-5500
web: www.sierraclub.org

Assets: $28,787,350 (Sierra Club, non tañexempt)
$24,780,906 (Sierra Club Foundation)
Income: $56,797,289 (Sierra Club, non tax-exempt)
$17,914,861 (Sierra Club Foundation)

(Sierra Club Foundation)
1995 Grants
Foundation for Deep Ecology	$23,000
Richard and Rhoda Goldman Fund	$10,000

1996 Grants
Rockefeller Brothers Fund	$30,000

World Resources Institute (WRI)
1709 New York Ave NW 7th Flr
Washington DC 20006-5206
tel. (202) 638-6300
web: www.wri.org

Assets: $46,826,470
Income: $17,565,180

1995 Grants
Wallace Genetic Foundation, Inc.	$90,000
John D. and Catherine T. MacArthur Foundation (3 yr.)	$400,000
John Merck Fund	$25,000
Geraldine R. Dodge Foundation, Inc.	$75,000
J.P. Morgan Charitable Trust	$10,000
W. Alton Jones Foundation	$200,000

1996 Grants
Amoco Foundation, Inc.	$20,000
David and Lucile Packard Foundation	$35,000
Bauman Family Foundation, Inc.	$10,000
Hitachi Foundation	$16,200
Joyce Foundation (2 yr.)	$140,000
McKnight Foundation	$100,000
Ford Foundation	$100,000
	$25,000
Andrew W. Mellon Foundation	$150,000
Surdna Foundation	$50,000

World Wildlife Fund (WWF)
1250 24th St NW
Washington DC 20037-1124
tel. (202) 293-4800
web: www.wwf.org

Assets: $89,515,224
Income: $165,300,493

1995 Grants
S.H. Cowell Foundation	$40,000
Ann and Gordon Getty Foundation	$65,000
John D. and Catherine T. MacArthur Foundation (4 yr.)	$375,000
(3 yr.)	$180,000
Chrysler Corporation Fund	$10,000
Geraldine R. Dodge Foundation, Inc.	$40,000
	$20,000
Hoffman-La Roche Foundation	$10,000
Howard Phipps Foundation	$25,000

	$25,000
AT&T Foundation	$25,000
Drue Heinz Trust	$10,000

1996 Grants

David and Lucile Packard Foundation	$15,000
Community Foundation for the National Capital Region	$100,000
Ford Motor Company Fund	$100,000
McKnight Foundation	$70,000
Rockefeller Brothers Fund	$20,000
Procter & Gamble Fund	$15,000
Alcoa Foundation	$20,000
Pew Charitable Trusts	$100,000

Worldwatch Institute
1776 Massachusetts Ave NW,
Washington DC 20036-1904
tel. (202) 452-1999
web: www.worldwatch.org

Assets: $4,084,714
Income: $3,827,824

1995 Grants

Wallace Genetic Foundation, Inc.	$130,000
John D. and Catherine T. MacArthur Foundation (3 yr.)	$450,000
Geraldine R. Dodge Foundation, Inc.	$100,000
Nathan Cummings Foundation, Inc.	$35,000

1996 Grants

William and Flora Hewlett Foundation	$300,000
V. Kann Rasmussen Foundation	$50,000
Ford Foundation	$200,000
Rockefeller Brothers Fund	$100,000
Surdna Foundation	$150,000
Weeden Foundation	$50,000

---

[1] *Grants data compiled from Grants for Environmental Protection and Animal Welfare, (Washington DC: The Foundation Center 1997). Assets and income data for 1996 derived from search of Form 990 series returns, IRS Charitable Organization Database, South Texas College of Law of Texas A&M University, Houston and National Society of Fund Raising Executives,* http://gateway.stcl.edu/nsfre.charity.irs/index.html. *Additional Form 990 assets and income data from Sovereignty International's exempt organizations database,* http://www.sovereignty.net/p/ngo/search-eo.cgi.

Directory of Significant Foundation Grants for International Environmental Advocacy

The Jenifer Altman Foundation
P.O. Box 1080
Bolinas, CA 94924
tel. (415) 868-2230
web: www.jaf.org

Established by Altman shortly before her death in 1991, the Foundation makes small grants for "a socially just and ecologically sustainable future." Altman was a researcher at Bolinas-based Commonweal, a health and environmental institute.

Selected 1995-1996 Grants

Center For International Environmental Law
$5000
Protecting marine and coastal biodiversity under the Biodiversity Convention

Citizens Network For Sustainable Development
$5000
Citizen participation in international negotiations

The Development Gap
$5000
"Mexico, the IFIs and the Spreading Crisis in Latin America" Workshop

Food and Agriculture Organization of the United Nations
$2000
NGO Participation at the World Food Summit

International Institute For Sustainable Development
$5000
"Principles of Sustainable Development Performance Indicators" conference

U.S. Network For Habitat II
$1500
United Nations Habitat II Conference

Urban Habitat Program/Earth Island Institute
$1000
Habitat II Oakland Regional Town Meeting

Women's Environment And Development Organization
$5000
Women's Caucus at the World Food Summit

Energy Foundation
P.O. Box 29905
San Francisco, CA 94129
tel. (415) 561-6700
web: www.ef.org

Created in 1991 by a joint decision of the John D. and Catherine T. MacArthur Foundation, the Pew Charitable Trusts and the Rockefeller Foundation, it distributed 268 grants in 1995-1997 totaling $26.7 million to 114 organizations.

Selected 1997 Grants

Alliance to Save Energy
1997 Amount: $720,000. Duration: Three years.
To support federal energy efficiency initiatives, as well as research demonstrating the benefits of U.S. Department of Energy and Environmental Protection Agency energy-efficiency programs.

1996 Amount: $75,000. Duration: One year.
To disseminate, through a targeted public outreach campaign, the "Energy Innovations" report, which addresses energy policy pathways to a sustainable energy future.

American Council for an Energy-Efficient Economy
1997 Amount: $165,000. Duration: Three years.
To support technical analyses and advocacy for federal and state energy efficiency policy initiatives, and to research the jobs and economic development benefits of efficiency investments.

1997 Amount: $230,000. Duration: Three years.
To develop analyses of federal and state policies to advance industrial energy efficiency.

1996 Amount: $15,000. Duration: Six months.
To provide research about the employment and economic growth ramifications of climate change mitigation measures for incorporation into the "Energy Innovations" report.

Business Council for a Sustainable Energy Future
1995 Amount: $40,000. Duration: One year.
To produce a forecast of the potential for sustainable energy technologies, and to sponsor workshops for policy-maker education on the topic.

Center for a Sustainable Economy
formerly the Economic Policy Institute
Environmental Tax Program
1996 Amount: $50,000. Duration: One year.
To analyze the industrial competitiveness impacts of energy taxes.

Environmental Information Center
c/o National Environmental Trust
1997 Amount: $125,000. Duration: One year.
To support public outreach regarding the benefits of public investments in energy efficiency and renewable energy policies as a means to cut U.S. carbon emissions and to help mitigate global warming.

Friends of the Earth
1997 Amount: $45,000. Duration: One year.
To support NewEngland tax shift efforts.

1997 Amount: $30,000. Duration: One year.
To support public education outreach and analyses regarding carbon taxes in Vermont.

Redefining Progress
1996 Amount: $100,000. Duration: One year.
To build business support for carbon tax shifting and energy efficiency investments.

Rocky Mountain Institute
1997 Amount: $25,000. Duration: One year.
To prepare and publicize research seeking to reframe the climate debate to be about policies to promote energy efficiency and renewable energy.

World Resources Institute
1997 Amount: $20,000. Duration: One Year.
To support dissemination and outreach activities for WRI's Climate Protection Initiative, including dissemination of the report, "The Costs of Climate Protection: A Guide for the Perplexed," by Robert Repetto and Duncan Austin.

William and Flora Hewlett Foundation
525 Middlefield Road, #200
Menlo Park, CA 94025
tel. (415) 329-1070
web:www.hewlett.org

Established in 1966 by the co-founder of Hewlett-Packard company, its international programs focus on population growth and family planning for which it authorized $11.6 million in 1996 grants.

Selected 1997 Grants

Environment Policy Analysis

Environmental Defense Fund, Oakland, CA
($200,000/2 years)
For the Western Water Resources program

Pacific Institute for Studies in Development, Environment and Security, Oakland, CA
($150,000/2 years)
For general support

Population

Environmental Defense Fund, New York, NY
($200,000/3 years)
For a policy evaluation and public education program on the links between population and climate change

National Audubon Society, New York, NY
($225,000/3 years)
For population activities

National Wildlife Federation, Washington, DC
($100,000/3 years)
For the population program

Parliamentarians for Global Action, New York, NY
($150,000/3 years)
For the Empowerment of Women and Population program

Planned Parenthood Federation of Canada, Ottawa, Ontario, Canada
($50,000/1 year)
For Action Canada for Population and Development

Population Action International, Washington, DC
($900,000/3 years)
For general support

Sierra Club Foundation, San Francisco, CA
($225,000/3 years)
For the international population program

International Family Planning and Development

Centre for Development and Population Activities, Washington, DC
($400,000/3 years)
For general support

Global Fund for Women, Palo Alto, CA
($225,000/3 years)
For family planning and reproductive health activities

International Women's Health Coalition, New York, NY
($405,000/3 years)
For general support

Planned Parenthood Federation of America, Family Planning International Assistance, New York, NY
($600,000/2 years)
For international family planning assistance

W. Alton Jones Foundation
232 E. High Street
Charlottesville, VA 22902
tel. (804) 295-2134
web: www.wajones.org

Established in 1944 by the founder of Cities Service oil company, it made 345 grants totaling $27 million in 1997, over half in its "Sustainable World" program. Year end assets were $370 million. (For more information, see the May 1998 *Foundation Watch*, published by Capital Research Center.)

Sustainable World Program
Selected 1996 Grants
American Communications Foundation
$173,000 over 2 years Mill Valley, CA
To develop environmental material for use on radio in "The Osgood Files."

Atmosphere Alliance
$30,000
A project of the Earth Island Institute
Olympia, WA
To develop a regional action plan in the northwestern United States to address climate change and reduce greenhouse gas emissions.

Bank Information Center
$200,000 over 2 years
Washington, DC
To provide information to nongovernmental organizations around the world about the policies and practices of MDB's, especially those of the World Bank and Inter-American Development Bank.

The Berne Declaration
$50,000
Zurich, SWITZERLAND
To promote environmentally sustainable lending practices at the World Bank.

Center for International Environmental Law
$60,000 Washington, DC

To ensure that joint implementation projects developed under the Framework Convention on Climate Change protect forests and biodiversity while reducing greenhouse gas emissions.

Environmental Defense Fund
$200,000 over 2 years
New York, NY
For public and policymaker education on global warming, and to pursue strengthening of international climate accords.

Foundation for International Environmental Law and Development
$50,000
London, ENGLAND
To provide legal research and analysis to small island and low-lying developing countries on the implementation of UN Framework Convention on Climate Change and opreation of the Global Environmental Facility.

Friends of the Earth Japan
$80,000
Tokyo, JAPAN
To monitor the Japanese government's bilateral and multilateral development bank aid policies, and to conduct a Siberian forest "hotspot" study.

Global Forest Policy Project
$50,000
A Project of Friends of the Earth
Washington, DC
To monitor international developments in forest policy and conservation.

International Project for Sustainable Energy Paths
$150,000 over 2 years
A project of the Natural Resources Defense Council
El Cerrito, CA
For analysis and dissemination of policy options to reduce greenhouse gas emissions.

IPS - Inter Press Service
$110,000 over 2 years
Rome, ITALY
For reporting and analysis of issues affecting the global environment.

Pacific Environment and Resources Center
$100,000
Sausalito, CA
To promote sustainable forestry policies and practices and advocate for new protected territories in Siberia and the Russian Far East.

Society of Environmental Journalists
$150,000 over 2 years
Philadelphia, PA
To improve the quality and visibility of responsible reporting on key environmental policy issues.

U.S. Climate Action Network
$100,000
A project of the Tides Center
Washington, DC
To increase understanding of climate change issues and to publicize the international scientific consensus about the destructive impacts of human-induced climate change.

World Resources Institute
$84,000
Washington, DC
To encourage the development of a renewable energy industry in Brazil.

Worldwatch Institute
$200,000 over 2 years
Washington, DC
To produce and distribute *Vital Signs 1997* and *Vital Signs 1998*.

Charles Stewart Mott Foundation
1200 Mott Foundation Building
Flint, MI 48502
tel. (414) 273-9643
web: www.mott.org

Established in 1926 by the long-lived (1875-1973) founder of General Motors, it made 464 grants totaling $64 million in 1996 from assets of $1.67 billion. (For more information, see the October 1997 *Foundation Watch*, published by Capital Research Center.)

Selected 1997 Grants

Reform of International Lending and Trade Policies:
Multilateral Development Banks

Bank Information Center
Latin America and Caribbean Program
To provide information and technical assistance to groups in Latin American dealing with multilateral development bank issues.
Amount granted this year: $5,600
Total granted to date: $425,600
Grant period: 03/01/1996 - 02/28/1998

Center for International Environmental Law
Monitoring MDB Inspection Panels
To test the independence and effectiveness of the inspection panels of the World Bank and Inter-American Development Bank.
Amount granted this year: $115,000
Total granted to date: $215,000
Grant period: 07/01/1997 - 06/30/1999

Conservation International Foundation
Policy Reform of Multilateral Development Banks
To reform the environmental policies of multilateral development banks.
Amount granted this year: $108,100
Total granted to date: $264,267
Grant period: 04/01/1997 - 05/31/1999

Friends of the Earth
World Bank Group and the Private Sector: A Campaign for Accountability
To effect positive changes in the World Bank's private-sector lending toward more sustainable, participatory and accountable development.

Amount granted this year: $15,000
Total granted to date: $165,000
Grant period: 04/01/1996 - 03/31/1998

International Institute for Energy Conservation, Inc.
Energy Efficiency at MDBs in Latin America
To create a strong market in Latin America for sustainable energy projects.
Amount granted this year: $150,000
Total granted to date: $335,000
Grant period: 05/01/1997 - 04/30/1999

Natural Resources Defense Council, Inc.
MDB Energy Policy Reform in Latin America
To promote energy efficiency and renewable energy sources in Latin America and improve multilateral lending for sustainable energy projects.
Amount granted this year: $150,000
Total granted to date: $549,000
Grant period: 08/01/1997 - 01/31/1999

Nature Conservancy
Global Environment Facility and Biodiversity Project
To support the conservation and sustainable use of natural resources by improving the transparency and effectiveness of the Global Environment Facility.

Amount granted this year: $38,000
Total granted to date: $170,000
Grant period: 03/01/1995 - 02/28/1998

Overseas Development Council
General Purposes
To support an organization that works to promote multilateral responses to global problems.
Amount granted this year: $375,000
Total granted to date: $375,000
Grant period: 01/01/1997 - 12/31/1998

United Nations Development Programme
Strengthening and Promoting Environmental Funds
To foster and support the development of national environmental trust funds.
Amount granted this year: $54,500
Total granted to date: $254,500
Grant period: 07/01/1995 - 12/31/1997

World Resources Institute
International Financial Flows and the Environment
To mainstream biodiversity conservation priorities into decisions made by the international financing community.
Amount granted this year: $350,000
Total granted to date: $350,000
Grant period: 01/01/1997 - 12/31/1998

Selected 1996 Grants
Bank Information Center
Latin America and Caribbean Program
To serve the information and technical assistance needs of groups in Latin America dealing with multilateral development bank issues.
Amount granted this year: $160,000
Total granted to date: $420,000
Grant period: 03/01/1996 - 02/28/1998

Berne Declaration
MDBs and Sustainable Development
To support efforts to effect significant policy changes in the major multilateral development banks.
Amount granted this year: $100,000
Total granted to date: $200,000
Grant period: 01/01/1996 - 12/31/1997

Development Group for Alternative Policies, Inc.
Global Economic Justice

To effect changes in the policies of international financial institutions.
Amount granted this year: $150,000
Total granted to date: $430,000
Grant period: 11/01/1995 - 10/31/1997

Environmental Defense Fund, Inc.
Technical Review of Hidrovia Studies by a Panel of Experts
To support a technical review of the Hidrovia waterway project in South America.
Amount granted this year: $30,000
Total granted to date: $30,000
Grant period: 05/01/1996 - 05/31/1997

Environmental Defense Fund, Inc.
Promoting Environmentally Sustainable Private Sector Investments
To support efforts to harmonize public- and private-sector environmental policies within the World Bank.
Amount granted this year: $120,000
Total granted to date: $120,000
Grant period: 04/01/1996 - 03/31/1998

Friends of the Earth
World Bank Group and the Private Sector: A Campaign for Accountability
To effect positive changes in the World Bank's private-sector lending toward more sustainable, participatory and accountable development.
Amount granted this year: $150,000
Total granted to date: $150,000
Grant period: 04/01/1996 - 03/31/1998

IPS - Inter Press Service
MDB Reform Media Project
To enable a worldwide media services organization to provide systematic coverage of multilateral development bank issues.
Amount granted this year: $185,042
Total granted to date: $185,042
Grant period: 06/01/1996 - 07/31/1998

International Institute for Energy Conservation, Inc.
Energy Efficiency at MDBs in Latin America
To increase energy-efficiency lending by the World Bank, the International Finance Corporation and the Inter-American Development Bank.
Amount granted this year: $20,000
Total granted to date: $185,000
Grant period: 05/01/1993 - 04/30/1997

International Rivers Network
Regional Communication on Hidrovia Project
To support the organization of an international campaign to promote debate and provide technical alternatives to the Hidrovia waterway project.
Amount granted this year: $25,000
Total granted to date: $265,950
Grant period: 05/01/1994 - 12/31/1996

International Union for Conservation of Nature & Natural Resources-US
Green Accounting Initiative
To promote the integration of environment and economics in systems of national accounting and lending strategies of multilateral development banks.
Amount granted this year: $360,000
Total granted to date: $360,000
Grant period: 07/01/1996 - 06/30/1998

Les Amis de la Terre
French NGO Involvement in MDB Reform
To enable a group of French organizations to address World Bank and International Monetary Fund accountability issues in France.
Amount granted this year: $204,000
Total granted to date: $204,000
Grant period: 01/01/1996 - 12/31/1997

Reform of International Lending and Trade Policies: Trade Agreements and Institutions

Selected 1997 Grants
Border Ecology Project
Reducing Negative Impacts of International Investment
To enable the organization to play a key role in future trade negotiations between the United States and Mexico.
Amount granted this year: $80,000
Total granted to date: $80,000
Grant period: 07/01/1997 - 06/30/1999

Canadian Environmental Law Association
Environment, Development and Trade Project
To explore links between international trade and environmental protection.
Amount granted this year $120,000
Total granted to date: $322,269
Grant period: 01/01/1998 - 12/31/1999

Center for International Environmental Law
Public Participation in Trade Negotiations in the Americas
To promote the integration of environmental protection and public participation in trade negotiations in the Western Hemisphere.
Amount granted this year: $110,000
Total granted to date: $532,139
Grant period: 08/01/1995 - 06/30/1998

Community Nutrition Institute, Inc.
Mutual Recognition Agreements Research and Education Project
To examine mutual recognition agreements and share findings with environmental and consumer non-governmental organizations and the public.
Amount granted this year: $140,000
Total granted to date: $140,000
Grant period: 10/01/1997 - 09/30/1999

Friends of the Earth
Research, Analysis & Education on Multilateral Agreement on Investment
To support an international investment liberalization accord currently in negotiation.
Amount granted this year: $60,000
Total granted to date: $60,000
Grant period: 07/01/1997 - 06/30/1998

Institute for Policy Studies
Global Economy Project: Monitoring North American Economic Integration
To monitor the effects of the North American Free Trade Agreement in the United States, Canada and Mexico.
Amount granted this year: $47,800
Total granted to date: $97,800
Grant period: 04/01/1995 - 03/31/1998

National Audubon Society, Inc.
Western Hemisphere Trade and Environment Program
To coordinate efforts of non-governmental organizations on trade and environmental issues throughout the Western Hemisphere.
Amount granted this year: $45,000
Total granted to date: $210,100
Grant period: 07/01/1996 - 06/30/1998

National Wildlife Federation
Quantum Leap Project
To support a capacity-building initiative designed to help environmental groups engage private international financial institutions.

Amount granted this year: $55,000
Total granted to date: $55,000
Grant period: 10/01/1997 - 09/30/1998

Sierra Club Foundation
Sierra Club's Responsible Trade Campaign
To educate the public about the need for environmentally responsible trade policies.
Amount granted this year: $200,000
Total granted to date: $410,000
Grant period: 07/01/1997 - 06/30/1999

Sierra Club of Canada Foundation
Canadian NGO Global Trade and Environment Campaign
To support a coalition of Canadian non-governmental organizations interested in issues that may be impacted by the World Trade Organization.
Amount granted this year: $116,600
Total granted to date: $176,600
Grant period: 08/01/1997 - 07/31/1999

World Wildlife Fund, Inc.
Building on the NAAEC and Its Public Participation Processes
To support a vehicle for international environmental governance that addresses the linkages between trade and environmental concerns.
Amount granted this year: $140,000
Total granted to date: $140,000
Grant period: 10/01/1997 - 09/30/1999

Selected 1996 Grants
Center for International Environmental Law
Public Participation in Trade Negotiations in the Americas
To promote the integration of environmental protection and public participation in trade negotiations in the Western Hemisphere.
Amount granted this year: $25,000
Total granted to date: $422,139
Grant period: 08/01/1995 - 07/31/1997

Centro Mexicano de Derecho Ambiental, A.C.
Trade and the Environment Program
To support the involvement of a Mexican public interest environmental law organization in international trade policymaking.
Amount granted this year: $100,000
Total granted to date: $170,000
Grant period: 01/01/1997 - 12/31/1998

Community Nutrition Institute, Inc.
Environmental Policy in Trade Liberalization Project
To develop consensus positions within the U.S. environmental movement and among environmental and business leaders on pending trade and environment issues.
Amount granted this year: $75,000
Total granted to date: $225,000
Grant period: 09/01/1996 - 08/31/1997

Development Group for Alternative Policies, Inc.
Project on Trade and Economic Integration in the Americas
To integrate environmental and social objectives into Western Hemisphere trade and economic integration policies.
Amount granted this year: $120,000
Total granted to date: $200,000
Grant period: 02/01/1996 - 01/31/1999

Institute for Agriculture and Trade Policy
Information Center on Trade and the Environment
To shape and promote environmentally and economically sound international trade policies and agreements.
Amount granted this year: $225,000
Total granted to date: $375,000
Grant period: 08/01/1996 - 07/31/1999

International Union for Conservation of Nature and Natural Resources
International Centre on Trade and Sustainable Development
To meet the information and communications needs of non-governmental organizations regarding the World Trade Organization.
Amount granted this year: $225,000
Total granted to date: $225,000
Grant period: 09/01/1996 - 12/31/1997

National Audubon Society, Inc.
Western Hemisphere Trade and Environment Program
To coordinate efforts of non-governmental organizations on trade and environmental issues throughout the Western Hemisphere.
Amount granted this year: $70,000
Total granted to date: $165,100
Grant period: 07/01/1996 - 06/30/1998

Sierra Club Legal Defense Fund, Inc.
International Trade and the Environment Campaign
To ensure that international trade policies, agreements and institutions promote domestic and global environmental protection.

Amount granted this year: $100,000
Total granted to date: $100,000
Grant period: 08/01/1996 - 07/31/1998

Sierra Club of Canada Foundation
Canadian NGO Global Trade and Environment Campaign
To organize a broad coalition of Canadian non-governmental organizations to work on environmental issues related to the World Trade Organization.
Amount granted this year: $60,000
Total granted to date: $60,000
Grant period: 07/01/1996 -06/30/1997

David and Lucile Packard Foundation
300 Second Street, #200
Los Altos, CA 94022
tel. (415) 948-7658
web: www.packfound.org

Established in 1964 by Packard (1912-1996), co-founder of the Hewlett-Packard company, it had $9 billion in assets at the end of 1997 and made more than $200 million in grant awards.

Selected 1996 Grants

International Planned Parenthood Federation (IPPF), London, England
$10,000
Support for training in the use of oral contraceptives and IUDs for emergency contraception by IPPF's affiliate, UMATI, in Tanzania

International Planned Parenthood Federation (IPPF), London, England
$20,000
Support for the Planned Parenthood Association of South Africa to initiate training in post-abortion care

International Planned Parenthood Federation (IPPF), London, England
$106,000
Support for the Pakistan Family Planning Association's project to reduce unsafe abortions

International Planned Parenthood Federation (IPPF), Western Hemisphere Region, New York, New York
$18,500
Support for translation, printing, and distribution of a Spanish-language version of prototype materials on emergency contraceptive pills developed by the Consortium for Emergency Contraception

Population Action International, Washington, D.C
$200,000
For general support

Population Council, New York, New York
$50,000
Support for Population and Development Review

Population Council, New York, New York
$199,716
Support for the introduction of emergency contraception in Maharashtra State, India

Women's Environment and Development Organization, New York, New York
$25,000
Support for the participation of women's advocates in the World Food Summit in Rome

Zero Population Growth, Washington, D.C.
$75,000
For the Population Education Program

Special projects

Population Action International, Washington, D.C.
$400,000
For expansion of communication programs about the importance of international family planning efforts

Population Reference Bureau, Washington, D.C.
$350,000
For expansion of the media program

United Nations Population Fund, New York, New York
$500,000
Support for a European media campaign about population

Conservation

World Resources Institute, Washington, D.C.
$35,000
Support for the Reefs at Risk program

World Wildlife Fund and the Conservation Foundation, Washington, D.C.
$15,000
Continued support for the Marine Fish Conservation Network

Rockefeller Brothers Fund
437 Madison Avenue, 37th floor
New York, NY 10022
tel. (212) 812-4000
web: www.rbf.org

Founded in 1940 by the daughter and five sons of John D. Rockefeller, Jr, it had 1997 assets of $454 million and made 352 grants totaling $10.4 million. Its major components are "Sustainable Resource Use" and "World Security."

Selected 1997 Grants

Greenpeace Environmental Trust
London, England
30,000
Toward The Solar Century, a project to encourage corporate investments in solar energy as an alternative to fossil fuel use.

International Rivers Network, *Berkeley, California*
$130,000 over 2 years
For general support of its Mekong basin project, including collaboration with civil society groups in Japan and capacity-building assistance for NGOs in the Mekong region.

Kiko Forum, *Kyoto, Japan*
$50,000
To support the public education efforts of this coalition of Japanese NGOs working on climate change issues at the 3rd Conference of Parties to the Global Convention on Climate Change.

National Environmental Trust, *Washington, D.C.*
$200,000
To continue public and media education efforts to build U.S. public support for climate protection.

Pacific Environment and Resources Center, *San Francisco, California*
$50,000
Toward efforts to promote a long-term conservation perspective in the North Pacific, focusing on bycatch reduction and fishery management reform.

Redefining Progress, *San Francisco, California*
$30,000
To disseminate the findings of a study on sustainable electricity futures in Europe to European and American policymakers, energy advocates, and the media.

The Tides Center, *San Francisco, California*
$80,000 over 2 years
For renewed support of the Biodiversity Action Network, an international clearinghouse for information on the protection of biological diversity.

Wilderness Society, *Washington, D.C.*
$50,000
For a public education and media campaign on sustainable forestry, designed to generate consumer demand for sustainably managed forest products.

World Resources Institute, *Washington, D.C.*
$50,000 over 2 years
For a forestry management project in Slovakia, designed to engage citizens in policymaking surrounding forestry use and protection and to involve a diverse group of participants in the region's forestry development issues.

Worldwatch Institute, *Washington, D.C.*
$100,000
Toward the institute's strategy for internal organization through the year 2000, to enable its continuation as an international publisher on environmental concerns.

Selected 1996 Grants
Environmental Defense Fund
$100,000 over 2 years
New York, New York
For a project to examine the impact of farmed seafood products on food safety and to design criteria for a possible "eco-friendly" shrimp certification program
$25,000
To review the World Bank's recent lending for agriculture and, in particular, its record of support for Integrated Pest Management programs.

Foundation for International Environmental Law and Development
$50,000
London, England
Renewed support for its efforts to encourage communication among countries involved in international climate change negotiation.

Stockholm Environment Institute
$30,000
Stockholm, Sweden
For support of its Climate Network Europe, which coordinates the activities of European NGOs working in the field of global climate change

Worldwatch Institute
$100,000
Washington, D.C.
Toward implementation of a new strategic plan

United States

The Energy Foundation
$12,000
San Francisco, California
To produce a report and a press packet on the economic benefits of greenhouse gas reduction

Environmental Information Center
$150,000
Washington, D.C.
Renewed support for an increased commitment to uniting the efforts of environmental groups working to expand public awareness of global warming.

Institute for Agriculture and Trade Policy
$100,000
Minneapolis, Minnesota
To support efforts to have state forest lands in Pennsylvania, Minnesota, Michigan, Indiana, and Wisconsin certified as sustainably managed.

Ozone Action
$25,000
Washington, D.C.
Toward its continued science-based commitment to increasing international public awareness and understanding of global warming.

Redefining Progress
$75,000
San Francisco, California
To encourage economic discourse and reevaluate current economic modeling tools in the climate change debate.

Sierra Club Foundation
$30,000
San Francisco, California
For a project to encourage regular coverage by broadcast meteorologists of the climate change issue

Tides Center
$150,000 over 2 years
San Francisco, California
Renewed support for its Environmental Media Services project, designed to improve the reliability and dissemination of environmental information among journalists through media education campaigns.
$50,000
Renewed support for its US Climate Action Network project, which coordinates U.S. environmental groups' launching of a nationwide public education campaign on climate change.

Union of Concerned Scientists
$60,000
Boston, Massachusetts
Renewed support for its efforts to ensure more and better news coverage of climate change by engaging scientists in public debate.

East Asia

Global Environment and Trade Study
$20,000
New Haven, Connecticut
Toward its conference, "Trade, Competitiveness, and the Environment," co-sponsored by the National University of Singapore and held in June 1996

International Institute for Environment and Development $10,000
London, England
To its work on sustainable resource use in the Mekong basin

International Rivers Network
$20,000
Berkeley, California
Toward its program on NGO support for sustainable resource use initiatives in the Mekong basin

Japan Center for a Sustainable Environment and Society
$45,000
San Francisco, California
For its project to monitor the involvement of Japan and the AsianDevelopment Bank in Mekong River basin development.

Nautilus of America
$150,000 over 2 years
Berkeley, California
For its Asia Pacific Regional Environmental Network (APRENet), an on-line information service available on the World Wide Web

Pesticide Action Network
$100,000 over two years
San Francisco, California
Toward efforts to monitor implementation of the sustainable agriculture policies of multilateral development banks in East Asia.

Rainforest Alliance
New York, New York
$1,500
For the reprinting and dissemination of two manuscripts concerning marine resource management in Southeast Asia at an international meeting on coastal mangagement.

World Wildlife Fund
$20,000
Washington, D.C.
To its work on sustainable resource use in the Mekong basin

Rockefeller Family Fund
437 Madison Avenue, 37th floor
New York, NY 10022
tel. (212) 812-4252
web: rffund.org

One of several family foundations, it had $54 million in assets in 1996 and made 77 grants totaling $1.9 million. Fund director Donald Ross also coordinates activities of the Environmental Grantmakers Association (EGA), a group of about 180 foundations. (For more information on EGA, see the April 1997 *Organization Trends*, published by Capital Research Center.)

Selected 1996 Grants

Environmental Information Center, Washington, D.C.
$50,000
The first installment of a two-year grant totaling $125,000 to support environmental campaigns to inform and mobilize the public.

Ozone Action, Washington, D.C.
$20,000
The first installment of a two-year grant totaling $40,000 for general support for a research, public education, and advocacy campaign to address the threat posed by depletion of the ozone layer.

Sierra Club Foundation, San Francisco, California
$25,000
Funding for the Environmental Public Education Project, which seeks to educate the public on a range of environmental issues.

Rockefeller Foundation
420 Fifth Avenue
New York, NY 10018.
Tel. (212) 869-8500
web: www.rockfound.org

Founded in 1913 by John D. Rockefeller, it has distributed during its existence more than $2 billion to thousands of grantees worldwide. The value of the endowment in 1997 was $3.1 billion. New president Gordon Conway is an agricultural ecologist who helped define the concept of sustainable agriculture. (For more information, see Martin Morse Wooster, *The Great Philanthropists and the Problem of 'Donor Intent,'* (Capital Research Center, revised edition, 1998).

Selected 1997 Grants
Brazilian Association for Leadership Development, São Paulo, Brazil
$25,000
Toward the costs of its workshop to prepare the Leadership for Environment and Development program's presentations for the five-year follow-up meeting (Rio+5) to the U.N. Conference on Environment and Development.

World Resources Institute, Washington, D.C.
$20,000
Toward the costs of the Solar Century component of its Climate Protection Initiative.

National Audubon Society, New York, New York
$150,000
To continue a public education program in the United States in support of international population and family planning programs.

International Planned Parenthood Federation, London, England
$55,000
Toward the costs of its educational initiative on international reproductive health and family planning issues for European parliamentarians, civil servants, the media, and others.

Population Action International, Washington, D.C.
$250,000
Toward the costs of publications and media activities that are designed to advance implementation of the Cairo Programme of Action.

Population Council, New York, New York
$296,090
For the third year of a study concerning the relationships between high fertility in developing countries and educational investments by parents.

Population Council, New York, New York
$338,480
For the third year of a study of the nature and causes of unmet need for family planning in Egypt, Ghana, Pakistan and Zambia.

Population Reference Bureau, Washington, D.C.
$248,980
For case studies in Brazil, India, Morocco and Uganda concerning implementation of the recommendations of the 1994 International Conference on Population and Development.

Planned Parenthood Federation of America, New York, New York
$132,000
For the planning phase of a new global partnership and leadership program to encourage affiliates to collaborate with their counterparts in developing countries.

Pew Charitable Trusts
2005 Market Street, #1700
Philadelphia, PA 19103
tel. (215) 575-9050
web: www.pewtrusts.com

With $4.5 billion in assets, the Trusts in 1997 made grants totaling $181 million to 320 nonprofits. Pew is a group of seven charitable trusts established by the children of Sun Oil Company founder Joseph N. Pew. (For more information, see Martin Morse Wooster, *The Great Philanthropists and the Problem of 'Donor Intent'* (Capital Research Center, revised edition, 1998).

1998 Grant
Pew Center on Climate Change, Washington, DC
$5,000,000/ 1 yr.
Supports work to put into effect Kyoto global warming pact, emissions trading schemes and to secure participation by developing countries. News reports indicate that about half the funding will be spent on advertising which cites promises by major corporations that they will seek ways to reduce their own emissions and invest in more energy efficient technologies and products. The new Center, announced on May 7, 1998, will be directed by Eileen Claussen, former deputy assistant secretary of state for environmental affairs.

Selected 1997 Grants
World Wildlife Fund, Inc., Washington, DC
$288,000/9 mos.
For B.C. Wild. To continue support for efforts to achieve protected-area

status for a minimum of 12 percent of British Columbia's threatened ancient forests and other wilderness areas.

American Council for an Energy Efficient Economy, Washington, DC
$100,000/2 yrs.
To develop and document energy efficiency programs suitable for a restructured industry.

Center for International Environmental Law, Inc., Washington, DC
$150,000/2 yrs.
For Eco-labeling. In support of a campaign to promote eco-labeling programs for consumers of environmentally sound products.

Environmental Information Center, Washington, DC.
$3,500,000/1 yr.
To educate the public on national environmental issues.

World Resources Institute, Washington, DC
$120,000/2 yrs.
For the Forest Products Buyer's Group. To establish a buyers' group of large purchasers of certified sustainable forest products.

Natural Resources Defense Council, Inc., New York, NY
$125,000/1 yr.
For the Project for Sustainable FERC Energy Policy. To participate in electric utility industry restructuring proceedings of the Federal Energy Regulatory Commission.

United Nations Foundation
1301 Connecticut Ave., NW, #700
Washington, DC 20036
tel. (202) 887-9040

Only UN agencies and programs may apply for grants from this new foundation to which Ted Turner has pledged $1 billion over the next ten years. UN agencies may invite NGOs to participate. In May 1998 the foundation announced its first 22 grants totaling $22.2 million.

Selected 1998 Grants
United Nations Population Fund (New York)
$300,000 over two years
To teach journalists about population issues by sending reporters on one to two week trips to visit health workers and clients in developing countries.

United Nations Environment Programme (Nairobi)
$350,000 over 18 months
To work with Rescue Mission, a British group, on a survey to gauge what young people think the world's top environmental priorities should be.

United Nations Development Programme (New York)
$900,000
To work with the World Resources Institute to reduce greenhouse-gas emissions in China without harming economic development goals.

INDEX

Abramowitz, Janet, 124
Abzug, Bella, 18, 19, 92, 99, 110
Action Aid, 113
Adams, John, 74, 82, 97
Adams, Patricia, 144
Advancement of Sound Science Coalition, 53
AFL-CIO Housing Investment Trust, 96
Agenda 21, 19, 20, 59, 69, 161
Aho, Michael, 70
Albright, Madeleine, 159, 162
Alcoa Foundation, 171, 174
Alliance for Responsible Atmospheric Policy, 59
Alliance for Responsible CFC Policy, 35
Alliance to Save Energy, 54, 176
Altman Foundation, Jenifer, 175
Amalgamated Clothing and Textile Workers Union, 69
American Communications Foundation, 179
American Council for an Energy Efficient Economy, 57, 59, 198
American Council for an Energy-Efficient Economy, 54, 176
American Gas Association, 57
American Rivers, 135, 138
American Soybean Association, 118
American Standard Companies, 57
American Wind Energy Association, 57
Amoco Foundation, 171, 173
Annan, Kofi, 160
Archer Daniels Midland, 117
Architects Forum, 97
Argentina, 49, 83, 162

Arrow, Kenneth, 54
Arzu Wilson, Mercedes, 101
Association for Women in Development, 96
AT&T, 56, 171, 174
Atmosphere Alliance, 179
Australia, 17, 49, 136
Babbitt, Bruce, 42, 58, 136
Bahai, 96, 97
Bailey, Ronald, 22
Baltimore Fannie Mae Partnership, 96
Baltimore Housing Roundtable, 96
Bank Information Center, 8, 179, 181, 183
Bank of America, 96, 145
BankAmerica Foundation, 165
Barratt-Brown, Elizabeth, 18
Basel Convention, 4, 162
Batra, Ravi, 67
Baucus, Max, 72
Bauman Family Foundation, 173
Beartooth Alliance, 135, 138
Becker, Daniel, 50
Becker, George, 82
Beinacke Foundation, 170
Beldon II Fund, 167, 168
Belgium, 117
Benedick, Richard, 34
Bentsen, Lloyd, 69
Berle, Peter, 74
Berlin, Kenneth, 73, 74
Berne Declaration, 179
Bibles, Dean, 133
Biodiversity Convention, 126, 162, 175
Biosphere Reserve, 133

Blackwelder, Brent, 76, 82
Block, Joseph, 82
Boeing, 56
Bolivia, 111
Border Ecology Project, 185
Border Information and Solutions Network, 96
Borlaug, Norman, 118
Boston Foundation, 166
Botts, Lee, 82
Boutros-Ghali, Boutros, 5
Bradley Foundation, Lynde and Harry, 166
Bradley, Bill, 150
Brazil, 17, 49, 79, 80, 83, 128, 144, 181, 196, 197
Brazilian Association for Leadership Development, 196
Bread for the World, 95
British Columbia Ministry of Forests, 125
British Petroleum, 56, 160
Brookings Institution, 59
Brown, Lester, 112
Browner, Carol, 58, 74, 77
Brueggemann, Ingar, 115
Brundtland, Gro Harlem, 15, 16, 21, 22, 24, 68
Bullitt Foundation, 167, 169, 171
Burkina Faso, 113
Burns, Conrad, 137, 138
Bush administration, 38, 39, 68, 71
Bush, George, 17, 18, 69, 70, 71
Business Council for a Sustainable Energy Future, 176
Business Council for Sustainable Energy, 57
Cable News Network (CNN), 51
Caldicott, Helen, 54
Canada, 17, 22, 37, 40, 49, 70, 71, 72, 73, 99, 101, 124, 144, 148, 150, 186, 187, 189
Canadian Environmental Law Association, 185
Canadian Parks and Wilderness Society, 135
Canadian Pulp and Paper Associations, 125
Capital Research Center, 181, 195, 196, 197
Cargill Foundation, 70
Carlsson, Ingvar, 21
Carnegie Endowment for International Peace, 22
Carrick, Roger, 82
Carson, Rachel, 10
Carter administration, 13
Carter, Jimmy, 19, 108
Cary Charitable Trust, Mary Flagler, 169
Castro, Fidel, 102, 108
Catholic Campaign for America, 110
Catholics for a Free Choice, 110
Cato Institute, 53
Caufield, Catherine, 152, 153
Center for a Sustainable Economy, 176
Center for Clean Air Policy, 59
Center for International Environmental Law, 8, 55, 59, 70, 77, 152, 165, 175, 179, 182, 186, 187, 198
Center for Marine Conservation, 83, 155
Center for Reproductive Law and Policy, 110
Center for Security Policy, 53
Center for Strategic and International Studies, 149
Center of Concern, 95
Centre for Development and Population Activities, 178

Centro Mexicano de Derecho Ambiental, 187
Chevron, 58
Chile, 79, 83
China, 48, 49, 59, 79, 103, 112, 199
Choucri, Nazli, 23
Christian Aid, 113
Christopher, Warren, 159
Chrysler Corporation Fund, 173
Ciba-Geigy, 117
Cisneros, Henry, 96
Citizens for a Sound Economy, 53
Citizens Network for Sustainable Development, 79, 91, 92, 95, 97, 175
Citizens Trade Campaign, 68
Clapp, Philip, 50
Clark Foundation, 171
Clausen, A.W., 145, 149
Claussen, Eileen, 160, 197
Climate Action Network, 4, 39, 40, 42, 54, 55, 181, 194
Climate Institute, 59
Clinton administration, 19-20, 33, 39, 42, 46-49, 51, 56, 67, 71- 85, 91, 93, 96-99, 103, 112, 123, 127, 135-139, 159-160, 162-163
Clinton, Bill, 42, 52, 70, 71,
Cloak of Green, 40
Club of Rome, 13, 14
Coalition for a Strong United Nations, 95
Collaborating Movements Towards Sustainability, 97
Columbia Foundation, 171
Commission on Environmental Cooperation, 73
Commission on Global Governance, 21, 109
Committee for a Constructive Tomorrow, 52, 53, 103

Community Nutrition Institute, 59, 186, 188
Competitive Enterprise Institute, 52, 53
Compton Foundation, 165, 167, 170, 171
Conable, Barber, 22, 145-147, 149
Concerned Women for America, 100, 116
Conservation Asia, 151
Conservation Foundation, 190
Conservation International, 18, 74, 152, 155, 165, 182
Consortium for Action to Protect the Earth '92, 16
Consumer Alert, 32, 53
Consumers Union, 82
Convention on Biological Diversity, 19
Convention to Combat Desertification, 162
Conway, Gordon, 196
Cooperative Housing Foundation, 96
Council on Foreign Relations, 70, 73
Countdown, 41, 125
Cowell Foundation, S.H., 166, 169, 170, 173
Cubin, Barbara, 138
Daly, Herman, 67
Danone, 117
Davis, Susan, 113, 116
Defenders of Wildlife, 3, 73, 77
DeLay, Tom, 152
Denmark, 22
Development Group for Alternative Policies (GAP) 146, 153, 175 183, 188
Dewar, Elaine, 23, 24, 40
Dillon-Ridgley, Dianne, 18, 93, 97, 112
Diouf, Jacques, 115

Dodge Foundation, Cleveland H., 169
Dodge Foundation, Geraldine R., 55, 166, 170, 173, 174
Dombeck, Michael, 127
Dow Chemical, 56, 58
Drue Heinz Trust, 174
DuPont, 56
Eagle Forum, 52
Earth Council, 161
Earth First, 3
Earth in the Balance, 46, 67, 159
Earth Island Institute, 68, 83, 97, 175, 179
Earth Negotiations Bulletin, 40, 41
Earth Times, 124
Easterbrook, Gregg, 118
Eco, 20, 32, 40, 41, 54, 55, 198
Ecological Society of America, 54
Economic Policy Institute, 176
Educational Foundation of America, 167
Edwards, Don, 93
Egypt, 79, 103, 109, 197
Ehrlich, Paul, 13
Ekey, Bob, 134
El-Ashry, Mohammed, 19
Energy Foundation, 176, 193
Energy Innovations, 54, 176
Enron, 50, 55, 57, 58, 160
Environment and Energy Study Institute, 16, 57, 70
Environmental Defense Fund, 2, 8, 14, 18, 31, 35, 43, 47, 55, 56, 57, 70, 71, 72, 73, 74, 77, 81, 82, 97, 144, 146, 166, 177, 178, 180, 184, 192
Environmental Grantmakers Association, 195
Environmental Information Center (see also National Environmental Trust) 31, 42, 43, 50, 51, 167, 177, 193, 195, 198
Environmental Investigation Agency, 125
Environmental Policy Institute, 145
Esty, Daniel, 23, 67, 71, 82
European Commission, 22, 78
European Community, 70
European Science and Environment Forum, 53
European Union, 47, 50, 78, 124
Family of the Americas Foundation, 110
Family Research Council, 110
Fannie Mae, 93, 96
Fannie Mae Foundation, 93
Fay, Kevin, 56
Finley, Mike, 137
Flavin, Christopher, 32, 161
Fletcher, Kathy, 82
Florio, James, 82
Focus on the Family, 110
Ford Foundation, 22, 96, 118, 166, 169, 173, 174
Ford Motor Company Fund, 174
Forest Stewardship Council, 9, 126
Forum for the Environment, 8
Forum of African Voluntary Development, 148
Foundation for Deep Ecology, 167, 172
Foundation for International Environmental Law and Development, 180, 192
Foundation on Economic Trends, 117
Fox, Sally, 82
Framework Convention on Climate Change, 19, 38, 55, 56, 179, 180
Frampton, George, 135-138
Fraser Institute, 53
Freeport McMoRan, 8

French, Hillary, 67
Friends of the Earth, 2, 8, 9, 46, 50, 52, 53, 55, 68, 75, 76, 77, 79, 81, 82, 95, 123, 125, 135, 146, 149, 152, 167, 177, 180, 182, 184, 186
Fuller, Kathryn, 74, 82
Gaines, Sanford, 71
Geffen Foundation, David, 171
General Agreement on Tariffs and Trade (GATT), 68-71, 74-78, 80, 83, 146
General Electric, 56
General Motors, 58, 181
Georgia Environmental Organization, 96
Georgia Pacific, 82
Gephardt, Richard, 69
Germany, 40, 117, 155
Getty Foundation, Anne and Gordon, 166, 173
Ghana, 21, 150, 197
Glickman, Dan, 58, 117
Global 2000 Report to the President, 13
Global Climate Information Project, 51
Global Commission to Fund the UN, 92
Global Environment and Trade Study, 59, 194
Global Forest Policy Project, 124, 125, 126, 180
Global Fund for Women, 178
Global Tomorrow Coalition, 14, 16, 93
Goldman Fund, Richard and Rhoda, 167, 172
Gore, Al, 42, 45-47, 52, 67, 72, 74, 80, 98, 159
Greater Yellowstone Coalition, 134, 135, 138

Greenpeace, 2, 3, 4, 6, 7, 8, 11, 32, 44, 45, 46, 50, 55, 57, 68, 75, 76, 79, 83, 117, 118, 123, 124, 125, 146, 147, 152, 155, 162, 168, 191, 199
Group of 77, 101
Guatemala, 83, 101
Gummer, John, 51
Gund Foundation, George, 169
Gupte, Pranay, 124
Guyana, 21
Habitat for Humanity, 92, 95, 96
Hagel, Chuck, 48, 49, 51
Hair, Jay, 74, 75, 76, 78, 97
Heinz Family Foundation, 166
Heinz Foundation, Teresa and H.John, 55
Heinz, Teresa, 18
Heitkamp, Heidi, 82
Hellinger, Doug, 153
Heritage Foundation, 53
Hershey, Jim, 118
Hewlett Foundation, William and Flora, 174, 177
Hitachi Foundation, 173
HKH Foundation, 168, 171, 172
Hoffman Foundation, Marian O. and Maximilian, 171
Hoffman-La Roche Foundation, 173
Hog Farm, 12
Holdren, John, 54
Honeywell, 57
Hong Kong, 79
Hoover Institution, 47, 118
Howard Phipps Foundation, 173
Howard, William, 82
Hudson, Stewart, 72, 74
Hufbauer, Gary, 72
Human Life International, 110, 116
Humane Society of the United States,

3, 14, 82, 83, 92
Hunt Foundation, Roy A., 167
Independent Institute, 53
India, 20, 22, 48, 49, 69, 79, 80, 103, 124, 128, 147, 151, 155, 190, 197
Indonesia, 8, 9, 22, 48, 79, 144, 155
Institute for Agriculture and Trade Policy, 70, 79, 82, 188, 193
Institute for International Economics, 23, 72
Institute for Policy Studies, 186
Inter Press Service, 180
InterAction, 148
Inter-American Tropical Tuna Commission, 83
International Biosphere Reserve Congress, 133
International Gay and Lesbian Human Rights Commission, 95, 97
International Institute for Energy Conservation, 59, 182, 184
International Institute for Environment and Development, 194
International Institute for Sustainable Development, 40, 125, 168, 175
International Ladies Garment Workers Union, 69
International Monetary Fund, 76, 146, 185
International Physicians for the Prevention of Nuclear War, 54
International Planned Parenthood Federation, 109, 110, 111, 112, 115, 116, 189, 196
International Rivers Network, 8, 185, 191, 194
International Union of Electricians, 68
International Whaling Convention (IWC), 12

International Women's Health Coalition, 178
Irwin, Paul, 82
Israel, 113
Ittleson Foundation, 169
IUCN-World Conservation Union, 14, 15, 16, 21, 55, 97, 125, 133, 135, 136, 138, 149, 155, 169, 185, 188
Izaak Walton League, 43
J.P. Morgan Charitable Trust, 173
Japan, 1, 9, 22, 29, 34, 39, 43, 47, 48, 49, 50, 103, 119, 143, 180, 191, 194
Japan Center for a Sustainable Environment and Society, 194
John Merck Fund, 167, 173
John Paul II, 110, 115
Johnson, Edwin, 82
Joint Council of Teamsters, 96
Jones Foundation, W. Alton, 55, 165, 167, 170, 171, 173, 179
Jorgenson, Dale, 54
Joyce Foundation, 166, 167, 168, 171, 173
Joyce Mertz-Gilmore Foundation, 166
Judd, Ron, 82
Kahn, Herman, 13
Kakakhel, Shafgat, 101, 102
Kane, Hal, 112
Kantor, Mickey, 71-73, 76-77
Karpatkin, Rhoda, 82
Kasich, John, 150
Katz, Abe, 82
Kenya, 11
Kiko Forum, 43, 191
Kimble, Melinda, 97, 112
Kirby Foundation, F.M., 166
Korean Federation of Environmental Movements, 44

Krupp, Fred, 47, 74, 97
Kyoto, 1, 29, 33, 39, 41-50, 52, 53, 55, 56, 57, 149, 162, 191, 197
Lake Michigan Federation, 82
Lamb, Henry, 52
Lannan Foundation, 168
Lash, Jonathan, 97
Lay, Kenneth, 50
Leadership Council of Metropolitan Open Communities, 96
League of Conservation Voters, 43
League of Women Voters, 96
Lebanon, 110
Leggett, Jeremy, 45
Les Amis de la Terre, 185
Levin, Gerald, 51
Lieberman, Joseph, 43
Limits to Growth, 13
Lindsay, James, 82
Liz Claiborne & Art Ortenberg Foundation, 169, 170
Local Environmental Initiatives-USA, 59
Lorma Community Development Foundation, 151
Lott, Trent, 49
Loy, Frank, 82
Lubchenco, Jane, 54
MacArthur Foundation, John D. and Catherine T., 21, 22, 23, 55, 96, 165, 166, 168, 170, 171, 173, 174, 176
MacNeill, James, 24
Magraw, Daniel, 72
Malaysia, 20, 79, 124, 128
Mankin, Bill, 124, 126
Marine Mammal Protection Act, 3, 68
Masters of Illusion, 152
Mathews, Jessica Tuchman, 22, 23, 38, 41, 78

McKnight Foundation, 166, 173, 174
McLeod, Laurel, 100
Mellon Foundation, Andrew W., 166, 173
Mellon Foundation, Richard King, 171
Mexico, 68, 70, 71, 72, 73, 83, 126, 175, 185, 186
Meyer, Alden, 55, 56
Miller, Henry I., 118
Mineral Policy Center, 135
Mitsubishi Corporation, 9
Mittermeier, Russell, 18, 74
Moffet, Jim Bob, 8
Mohamad, Mahathir, 79
Monsanto, 82, 117, 171
Montreal Protocol, 33, 35-38, 56
Moore Family Foundation, 165
Moore, Patrick, 125
Moore, Thomas Gale, 44, 47
Morocco, 79, 113, 197
Mortgaging the Earth, 144, 152
Mott Foundation, Charles Stewart, 166, 168, 169, 171, 172, 181
Nader, Ralph, 32, 68, 75
Nathan Cummings Foundation, 167, 174
National Association of Evangelicals, 110
National Audubon Society, 2, 14, 16, 73, 74, 77, 81, 135, 152, 169, 178, 186, 188, 196
National Council of Churches, 96
National Environmental Trust (see also Environmental Information Center) 46, 50, 53, 167, 177, 191
National Family Farm Coalition, 68
National Farmers Union, 68
National Fisheries Institute, 82
National Law Center on Homelessness and Poverty, 96

National League of Cities, 96
National Low-Income Housing Coalition, 96
National Organization for Women, 110
National Parks and Conservation Association, 135, 138
National Religious Partnership for the Environment, 43
National Review, 22
National Wildlife Federation, 2, 8, 16, 43, 57, 69, 70, 71-74, 76-79, 81, 82, 92, 94, 95, 125, 135, 145, 152, 170, 178, 186
NationsBank, 93
Natural Resources Defense Council, 2, 8, 14, 16, 18, 31, 33, 39, 42, 43, 54, 55, 57, 59, 70-74, 77, 81, 82, 97, 135, 145, 152, 170, 180, 182, 198
Natural Step, 10
Nature Conservancy, 16, 55, 57, 59, 73, 97, 155, 171, 182
Nautilus of America, 194
Nautilus Pacific Research, 82
Navarro-Valls, Joaquin, 101
N'Dow, Wally, 93, 99, 102
Nepal, 103, 128, 148, 151
Nestle, 117
Netherlands, 22, 40
New Guinea, 8
New International Economic Order, 12
New York Times Company Foundation, 169
New Zealand, 49
Niger, 103, 110
Nigeria, 79
Nixon, Richard, 131
Nordhaus, William, 54

Norris Foundation, Kenneth T. and Eileen L., 170
North American Development Bank, 74
North American Free Trade Agreement (NAFTA), 68, 70, 71-77, 81-83, 85, 186
North, Robert C., 23
Northeast Denver Housing Center, 97
Northwest Area Foundation, 71
Norway, 15, 22, 68
Nuclear Energy Institute, 45
Nutter, Franklin, 57
Odious Debts, 144
Ologa, Margaret, 111
Olson, Molly Harriss, 10
Oppenheimer, Michael, 42, 55
Our Common Future (Brundtland Report), 15, 16, 22
Our Global Neighborhood, 22, 109
Oxfam, 113, 143, 147, 148
Ozone Action, 32, 53, 54, 55, 172, 193, 195
Pacific Environment and Resources Center, 180, 191
Pacific Gas and Electric, 58
Pacific Institute for Studies in Development, 59, 178
Packard Foundation, David and Lucile, 165, 169, 171, 173, 174, 189
Pakistan, 101, 102, 189, 197
Panama Declaration, 83, 84
Paraguay, 113
Parliamentarians for Global Action, 178
Partizans, 8
Penzance Foundation, 170
People for Puget Sound, 82
People-Centered Development Forum, 92

Perrault, Michelle, 97
Peru, 111
Pesticide Action Network, 195
Pew Center on Climate Change, 160, 197
Pew Charitable Trusts, 50, 160, 167, 170, 171, 174, 176, 197
Philippines, 20, 111, 151
Physicians for Social Responsibility, 43, 54, 96
Planned Parenthood, 109, 110, 111, 150, 178, 179, 197
Pomerance, Rafe, 125, 127
Population Action International, 95, 178, 190, 196
Population Bomb, 13
Population Council, 190, 196, 197
Population Reference Bureau, 190, 197
Population Research Institute, 110
Porter, Gareth, 82
President's Council on Sustainable Development, 10, 20, 57, 92, 93, 96, 97
Preston, Lewis, 147, 149
Pritzker Foundation, 165
Probe International, 144, 148, 150
Procter & Gamble Fund, 170, 174
Progress and Freedom Foundation, 96
Prospect Hill Foundation, 165, 170
Prudencio, Rodrigo, 72
Public Citizen, 68, 69, 71, 81, 83
Public Welfare Foundation, 166, 168, 171
Rainforest Action Network, 9, 11
Rainforest Alliance, 195
Ramphal, Shridath, 21
Rao, P.V. Narasimha, 79
Rasmussen Foundation, V. Kann, 174
Reagan administration, 13, 132
Reagan, Ronald, 12, 13, 34, 47

Redefining Progress, 54, 55, 177, 191, 193
Reinsurance Association of America, 57
Resourceful Earth, The, 13
Resources for the Future, 59
Rich, Bruce, 144, 152, 153
Rifkin, Jeremy, 117
Rio + 5 Meeting, 123, 161, 162
Rio Earth Summit, ii, 17-19, 38, 46, 92, 123, 153, 160, 161
Ritchie, Mark, 82
Rockefeller Brothers Fund, 166, 167, 172, 174, 191
Rockefeller Family Fund, 195
Rockefeller Foundation, 168, 170, 176, 196
Rockefeller, Jr., John D., 191
Rockefeller, John D., 196
Rockford Institute, 110
Rockwell International Corporation Trust, 171
Rocky Mountain Institute, 177
Rostenkowski, Dan, 69
Rothbard, David, 52, 102
Rowland, Sherwood, 30
Royal Dutch Shell, 7-8
Rucker, Craig, 102
Rue, Michael, 82
Runge, C. Ford, 70
Russia, 49, 59, 124
Rwanda, 103
San Francisco Foundation, 165
Saro-Wiwa, Ken, 7
Saudi Arabia, 110
Save the Children Fund, 143
Sawhill, John, 97
Scherman Foundation, 167
Schlafly, Phyllis, 52
Schmalensee, Richard, 33

Schott, Jeffrey, 72
Schumann Foundation, Florence and John, 169
Science and Environmental Policy Project, 46, 52
Scrace, Richard, 45
Sea Shepherd, 3
Seaver Institute, 172
Sedjo, Roger, 128
Senegal, 115
Shabecoff, Philip, 10, 55, 161, 199
Shapiro, Robert, 82
Shell Oil Company Foundation, 172
Sierra Club, 2, 8, 14, 16, 30, 42, 43, 47, 50, 55, 57, 70, 71, 72, 75, 81, 83, 92, 95, 97, 125, 135, 145, 146, 153, 172, 178, 187, 188, 189, 193, 195
Silent Spring, 10
Simmons, Adele, 22
Simon, Julian, 13
Simpson, Alan, 138
Sims, Arden, 82
Singapore, 80, 103, 116, 194
Singer, S. Fred, 46, 52
Smith, Frances, 32
Smith, Fred, 52
Smith, Michael, 71
Society of Environmental Journalists, 181
Solar Energy Industries Association, 57
Solorzano, Elida, 111
Solow, Robert, 54
South Africa, 103, 189
South Korea, 48, 69, 79, 119
Southern California Council on Environment and Development, 96
Southern California District Council of Laborers, 96

Southern California Nuclear Freeze Foundation, 96
Sovereignty International, 52
Speth, James Gustave, 19, 108, 146
Stanley Foundation, 97
Starr Foundation, 166, 171
Stockholm Environment Institute, 192
Stratospheric Ozone Depletion, 35
Strong, Maurice, 11, 12, 14, 17, 21, 24, 41, 109, 148 160, 161
Study Group on Trade and the Environment, 70
Sudan, 110
Surdna Foundation, 166, 167, 168, 172, 173, 174
Sustainable Seattle, 97
Sweden, 10, 11, 21, 22, 192
Switzerland, 22, 117
Taiwan, 103
Tanzania, 111, 189
Technology Sciences Group, 82
Tellus Institute, 54
Texas Commerce Bank, 96
Thailand, 48, 113, 137
Thibodeau, John, 148
Thomas, Lee, 82
Tides Center, 181, 192, 194
Time-Warner, i, 51
Tobin, James, 22
Trade and Environment Policy Advisory Committee, 81, 82
Train, Russell, 18
Trout Unlimited, 135
Turkey, 91
Turner, Ted, ix, x, 51, 112, 160, 162, 198
Udall, Lori, 8, 146, 147
Uganda, 197
Unilever, 117

Union of Concerned Scientists, 43, 46, 54, 55, 56, 57, 194

Union Pacific Foundation, 172

United Kingdom, 128, 189, 191, 192, 194, 196, 199

United Nations Association-USA, i, 91, 92, 93, 96, 97

U.N. Commission on Sustainable Development, 19, 124

U.N. Conference on Environment and Development (UNCED), 17-20 (see also Rio Earth Summit)

U.N. Conference on the Human Environment (Stockholm), 11-12

U.N. Conference on Human Settlements, Habitat II (Istanbul) 91-96, 99-103

U.N. Conference on the Law of the Sea, 12

U.N. Conference on Population and Development (Cairo), 109-112, 197

U.N. Conference of the Parties (COPS), 4, 38, 39, 49, 162, 191

U.N. Convention on Climate Change (Kyoto), 41-53 (see also Kyoto)

U.N. Department of Public Information, 5

U.N. Development Program, 19, 108, 199

U.N. Economic and Social Council, 5

U.N. Educational, Scientific, and Cultural Organization (UNESCO), 13, 14, 131-133, 135-136, 139

U.N. Environment Programme, ii, 11, 14, 34, 199

U.N. Food and Agriculture Organization (FAO), 14, 107, 175

United Nations Foundation, i, ii, 160, 198

U.N. Fund for Population Activities, ii, 116

U.N. General Assembly, 12, 22, 54, 123, 125

U.N. Intergovernmental Panel on Climate Change, 41

U.N. Intergovernmental Panel on Forests, 124, 125, 127

U.N. Secretary General, 15, 160

U.N. Security Council, 22

U.N. World Food Summit (Rome), 107-109, 113-117

U.N. World Heritage Committee, 131-132, 134-139

U.S. Agency for International Development, 8, 70, 93, 111, 160, 163

U.S. Citizens Network for UNCED, 16, 93

U.S. Constitution, 115

U.S. Council for International Business, 82

U.S. Council on Environmental Quality, 11, 19, 108

U.S. Department of Agriculture, 109, 112

U.S. Department of Commerce, 57, 70

U.S. Department of Energy, 57

U.S. Department of Housing and Urban Development, 93, 96-99

U.S. Department of Interior, 71

U.S. Department of State, 57

U.S. Department of the Interior, 133, 135, 136, 138

U.S. Environmental Protection Agency, 11, 33, 55, 57, 58, 59, 60, 67, 69, 70, 71, 72, 74, 77, 81, 82, 160, 176

U.S. Food and Drug Administration, 71

U.S. Forest Service, 125, 127, 131

U.S. House of Representatives, Resources Committee, 139

U.S. National Committee for the Man

and the Biosphere Program, 133
U.S. National Oceanic and Atmospheric Administration, 11, 71
U.S. National Park Service, 134, 136, 137
U.S. Network for Cairo '94, 93
U.S. Network for Habitat II, 91-93, 95-97, 175
U.S. Office of Technology Assessment, 70
U.S. Overseas Private Investment Corporation, 8
U.S. Public Interest Research Group, 43
U.S. Senate, 47, 49, 70, 126, 152, 162
U.S. State Department, 52, 70, 72, 111, 112, 133, 159
U.S. Trade Representative, 70, 71, 72, 73, 77, 82
United Nations Population Fund, 110, 190, 199
United Steelworkers of America, 82
United Technologies, 56, 160
Valley Proud Environmental Council, 96
Vatican, 20, 100, 101, 110, 111, 112, 115
von Droste, Bernd, 135, 136, 137
Waldheim, Kurt, 15
Wallace Genetic Foundation, 165, 166, 167, 168, 169, 170, 171, 173, 174
Waller, J. Michael, 110
Wallis Foundation, 172
Wallis, W. Allen, 34
Wapenhans, Willi, 146
Ward, Justin, 72
Wathen, Tom, 50, 51, 52
Watson, Robert, 29, 149
Weddig, Lee, 82

Weeden Foundation, 167, 174
Wichiencharoen, Adul, 137, 138
Wilderness Society, 14, 16, 135, 137, 192
Wirth, Tim, i, 50, 72, 111, 112, 160
Wolfensohn, James, 148, 149, 153
Women's Environment and Development Organization, 18, 91, 95,110, 175, 190
Woodwell, George, 54
Wooster, Martin Morse, 196, 197
World Affairs Council, 97
World Bank, 19, 22, 70, 74, 76, 108, 113, 118, 143-155, 163, 179, 182, 184, 185, 192
World Bank Global Environment Facility, 19, 151, 152, 155, 160, 163, 182
World Commission on Environment and Development, 15, 16, 24, 68
World Conservation Strategy, 14
World Heritage Convention, 131, 132, 136, 137
World Meteorological Organization, 35, 38
World Resources Institute, 3, 16, 19, 23, 29, 30, 38, 43, 55, 57, 59, 67, 70, 78, 91, 92, 97, 108, 125, 145, 146, 155, 173, 177, 181, 183, 190, 192, 196, 198, 199
World Trade Organization, 68, 76-78, 80, 83, 116, 187, 188, 189
World Wide Fund for Nature, 46, 49, 50, 53, 55, 78, 123, 125, 128, 155
World Wildlife Fund, 2, 9, 14, 15, 18, 31, 43, 60, 73, 74, 76, 78, 79, 81, 82, 126, 135, 153, 173, 187, 190, 195, 198
Worldwatch Institute, 3, 11, 14, 29, 37, 57, 67, 107, 112, 124, 153, 161, 174, 181, 192, 193
Young, Don, 139

YWCA International, 18
Zambia, 197
Zarsky, Lyuba, 82
Zero Population Growth, 92, 93, 95, 97, 112, 190